The Birth of Europe

The Birth of Europe

II
The History of the Christian Church
from John Chrysostom to the
Conversion of Russia (AD 398–999)

Church history unfolded, through the stories
that are the inheritance of all believers

Leigh Churchill

paternoster
Lifestyle

Copyright © 2001 Leigh Churchill

First published in 2001 by Paternoster Lifestyle
Reprinted 2002

08 07 06 05 04 03 02   8 7 6 5 4 3 2

Paternoster Lifestyle is an imprint of Paternoster Publishing,
P.O. Box 300, Carlisle, Cumbria CA3 0QS, UK
and Paternoster Publishing USA
Box 1047, Waynesboro, GA 30830-2047
www.paternoster-publishing.com

British Library Cataloguing in Publication Data

A catalogue record for this book is available from the British Library

ISBN 1–84227–081–8

Cover design by Campsie, Glasgow
Typeset by Textype Typesetters, Cambridge
Printed and bound in Great Britain by
Cox & Wyman Ltd, Reading, Berkshire

Table of Contents

Volume II: The Birth of Europe

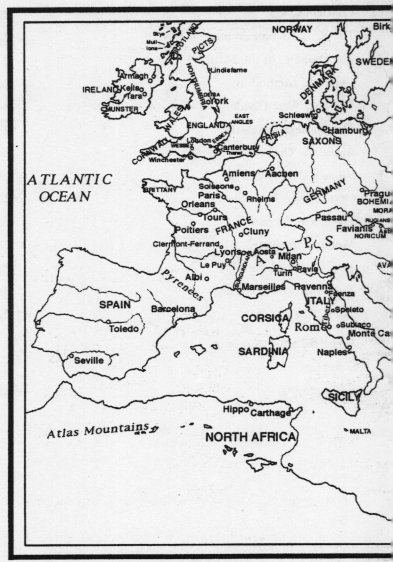

Infant

Over the centuries the locations of the tribes of northern Europe varied greatly.

The locations given for the various peoples indicate their position at the time of chief relevance to the narrative.

Europe

The Golden Mouth

In 398, the year after the death of Ambrose, John of Antioch became bishop of Constantinople.

John, son of a noble Antiochian family, was born in 347. His father, a leading officer of the imperial army, died when John was a baby, and John's mother Anthusa was left a widow at the age of twenty. A deeply Christian woman, Anthusa refused all offers of a second marriage and instead devoted herself to raising and educating John and his elder sister. John proved to be a brilliant student, and in his teens he entered the school of Libanius, the empire's leading literary scholar and rhetorician. The teacher, a pagan, was highly impressed with the young Christian.

'From whom did you receive your earlier education?'

'From my mother Anthusa.'

Libanius shook his head in wonder at the story of Anthusa's faith and dedication.

Rhetoric, or oratory, was one of the most important subjects in ancient education. It was the art of speaking well and persuasively, and no one could be considered a gentleman without some skill in it.

Persuasive speech, of course, was especially useful to the lawyer or teacher, and also in some degree to the Christian preacher, but Christians were unhappy with the way that the subject was taught in the schools. Orators were taught how to convince people through cunning speech, but they were not at all encouraged to have a respect for the truth, and as a result most pagan orators were perfectly happy to use their skills to defend falsehood. The pagan law courts were often chaotic, and it was common for juries to give their verdict in favour of anyone who pleased them with a flowery speech, regardless of the merits of his case.

'What women these Christians have!'

After the completion of his studies John began a profitable career as a lawyer, and his name was soon widely respected. His speeches were models of the art, and clients flocked to his door. But John was not happy.

'Is this what my mother raised me for?' he asked himself. 'Is this what God wants of me? What a life! I stand in court all day, defending this one, accusing that one, not even caring who is right and who is wrong. To accept money for making the worse cause seem the better is surely the devil's work!'

John began to search the Scriptures daily, and it seemed that the more he learned about Jesus Christ, the less his lifestyle satisfied him. He finally made the decisive break and left the law courts behind. He was baptized at the age of twenty-two.

> Libanius remained an idolater to the end, and lived to see the destruction of most of his beloved pagan society. The conversion of John was one of many disappointments for him. Late in life, when asked whom he wished to succeed him as head of the rhetorical school, he answered that only one was fit for the job: 'John, if only the Christians hadn't stolen him!'

Immediately John began to think of retiring to a monastery. Like so many others he wished to escape his past life and all of the temptations of pagan society, but it was his mother who halted his plans.

'I have, my son, been widowed once already. To lose you also will be more than I can bear. I beg you not to enter a monastery while I live.'

John listened to Anthusa's pleas, and rightly so, and he found a satisfactory compromise by living in strict monastic discipline in his mother's home. When Anthusa died four years later, he moved to the mountains south of Antioch.

John spent the next six years in the mountains, dividing his time between a small community of monks and a cold and remote cave to which he retreated for greater quiet. He spent his days and nights in prayer and meditation, and in the study of Scripture and theology. John's pen began to flow at this time, and his quiet cave saw the composition of several important works. But the harsh ascetic life and the constant assaults of hunger and cold eventually caught up with him, and at the age of thirty-three a severe bout of illness forced his return to the city.

The barren mountain's loss was Antioch's gain. John was immediately ordained deacon, and when he was later raised to the priesthood his gift as an orator could again shine forth. The skills that had been misused in the law court now found their fulfilment in the pulpit, and John's sermons were soon the talk of the town. He alone among the church's leaders has been universally nicknamed 'Chrysostom' – the golden mouth.

John had fled Antioch to save himself from the temptations lurking within the great city. This may have been well enough for him, but it was not what Antioch itself needed. The city needed its Christian sons at home, striking at the heart of its problems by converting sinners from their ways. Thankfully John returned to do just that.

In all, John laboured some 17 years in Antioch. Through his sermons the Spirit turned the hearts of countless hardened sinners, and the people flocked to him in their thousands. The church was usually so densely packed – the people hanging on every breath in rapt silence, and occasionally bursting out into applause – that the presbyter had to warn against the pickpockets who came for the easy takings! It was no small achievement that John made sermons rival the theatre and circus as attractions for the idle masses. In time the eloquent minister's fame spread far beyond his homeland.

In 397, Bishop Nectarius of Constantinople died. The spiritual leadership of this mighty city was a powerful position, and immediately after Nectarius' death a crowd of hopefuls began choking the path to the emperor's presence. Arcadius, Theodosius' son, had recently risen to the throne of the eastern empire, and he was dismayed by the character of the majority of those pushing for the position.

'Some have offered bribes, some have promised favours,' he snorted, 'what sort of men are these to become bishops!'

The citizens of Constantinople were likewise unimpressed with the prospective 'shepherds', and they urged the emperor to find them a real bishop. The king's chief counsellor, Eutropius, had spent time in Antioch and knew well of the presbyter John.

'Send for John,' he advised. 'He is a man of integrity, and such an eloquent orator that he will be like a jewel in the capital.'

Arcadius was delighted with the advice.

'But I warn you,' Eutropius added, 'the citizens of Antioch won't like it. Neither will John himself. They might riot if we try to deprive them of their favourite minister.'

So the crafty Eutropius hatched a plan, to which the emperor agreed.

Asterius, governor of the east, lived in Antioch, and he was instructed to invite John to a small chapel just outside the city. There government officers confronted the unsuspecting preacher.

'You will come with us.'

'Where are you taking me? What is the meaning of this?'

But his questions were met with silence, and the prisoner was placed in a carriage and carried over the eight hundred miles to the capital with the greatest speed. Upon his arrival in Constantinople, John quickly heard of the emperor's wishes, an assembly of bishops was called, and on 26 February 398 John was consecrated bishop of the capital.

Theophilus, Bishop of Alexandria, was one of those summoned to the consecration. He had come to Constantinople in the hope of winning the bishopric for his friend Isidore, and he was greatly annoyed that his recommendations had been ignored. He performed the consecration reluctantly, and left Constantinople with his mind set against the newcomer.

John set about his work as bishop with great energy, and the city soon saw it had acquired more than just a skilful preacher. Like Gregory Nazianzen 20 years earlier, he refused the luxury to which many other bishops had become accustomed. He collected together the gold plate, the expensive furniture, indeed all of the trappings of his official residence, and sold them and gave the proceeds to hospitals and the homeless. He kept a much stricter watch on the local ministers than had Nectarius before him, and he soon discovered and dismissed several unworthy priests. He also, accidentally, became responsible for the Arians being finally banned from teaching their heresy in Constantinople.

There were still considerable numbers of these heretics in the city, and their leaders still dreamed of regaining the power they had once enjoyed. At least twice a week the Arians would assemble in the streets to spend the evening chanting hymns that taught their heresy.

'If we can't have the churches,' said their leaders, 'we must regain the people's ear some other way!'

Urged on by their ministers the Arians would cry out insults against the Christians, taunting them bitterly in the empty streets.

'Where are you?' they would sing. 'Where are they who believe in the three?'

John was not content to sit back and allow the Arians to go unchallenged. He formed a choir of true believers, and with the support of Arcadius' young wife, Empress Eudoxia, arranged an even greater evening ceremony. The Christians, carrying silver crosses and candles, made a procession through the streets and squares and drowned out the noise of the heretics with Christian hymns. But the Arians were not to be defeated without a struggle.

'Perhaps they can defeat us in song,' the Arian leaders cursed, 'but their crosses and candles will do them no good against cold hard steel!'

When the Christians gathered again the next Sunday night, their Arian opponents were nowhere to be seen. Briso, a servant of Eudoxia and a talented singer, was leading the crowd in song.

'Have we defeated them so easily?' he asked the crowd in delight.

He soon received an answer. A shower of stones rained down upon the Christians from the darkness, and Briso himself was knocked to the ground. The Arians soon emerged from the shadows, hurling stones and attacking the believers with knives and all manner of weapons. The Christians turned on their assailants, and when the sun rose the next morning it was seen that several from both sides lay dead.

'Enough!' said Arcadius. 'No more Arian chants in this city.'

> The Novatian sect, which had arisen after the Decian persecution, still had churches in many places, and it existed fairly peacefully alongside the mainstream church. (These Novatians, of course, were not heretical – the difference between themselves and the main church being one of discipline.) In the time of John a bishop named Sisinnius, a popular man who was famed for quick wits and amusing comebacks, led the Novatians of Constantinople. His rival bishop once confronted him.
>
> 'You realize that a city cannot have two bishops,' John challenged.
>
> 'Then it is just as well that ours doesn't,' Sisinnius replied.
>
> 'Do you mean to say that you alone are bishop?'
>
> 'No, but all agree that this city has only one bishop, they just don't agree on which of us it is!'
>
> Sisinnius was sometimes criticized for living too richly for a bishop. Fine food was always served at his table, and he was known to visit the baths to relax twice a day.
>
> 'Why do you, a bishop, bathe twice daily?' a critic once asked.
>
> 'Because it is inconvenient to do it three times,' was the instant reply.

So the contention with these Arians was over, but much greater problems were brewing in the city of Constantinople.

JOHN CHRYSOSTOM, *ON THE PRIESTHOOD*; SOZOMEN, *CH* 8.2–8

A Guard of Angels

Eutropius, Arcadius' chief adviser, had risen from the depths of slavery to the very pinnacle of power. A master of cunning, his very greatest coup had been the introduction of Arcadius and the beautiful Eudoxia, now empress. We shall hear a little more of his rise in a later story, but for the moment we are concerned with his fall.

Eutropius was a eunuch, and as was the case with many eunuchs, this sad fact embittered and twisted his whole life. It seemed that his only pleasure lay in the pursuit of power, and he carried his passion to such lengths that he could not bear to see anyone but himself sharing the emperor's confidence. He was forever hatching plots against Arcadius' closest friends, and many worthy men fell victims to his jealousy.

Sanctuary was a custom that allowed some criminals to take shelter in church buildings. So long as they stayed within they were safe from the executioner and could plead their case with the help of the priests. But when certain enemies of Eutropius took advantage of this right and sheltered in a church, Eutropius pushed Arcadius into banning Sanctuary altogether. The church's complaints were ignored, but justice (poetic justice) caught up with the cruel eunuch soon enough.

Tribigild, a hot-headed young Gothic ally of the Romans, had been given a command in the imperial forces. He had won Arcadius' admiration, and had good prospects of promotion. But he knew that it was Eutropius who held the real power, so he paid the adviser a respectful visit in the hope of currying favour. His reception was far from his expectation, and after being treated with every sign of disrespect the slighted barbarian departed to meditate drastic revenge on the aged eunuch.

In 399, Tribigild and the Goths under his command rose in revolt against the empire. Not long afterwards they were joined by the forces of Gainas, an even more formidable barbarian ally. Both men were inspired by the same wish, and offered Arcadius the choice of war or the sacrifice of his vicious minister.

Arcadius was in a fix. He was attached to his unworthy adviser, and Eutropius may have survived the crisis had it not been for his own savage temper. He happened to argue violently with Eudoxia, and in the heat of the moment cursed her bitterly.

'I brought you here,' he screeched in a rage, 'watch that I don't throw you out again! I made you empress. Careful I don't send you packing!'

Eudoxia could not take such an insult lightly. She fled from the eunuch's presence, and snatching up her two babies she burst in upon her husband.

'Do as the Goths command you!' she cried. 'Get rid of the wretched Eutropius. Just now he has abused me to my face, and threatened to throw me out of the palace! It is him or me!'

Arcadius reacted swiftly, as did Eutropius. Before the order for his arrest had been proclaimed the old eunuch was out on the street, running as swiftly as his legs would carry him. He burst into the city's major church, Saint Sophia (literally 'church of the Holy Wisdom', i.e., the Word, Jesus Christ), and throwing himself beneath the altar clung to it for dear life. Bishop John discovered him in this position.

'What do you seek here Eutropius?'

'Sanctuary!' came the feeble reply. 'Protect me from the emperor's anger!'

'Have you yourself not banned Sanctuary?'

'Please Bishop John,' Eutropius moaned. 'Save me!'

'Very well.'

Soldiers were soon heard in the outer part of the church.

'He went in here, did he?'

'Come no further,' John commanded. 'Eutropius has thrown himself upon God's mercy, and under the church's shelter. Leave. I will plead his cause with Arcadius myself.'

As good as his word, John managed to protect Eutropius from his enemies' anger. The whole city loathed the cruel old man, and it took all the authority of emperor and bishop to stop the soldiers from dragging him out to face rough justice. On the following day the crowds gathered early at Saint Sophia. What would the eloquent John have to say on such an occasion? Wretched Eutropius was still crouching beneath the altar as John began his sermon.

'Vanity of vanities,' the bishop declared, 'all is vanity! These words are ever true, and how well do we see them illustrated today! Where is the applause that once greeted the steps of Eutropius? Where the flattery and the banquets? A wind has blown upon the tree of human pride, and all its leaves are gone.

'Like smoke the friends of Eutropius have dispersed, like a cobweb his world is rent in pieces. Were you not warned of this outcome? Did I not point out the deceitful allurements of wealth? Events have proved my words. Eutropius was great, he trusted in money and power to provide happiness, but now with empty hands he lies here fearing for his life. I say this not to insult the fallen, but to excite the pity of each of you, that through your pity his life might be saved. Take to heart the lesson of Eutropius' fall, and remember that true happiness is found in God alone.'

And so it was that John used the power of Sanctuary to preserve the very man who had sought to destroy it. But even Chrysostom could not defend the old man indefinitely, and when Eutropius ventured to leave the refuge he was apprehended and sent into exile. Even so the eunuch's enemies were not satisfied, and Eutropius eventually paid the deserved penalty of his crimes with his blood.

The fall of one tyrant, however, only served to bring another to the fore. The Gothic chief Gainas, aware that Arcadius was weak and easily controlled, began demanding for himself a privileged position such as Eutropius had held. Was he not, after all, commander of the brave Gothic troops? As allies the Goths were very desirable, as enemies they were terrifying. Gainas demanded that the Romans surrender as hostages several of the nation's greatest citizens, all personal friends of the royal family.

'They will be the pledge of our friendship,' he menaced. 'That is, if you want the friendship of the Goths.'

John was summoned before the nervous emperor.

'Go, please, and use your famous eloquence to soften his demands.'

John enjoyed only moderate success in his embassy to the barbarians. Gainas withdrew his demand that the emperor's friends be given into his hands, but he still insisted on their exile. Even this, however, did not bring lasting relief, and early in the following year Gainas' Goths crossed the Bosphorus and marched into Constantinople itself, making camp in the very streets of the capital.

'Where is your respect for your guests?' Gainas challenged Arcadius. 'We are Arians, and we cannot worship alongside you. Empty some of your churches and hand them over immediately.'

The weak Arcadius would have bent but for his bishop.

'Emperor, we cannot abandon our churches to the enemies of God. Trust the Lord.'

The city trembled at the Gothic presence within its walls: how long could these 'allies' be trusted? For some weeks there was an uneasy stalemate, but it ended in open panic when Constantinople's evening sky was lit by a comet, a sure sign, many said, of coming calamity. Gainas did not want to disappoint the doomsayers.

'If there are no churches for the Goths there will be no residence for the emperor. Go, and burn Arcadius' palace to the ground.'

A large detachment left the Gothic camp, but it was halted some distance from the palace by the sight of an opposing army in front. They turned, and quietly returned to their leader.

'Arcadius has a force on duty before the palace,' they declared, 'they are all mighty men, tall and well equipped for battle.'

'Nonsense!' Gainas roared. 'Arcadius has scarcely a soldier in the whole city, much less an army. His men are on campaign elsewhere, for how otherwise could we have entered the city without dispute?'

'Go and see for yourself!'

The following night Gainas did just that, and he was dumbfounded to see the army with his own eyes.

'Where did Arcadius find such men!' he whispered in awe. 'He must have brought his choicest troops back from the east to protect Constantinople against me.'

The barbarian was now unnerved. Weeks had slipped into months, and far from capturing the government he had not even managed to acquire a solitary church!

'We had better leave while the going is good,' he charged his men. 'We must evacuate before we provoke the emperor's army.'

There was actually no danger from Arcadius' army, because as Gainas had thought the Roman troops were miles away. When news of the army seen by the Goths spread, the people of Constantinople had only one answer:

'We have been saved by angels!'

But nothing was going to save the Goths. Many of Gainas' men, disguised as travellers, attempted to leave Constantinople secretly, but they were stopped by officials at the city gates and their baggage inspected.

'Why do you have all of these weapons? Who are you?'

Boiling with frustration, the Goths dropped the pretence and took up their arms.

'Death to the Romans!'

A scuffle soon became a full-scale riot. Civilians came from all directions to aid the city guards, and before long many Goths lay dead in the streets.

'We are rid of the barbarians!'

Gainas himself managed to escape with the bulk of his troops, and fearing pursuit he hastily prepared rafts in order to cross into Asia. Once on the water, however, the Goths were dismayed to see Roman ships nearby, and when a strong wind descended on the Hellespont the makeshift craft of the Goths were thrown into complete disorder, while the Roman navy was enabled to bear down on them with great speed. Almost to a man the Goths were tossed into the sea and drowned, and very few survived for the Romans to attack.

Gainas, however, again proved a survivor. He struggled ashore and fell in with a tribe of Huns. Nothing could be more pleasing to Uldin, the Hun chief, than this visitor.

'Gainas,' he cried, 'you will be of great assistance to me!'

'How so?' asked the Goth in surprise.

'You will be a bond of friendship between myself and Arcadius!' he replied, turning to his attendants. 'Off with his head! It will be a most pleasing gift for the emperor!'

So the east was again safe, and Constantinople rejoiced in its deliverance.

JOHN CHRYSOSTOM, 'ON EUTROPIUS', 'HOMILY I'; SOCRATES, *CH* 6.5–6

'Again She Dances'

Bishop John's popularity among the common people continued to soar. His sermons against greed, luxury, vanity and all the other sins of the capital were unceasing, and it seemed that a great reformation was getting underway amongst the citizens. It looked as though John's labours might well lead to something altogether new – a great city wholly dedicated to Christ. How could anyone fail to admire this earnest minister, who preached like an angel and lived as he preached?

Easily enough, it turned out, if one felt that the preacher's criticisms hit rather too close to home. When John preached against gluttony and greed the poor folk cheered, while many of the aristocrats sneered and stewed.

'Who is this priest to tell us what to do?'

Another group of enemies was also growing – the greedy and incompetent priests whom John had either dismissed or rebuked.

'How long must we suffer this nosy monk prying into our business? The sooner he's gone the better.'

Most dangerous of all, as it finally appeared, was Empress Eudoxia herself. Though she was a pious woman who considered herself strongly Christian, Eudoxia was angered by John's rebukes of her wealthy friends. She felt that several points in the preacher's sermons fitted herself rather too neatly. All of this bad feeling, however, would have come to nothing without the interference of Theophilus, Bishop of Alexandria.

Theophilus and John were the two most important figureheads of the eastern church, just as their cities were the two greatest of the eastern empire. Theophilus was an energetic and strong-willed man, but one who all too often put his gifts to the wrong use. He knew no moderation in the use of power, and he acquired a reputation for greed and injustice. He seemed the opposite of much that John stood for, and he must have been uncomfortable with a man of John's character leading the church of the capital – a living rebuke to himself and his cronies.

The bishops of the empire's major cities, namely Rome, Alexandria and Antioch, were known as 'patriarchs', and from early times these three bishops had been treated as high authorities to whom members of smaller congregations could appeal in difficult cases. For example, Christians from Syria and Asia Minor commonly appealed to the Patriarch of Antioch, Egyptians to Alexandria, Italians or Gauls to Rome.

Constantine gave his new capital, Constantinople, equal rights with the older great cities, and he made the bishop of Constantinople a fourth patriarch. This caused jealousy in Alexandria especially, which had formerly been the chief city of the east. Many Alexandrians resented their new rival, and this showed itself over the years in both politics and religion. We shall hear more of it later, but Theophilus' attack on John was an early sign of the troubles to come.

Trouble arrived at Theophilus' door when a new heresy, 'anthropomorphitism', began to spread in Egypt.

'God,' certain rustic monks decided, 'has a body like men, a human physical form. Doesn't the Bible say that man is made in the image of God?'

Theophilus of course rejected such nonsense, and he made the correct doctrine clear in his sermons.

'Man is made in the image of God,' he said, 'but that image refers to our minds, not our bodies. God, like us, has a mind, but he does not have fingers and toes!'

When the monks learned of this attack on their ideas they marched upon the city and threatened to lead a mob against the bishop.

'Theophilus is unworthy to lead this church!'

Faced with this hostility, Theophilus did a swift about-face.

'Let there be no argument between us,' he pleaded. 'I hold to the same beliefs as you.'

'Is that the truth?' the monks demanded. 'What about God's body?'

'In seeing you,' Theophilus replied, 'I see the face of God!'

The simple-minded monks were satisfied with this answer, and it was not long before the crafty bishop found a means to use this defeat to his own advantage.

Anthropomorphitism was the vulgar face of a much broader controversy.

Certain writings of Origen had recently become the subject of intense debate. The theological warfare of the fourth century had inspired a dislike of Greek philosophy among many Christians, and they had become wary of those theologians whose writings showed too much sympathy for Greek ideas. Epiphanius, a Cypriot bishop and renowned warrior against heresy, had come to believe that Origen was responsible for many recent heresies, and that his writings had provided the heretics' chief inspiration and support. He urged that Origen's books be put under a ban and argued vigorously against all who admired the Alexandrian's work.

Others went further. Lacking the nous to carefully weigh the questions of theology, and to use Greek philosophy with discrimination, they launched an attack upon all whose faith had any semblance of 'suspicious' intellectual depth. Ironically they ended up in heresy themselves, embracing such absurdities as anthropomorphitism – no bodiless and spiritual God for them!

There were four leading Egyptian monks – Ammonius, Dioscorus, Eusebius and Euthymius – wise and pious men, who were nicknamed the 'tall brothers' on account of their extraordinary height. They had been of service to Theophilus and his church for a long time, but at this time all four revealed a wish to retire permanently to the desert. Nothing the patriarch could say or offer would induce them to change their minds. Theophilus was irritated by their firmness, and he guiltily sensed that their decision was the result of dissatisfaction with his personal conduct.

'I'll fix them some day,' he promised himself as the tall brothers departed.

Soon afterwards Isidore, for whom Theophilus had once tried to win the bishopric of Constantinople, received a large donation for the purpose of extending a hospital. Theophilus demanded that the money be put into his own hands, and he was incensed by the priest's reluctance.

'Do you doubt my honour?' Theophilus demanded. 'I need extra funds for a grand new church building, so you can be assured that it will be money well spent.'

'But you know as well as I do that the money is earmarked for the hospital. Surely it is better to heal the bodies of the suffering, the true temples of Christ, than to build fine walls of stone?'

Theophilus was enraged by Isidore's defiance, and the younger priest was forced to flee the city to escape the patriarch's wrath. Fatefully he chose Nitria, the desert retreat of the tall brothers, as his place of refuge.

'Aha!' Theophilus cried. 'I can kill two birds with one stone!' Quickly he assembled the anthropomorphites who had so recently threatened his own safety. 'Come with me to Nitria. The tall brothers and their followers must be destroyed.'

'Why? What have they done?'

'They are teaching the lie that God does not have eyes, ears, hands and feet!'

And so it was that the bishop led a crowd of the simplest and most vicious rabble to attack the Nitrian monastery. The tall brothers could not deny the charge – it was of course perfectly true – and in peril of their very lives the monks of Nitria fled to Constantinople.

In Constantinople they received a kindly welcome from John. Knowing of the trouble that had raged in Alexandria, John was inclined to be cautious. He asked the advice of some Alexandrian priests who were visiting Constantinople.

'Be careful of offending Theophilus,' they said. 'Treat them well, but do not admit them to full church membership. Theophilus himself has excommunicated them, and he is not a man to be trifled with.'

John heeded the advice, and took it upon himself to make peace between the warring parties. In a letter to Theophilus he pleaded for mercy on the Nitrians.

'Never!' was the immediate response.

John urged the case in a second letter, but again Theophilus was adamant. The monks themselves now wrote up an account of their unjust sufferings, and presenting it to Eudoxia they pleaded that Theophilus be forced to face their charges. Eudoxia consented, and Theophilus was summoned to Constantinople.

Theophilus was enraged at this public embarrassment, especially at the interference of John, and the Nitrian monks were all but forgotten as he began plotting revenge against his rival patriarch.

'I'm not going to Constantinople to be put on trial for my attack on the Nitrians,' he assured his city. 'It is John himself who will be in the hot seat!'

Theophilus was as good as his word. Within days of his arrival in Constantinople he had rallied the many aristocrats and corrupt priests whom John had angered, and under his own leadership held a synod in a suburb of Chalcedon called 'the Oak'.

'We put John, Patriarch of Constantinople, on trial for high treason.'

Every stray word John had ever used in the pulpit was now brought against him.

'All these attacks on the wicked,' said Theophilus, 'are nothing more than thinly disguised attacks on Empress Eudoxia, and on the best people of the empire!'

Four times John was summoned to answer the charges, but each time he refused.

'This "Synod of the Oak" is complete nonsense. I refuse to be tried by a mob of sinful priests, all of them my personal enemies!'

This was just what Theophilus had hoped for. 'We are left no choice,' he declared. 'We find John guilty of failing to obey our lawful summons, and depose him as bishop from this moment.'

News of the verdict reached the capital late one evening. Within minutes an angry mob was surrounding the cathedral where John was ministering.

'Injustice!' the crowd cried. 'The synod is a farce! Bishop John! Bishop John!'

Eudoxia, however, was pleased with the decision, and at her insistence Arcadius ordered John's arrest and exile. The command may as well have fallen on deaf ears. All through the night the people surrounded Saint Sophia, shouting defiance at the emperor's soldiers, and for three whole days the city was frozen. Fearing to attack the crowd, and equally unwilling to back down, the emperor finally sent the patriarch a secret message.

'Please come quietly. Who knows how much trouble we may cause otherwise.'

John obeyed Arcadius' request with a heavy heart, and he secretly slipped from the church and was soon on his way into exile. Word of his disappearance whipped the crowd into even greater violence. Until now their anger had been mainly directed at Theophilus and his cronies from the synod, but now the emperor and empress became equally the targets of their rage. A priest from 'the Oak', sent to calm the crowds, tried to deliver a sermon against John.

'John made many enemies because of his hard-headed ways,' he declared. 'His arrogance has seen him rightly deposed. Scripture itself tells us that "God opposes the proud."'

This infuriated the crowds all the more.

'Shame on you! Shame on Theophilus and all his cronies!'

Throughout the night the crowds filled the streets. They surrounded the churches and the emperor's palace, filled the markets and squares, and everywhere sent up to the skies the same demand.

'Bring back the bishop!'

Inside the palace Arcadius and Eudoxia paced about in dread, unable to sleep for the riotous noise which assaulted their ears.

'SHAME! SHAME! SHAME!'

They feared that the crowd might attempt to break in, or set fire to the building, and both anxiously wondered how the crisis would end. About the middle of the night an earthquake shook the palace, and the terrified empress gave in.

'Briso,' she called her trusted servant, 'pursue the soldiers immediately. Bring John back!' In haste she drew up a personal letter to the bishop. 'I am innocent of the plots against you. Please return immediately.'

John soon received this message, but he was not so quick to obey as Eudoxia might have hoped. He returned as far as the outer suburbs of the city, but he refused to go farther until a new synod had found him innocent.

'There is no time,' Arcadius replied. 'Come back now or the people will riot, and the blood will be on your hands.'

Seeing the truth of this John obeyed, and nearly the whole city turned out to greet him. The streets were lit as though for a great festival, and the people carried candles and sang hymns written especially for the occasion. The crowd pleaded with John to resume his duties immediately, but the minister was wary.

'I have been deposed,' he said. 'If I am not properly reinstated now it could mean trouble later.'

But the people would not be refused, and John eventually mounted the pulpit and delivered a celebratory sermon. He thanked the people for their strength and courage, and he praised their determination to do right. He praised God for the difficulties he had suffered, as they had brought the whole city together in such spectacular fashion.

'Before this trouble I knew that my people loved me, but now I find even the Jews paying me honour. Today there are pagan games at the circus, but not a soul is there! All have been seized by the flood of thanksgiving and brought here to rejoice with us.'

The patriarch even had kind words for the empress, and he praised Eudoxia for bowing her will to God as he read aloud the letter she had sent him in exile.

Theophilus was enraged by this turn of events. Swiftly he clutched the last straw, as John had suspected he might.

'John has compounded his sins by illegally resuming the bishopric!'

But his folly was not going to win any support this time, and hearing that some citizens were plotting to throw him into the sea, Theophilus beat a hasty retreat to the safety of Alexandria. Many other enemies remained, however, and greater tribulation yet lay ahead for the fearless preacher of righteousness.

Later in the same year, 403, a silver statue of Empress Eudoxia was erected before the Senate building. A wild party accompanied its dedication, and the streets around the Senate and nearby Saint Sophia were filled with revelry – much of it crude and immoral. It was a Sunday, and Bishop John was not impressed.

'Must we celebrate like pagans?' he asked from the pulpit. 'Is this statue, dedicated on our holy day, any better than a return to the ways of old? Those responsible for these obscene dances and displays have some serious explaining to do.'

Eudoxia fell into a rage at these words. John's attack on her statue, she felt, was an attempt to turn the people against her. She was furious at this disrespect and began looking for a way to exile the patriarch for good.

'Another synod!' she demanded of Arcadius. 'We must get rid of him properly this time!'

Seeing the plots afoot against him, John was not inclined to play it safe. He knew that the empress was determined to remove him, and he mounted the pulpit on the following Sunday to begin his sermon with fiery words:

'Again Herodias raves, again she is disturbed; watch her dance, as she again desires to receive John's head upon a platter!'

Though nothing was said directly against Eudoxia, most thought the meaning clear enough. Chrysostom, like John the Baptist, was going to be the victim of a woman's malice (see Mk. 6:17–28).

His enemies jumped at the chance, and with Eudoxia back on their side they began arranging for another trial. The old charge, illegal resumption of the bishopric, was again put to service. Christmas was approaching, and Arcadius advised John that he would not attend his services until the bishop cleared his name. John accepted the slight without murmur, but legal proceedings dragged on slowly, and it was not until just before Easter that John was formally deposed and forbidden to minister. Again he humbly obeyed, but when Holy Week came it found him still living in the bishop's residence. The emperor had not yet raised courage to send him into exile again!

'John must go before Easter,' the patriarch's enemies demanded. 'His followers might riot if he is still here but forbidden to minister.'

Arcadius was finally prodded into action, but John would go no further without a struggle.

'The care of this city is my calling from God. I have been put here for the people, not for you. Push me out by force if you wish, but I cannot desert my flock.'

At the last minute, on Good Friday, John's supporters made a solemn appeal to Arcadius and Eudoxia.

'Restore the bishop! Do not risk bloodshed in this holiest of seasons!'

But there was no answer.

On Saturday night Saint Sophia was filled with people. The Easter vigil was an awesome occasion. It was a traditional time for the baptism of new believers, and thousands of catechumens, converts under the ministry of John Chrysostom, eagerly awaited the seal of their spiritual rebirth. The occasion was slightly dampened because John himself could not be there, but there was still great joy and celebration.

Suddenly terrible screams resounded through the great cathedral. The ministers performing baptism stopped in shock, and the catechumens and their friends fled in horror.

'Soldiers!'

John's enemies, determined to prevent any uprising, had sent a large force to expel John's supporters from the cathedral. Deacons and presbyters were struck to the ground, young catechumens were knocked down and trampled, and many believers fled to their homes in dismay.

'Fear not!' some of John's supporters cried. 'They will not defeat us!'

Some ministers began running through the crowd, inside the church and on the street, calming the panicked flock.

'Let them have the cathedral! We shall finish the baptisms at the public bathing house.'

Soon the congregation, a little the worse for wear, was reassembled at the Baths of Constantine.

'It may not be a holy place,' said the deacons, 'but God will make holy any place where there are hearts which call on Him.'

John's enemies were enraged by this display of patience.

'Leave the baths immediately!'

The command was ignored, so again the soldiers were sent into action.

'Crush them!'

The soldiers struck at about three o'clock in the morning.

Most of the congregation was sent fleeing into the night, many still in their baptismal gowns, while the ministers were beaten and arrested. Young and old, men and women were assaulted, and the baptismal waters could be seen tinged with blood. A persecution had begun.

On Easter Sunday Arcadius, on his usual morning walk, was amazed to see a crowd of men and women, many dressed in only their white baptismal gowns, gathered in a field. In all there were some three thousand of them.

'Who on earth are these people?' he asked his escort.

Arcadius was quite in the dark about the extent of what had happened the night before, and his aides wanted him to stay that way. The crowds, of course, were John's followers, celebrating Easter out of doors now that their enemies held the cathedral.

'They are heretics your majesty,' was the quick response, 'this is how they celebrate Easter.'

'I had no idea there were so many heretics in my city!' said the emperor in dismay.

The followers of John were attacked repeatedly in the weeks ahead. Many suffered torture and prison, but still their courage was unsubdued. John remained in his official residence, and a guard of the faithful constantly defended his door.

'Arcadius,' John's enemies insisted, 'there can never be peace while John remains. Exile him now, and let the guilt be on our heads!'

A messenger was again dispatched to the bishop, and John, knowing that further resistance would only harm his flock, obeyed immediately. It was just after Pentecost.

Word of John's departure spread quickly. Many took to the roads out of a desire to follow their beloved pastor into exile, while others, dreading an imperial crackdown, went into hiding. Normal city life ground to a halt. A terrible fire that raged in the city's centre that night only increased the people's consternation of the city. The fire began in Saint Sophia and spread widely from there.

Persecution against John's followers continued, but John himself retained a great influence in exile. With an incessant stream of letters to his supporters and friends, and support from bishops across the empire, John remained his city's true spiritual head, and his successor Arsacius was scorned as a mere usurper.

A couple of months into John's exile, Constantinople was struck by a freakish hailstorm – and the citizens had few doubts as to its message. Four days later, Empress Eudoxia died in childbirth. This time the signs were ignored, and John's enemies remained implacable. When three years had passed, and John's influence showed no signs of waning, they resolved on even more drastic measures.

'John must be pampered no longer,' they demanded of Arcadius. 'We must prevent his communications with his friends. He must be sent further away, preferably to the grave.'

Arcadius bowed to the demand, and ordered that John be removed to Pityus, the empire's most remote and inhospitable outpost. The bishop's enemies ensured that he never arrived. The soldiers sent to escort him were commanded to make the journey John's last.

'March him at a cracking pace, through storms and blazing heat. He must do the whole distance on foot. Don't allow him a single bath, and give him the poorest food. A man of his age will break down in no time under such conditions.'

The guards obeyed, and for three months John followed the painful road to martyrdom. Never had the words of Jesus, 'take up your cross and follow Me', been so real to him before. On 13 September 407, John and his guards stopped for the night at a church in Pontus that was dedicated to Basiliscus, a martyr under the Diocletian persecution. In a deep sleep John dreamed that Basiliscus came to him.

'Have courage, brother John, for tomorrow we shall be together.'

When morning came, John knew that he was dying.

'Please, let us stay here at the church this morning.'

The guards refused, and they marched the unhappy bishop on his way. But John was soon overpowered by terrible pains in the head, and after only four miles it became obvious that he was dying. The soldiers relented and took him back to the church.

The minister of St Basiliscus pleaded permission to look after the bishop's needs. John was given fresh white garments and received Holy Communion.

'Glory to God for all things,' he softly prayed. 'Amen.'

With his last prayer still sounding, the bishop bowed his head and died. He was buried there at the church, beside the remains of Basiliscus.

Arcadius outlived his victim by only a few months, and dying at the age of thirty he left a seven-year-old to take his throne. It was to be left to this son, Theodosius II, to set things right. Christians across the empire cherished John's memory, and after years of controversy the patriarch's enemies were finally silenced. In 438 John's remains were transported from Pontus to Constantinople, and there interred in their rightful place among the city's bishops. Emperor Theodosius and his sisters accompanied the procession.

'Bishop John,' Emperor Theodosius cried aloud, before resting his head upon the great man's coffin, 'forgive the folly of my parents! Forgive the sin of my family against you!'

Finally there was justice for John Chrysostom, from the city for which he had done and suffered so much.

SOZOMEN, *CH* 8.9 – 9.1; THEODORET, *CH* 5.34–36

Rome's Last Defender

We turn back now to the period just after the death of Theodosius I, and the events more closely associated with the western empire, the realm of Arcadius' younger brother Honorius.

Honorius was little more than ten years old when raised to the throne, and his father had appointed Stilicho, the empire's greatest general, as regent. Son of a barbarian cavalry officer in the army of Emperor Valens, Stilicho had risen to his position from the very humblest beginnings.

Stilicho was stationed in Italy when Theodosius passed away, commanding a mighty army of Romans and barbarians which comprised both the troops Theodosius had brought from the east against Eugenius, as well as the army which had formerly followed Eugenius himself. When news reached Italy that a Visigothic army led by Alaric, a former Roman ally, was devastating a wide area of Greece, Stilicho immediately marched to the defence of the province. But before he could engage the enemy he received most unusual imperial orders:

'Do not enter battle with the Goths,' came word from Arcadius in Constantinople. 'Divide your army, send the eastern troops back to Constantinople, and return to Italy with the western troops immediately.'

The Goths were divided into two main peoples, the Ostrogoths, or eastern Goths, and the Visigoths, or western Goths. They were the first, but far from the last, major barbarian threat to the Roman Empire. Following in their footsteps in the invasion of Rome came many other tribes, the most important of which were the Vandals, Sueves, Huns, Burgundians, Alans, Rugians, Franks, Saxons, Lombards and Arabs.

Was it possible? The combined forces could easily account for the mutinous Visigoths – why would the emperor throw such an opportunity away?

The answer was that it was not the emperor's command at all. Arcadius had given the order under the influence of Rufinus, a former chief adviser to Theodosius. Rufinus resented Stilicho's position in the west, and he was hoping to gain a similar degree of authority over Arcadius in the east. He had recently been thwarted in a plan of marrying his daughter to Arcadius (with Eutropius upsetting the projected match by introducing the young emperor to Eudoxia). And, beaten once in palace politics, Rufinus wanted to ensure that Stilicho did not gain any greater prestige or perhaps permanently establish himself as commander of all military, east and west.

After much hesitation Stilicho decided that he could not disobey Arcadius. He, and his troops, were quite aware of who really lay behind the orders, but Stilicho was eager that his proceedings should carry no appearance of insubordination.

Gainas the Goth led the eastern troops back to Constantinople, Stilicho returned to Italy as commanded, and Alaric, exulting in his escape, went on a rampage of plunder and murder.

The eastern troops were welcomed to Constantinople with a great ceremony. Arcadius and Rufinus saluted the men, and then strolled through the ranks to thank the leaders of the various divisions individually. No one noticed as certain soldiers slowly left their positions, and began to enclose Rufinus in a ring. Rufinus was put off guard by friendly greetings and a stream of questions about the state of affairs at home, about the health of family and friends, until suddenly swords were drawn.

'Stilicho strikes you!' And with that the counsellor fell dead beside the startled emperor.

In the western empire to which Stilicho returned, the tale of the next few years is one of slow decay. By 401 Alaric was bold enough to march into Italy, and Honorius himself was besieged in Milan, a city which had long since replaced Rome as the western imperial residence. Stilicho, already engaged with another invading army, flew to the emperor's rescue, and after a bloody but indecisive battle Alaric withdrew from Italy.

The west was falling, and Honorius knew it. Rather than return to Milan the young emperor retreated to Ravenna, a city which was recommended to him only by the wide marshlands which surrounded it, and which presented a mighty natural barrier to the invasions which he knew would continue. This action of caution, or cowardice, was a sure sign to the barbarians.

'Rome will soon be ours!'

But for a few years more there was still some hope, at least for Italy itself. A stream of invasions and internal rebellions crushed the provinces, but Stilicho preserved the empire's heart from a succession of barbarian assaults, until in 408 the thread that held the empire together snapped. Honorius, now in his twenties, was an even weaker man than his brother Arcadius, and he now fell under the spell of Olympius, a bitter enemy of Stilicho.

'Your majesty, it will not do for you to constantly use Stilicho to fight your battles for you. The people will begin to see him as the true ruler. Beware!'

But Honorius had no other option, no one else to fight his battles – certainly not himself! He hesitated until news of Arcadius' death and the accession of his infant son reached Ravenna.

'Now will be Stilicho's moment!' Olympius warned. 'Though he may not attack you directly, he will certainly dispose of your nephew Theodosius and establish himself on the throne of the east. If you don't move now you will never have another opportunity to stop him.'

The cowardly Honorius was swayed by this advice, and Olympius swung into action. He decreed death for all supporters of Stilicho, and with a band of brutal assassins slaughtered many of the empire's leaders. Honorius was horrified at the bloodbath he had unwittingly caused, and as he hid in the imperial palace and feared for his own safety he received reports by the minute of the carnage being wreaked amongst the military and civil rulers. Finally even Honorius' feeble soul found a streak of courage, and throwing off his imperial robes he rushed into the streets and confronted Olympius' mob.

'Stop the massacre!' he cried. 'I am your emperor!'

For a moment there was a startled pause to the outrage. But only for a moment.

'Death to the supporters of Stilicho!'

The trembling emperor was ignored, and the soldiers finished their dirty work. Even a chief adviser, clinging in tears to the emperor's feet, was struck and killed.

At first only confused reports got through to Stilicho. Thinking that Honorius himself had been killed in an uprising he prepared to march against the guilty soldiers, but when he learned that it was Honorius himself who had commanded the massacre he hesitated. Should he stand against the emperor, who for some reason was obviously now his enemy, or should he again submit to Honorius and accept his fate?

Again Stilicho chose obedience, and leaving his army he

hastened with all speed to Ravenna. Once there, hearing that orders were already given for his arrest, he sought Sanctuary in a church. Soldiers soon arrived from Honorius.

'The emperor does not wish your death,' they promised, showing the fallen general a written pledge from Honorius. 'Come with us and you will be safe.'

Stilicho submitted, and left the safety of the church. Immediately a messenger ran up with a second letter from the emperor, overriding the first.

'Kill him.'

Word of the deceit spread in an instant – the great general still had many friends left even in Ravenna! Soldiers and servants ran to his assistance, and Honorius' men were outnumbered.

'Go!' Stilicho said to his rescuers. 'Leave me to my fate. The emperor has commanded it, and I will obey.'

His friends backed away, and Rome's last defender bowed his head to the axe.

CLAUDIAN, 'AGAINST RUFINUS', 'THE GOTHIC WAR'; ZOSIMUS, *THE NEW HISTORY* 5.1–34

'Greater Love Has No Man'

The long task of destroying the pagan culture of Rome had begun under the reign of Theodosius. The old idol temples now lay silent and neglected, and many pagan ceremonies and festivals were gone.

The ancient pagan games, including the famous Olympic games, were among the pagan festivals to which Theodosius put an end. This may sound harsh to us, accustomed as we are to the modern games, but we should not forget that the ancient games were entirely pagan, and the whole occasion was given to idol worship and perversity. The Olympic games, banned in 393, were the high point of the pagan calendar, the chief festival for the worship of Zeus.

But the bloody entertainment of the amphitheatre remained, and laws limiting the gladiatorial shows had proved largely ineffective. Evidently, if the emperors could not remove the disgrace, someone else must take a stand.

Telemachus was a monk from Asia, a monk with a lofty mission burning in his heart. He knew of the Roman arena, of the cruel scenes that delighted the pagans there, and his mind could not rest while he knew that such wickedness still lived in the world. But what could one man do about it?

Nothing. Not if he stayed in Asia anyway. So with no clear plan in mind, but with the sure knowledge that he had been called by God, Telemachus departed on foot for the western capital. Hundreds, then thousands, of miles he travelled, through heat and cold, wind and rain, alone with his God and his mission.

'Lord, I know not what You plan for me, but I ask only one thing – that You find me not unworthy of this mission.'

It was New Year's Day 404 that Telemachus finally arrived in the city of Rome.

'Lord, I am here. What am I to do?'

Telemachus made his way to the arena, and like everyone else was soon seated inside as the day's entertainment began. The scene can hardly be imagined. The cruel Romans delighted in the sight of bloodshed, but to the most bloodthirsty fiend simple murder can become boring rather quickly. The pagans had developed a variety of means to make death more interesting.

Gladiators with a short sword and full body armour would be pitted against others who were without armour, but provided with a long trident (a three-pointed pitchfork) and a strong net. The crowd would roar with delight as the cumbersome armoured man became trapped in the net, trying to avoid his enemy's trident and get in a blow with his short sword at the same time.

Some of the gladiators were forced to wear bronze helmets with no eyeholes. Two poor souls dressed in such helmets could provide endless amusement to their cruel audience as they swung at each other wildly, dodging blows when none were coming and then being struck totally unawares. It could be a long time before one was finally vanquished by his opponent's random blows. Even women were thrown into the arena to fight before the insane crowd.

'O Lord!' Telemachus cried. 'No!'

The monk watched in helpless exasperation as two young men attacked each other with a savagery that only certain death can provide.

'Lord, bring this horror to an end!'

Unable to sit a moment longer, Telemachus began to push his way through the cheering crowd. A look of grim determination was etched upon his face as he made his way to the lowest tier, oblivious to the shoves and curses that came his way. He sprang over the partition, and a second later was dashing across the arena floor towards the two combatants.

For a few seconds the crowd roared with laughter at the unusual sight, this shabbily dressed foreigner running wildly into the danger zone on the Colosseum floor, but silence fell as Telemachus separated the warriors, stood between them, and addressed them in a powerful voice.

'For the sake of Christ I beg you to show true bravery,' he cried. 'Don't fight like animals to amuse these savages! If you must, offer your neck to the sword of the foe, but do not bring this guilt upon yourselves! Put your trust in the eternal life which Christ offers, and do not fear what men can do to you!'

The weary gladiators stood silent and uncertain. Exhausted and bloody, they listened with full attention to the earnest Christian's words. The crowd also was silenced – but not for long.

'You filthy beast!' Enraged at the interruption of their vile pleasures, the crowd exploded with demonic fury. 'Kill him!' They began to throw stones and whatever rubbish came to hand at the defenceless monk, as he turned his attention to them.

'Only Jesus can set you free!'

With a roar the crowd burst over the barricades, and within seconds they were upon him. The monk soon collapsed beneath their blows.

'Lord forgive them! They know not what they do.'

Telemachus breathed his last, and entered the life that knows no horror, no pain. But what had he achieved? What had God accomplished in sending him across the world to die on the Colosseum floor? The answer was soon revealed.

'Gladiatorial combats are prohibited,' came the imperial order. 'Organizers of such events shall be severely punished.'

Telemachus had not died in vain. News of his death had drawn an immediate and furious response from the Christian population, and their clamour had galvanized the emperor into action. Not a few pagans, brought to their senses by this last victim of the amphitheatre, were converted soon after the fateful day. The chief attraction of the great Roman arena, the Colosseum, was outlawed, and the scene of untold suffering eventually fell into disuse, and was left to slowly crumble. Its remains stand to this day as a reminder of the horrors of the pagan past.

Telemachus' death is commemorated on the first of January. At the beginning of each year we should perhaps spare a thought for all those Christians who have given their lives to give us something much more significant than a new year. They have bought with their blood a new world.

THEODORET, *CH* 5.26

Jerome

In the cities of the decaying empire the call of the monasteries became louder every day. Life was uncertain, and each new day brought new problems to the Roman world. Why cling to possessions that the barbarians might any day be expected to plunder? Why marry and raise children when the future seemed so bleak? One of the period's greatest scholars, Jerome, was also one of its leading monks, and his voice resounded in the great cities of the empire.

'Escape the coming wrath! Abandon the riches of this world, riches that are vanishing as we speak, and set your sights on the riches of the world to come!'

Many of the empire's leading men and women responded to

the call, and they gave their riches to the poor and entered into the monastic life.

Jerome himself was the son of a wealthy Christian family. He had studied in Rome as a young man, and read widely in classical Roman literature, but at the time of his baptism he had determined to leave pagan literature behind and dedicate himself wholly to the work of the church. Scripture, not the pagan thinkers, would fill his leisure hours.

These were his first intentions, but as time went by Jerome found himself frequently returning to his former favourites. He was experimenting with the life of a monk, but even in times of fasting and prayer found himself unable to put down the comedies of the pagan Plautus and the philosophical works of Cicero.

While visiting Antioch in early 374 Jerome was bedridden with a fever. The season of Lent arrived, and in spite of his poor health and the cautions of friends, Jerome insisted on observing the fast.

Lent is a time of fasting prior to Easter. In different times and places it has been observed in different ways, with the period of the fast lasting from seven to 40 days. The 40-day Lent, commemorating Christ's 40 days in the desert, is the most common.

Lent, of course, is not a complete fast for 40 days, and most people who observe Lent only abstain from certain foods, usually sweets and meat. Some eat less than usual and spend several days in total fasting. The 40 days of hardship before Easter, culminating in the remembrance of the crucifixion on Good Friday, help us appreciate the wonderful celebration (and feasting!) of Easter Sunday, the joy of Christ's resurrection, all the more.

Lent begins 46 days before Easter Sunday, on Ash Wednesday. The six extra days are Sundays, as by an ancient tradition Christians have avoided fasting on Sundays. Ash Wednesday gets its name from a practice of the ancient church. The beginning of Lent was the day on which Christians under temporary excommunication were readmitted to the congregation. They would attend church in 'sackcloth and ashes', hence Ash Wednesday.

Fasting makes us uncomfortable. We feel different in both mind and body, and the persistent sense of being in an altered state can serve to sharpen our attention. A true fast is a time to commune with God and study His word. Our thoughts often wander when we are meant to be praying or studying the Bible, but fasting can be used as a tool to limit the mind's meandering. It is a spiritual discipline which most great servants of God, both in the Bible and in later times, have used to grow in commitment to God.

Jerome, however, spent his Pharisaical fast in reading his favourite pagan authors, for even on his sick bed he could not keep himself amused without such books. Fasting when good food and rest were more in order, Jerome slowly wasted away, until one day, still holding Cicero in his weakened hands, he fell unconscious. A thundering voice filled his mind.

'Who and what are you?'

Looking up, Jerome was nearly blinded, as on a glorious throne before him he saw the Judge of all the world surrounded by radiant angels. In terror he threw himself to the ground.

'I am Jerome, a Christian.'

There was a terrible pause.

'You lie. You are a follower of Cicero, not of Christ!'

The strokes of a lash began falling across his back and shoulders, and Jerome cried out in agony. In his disordered state of mind he felt horrible pain throughout his body.

'Have mercy on me, Lord! Have mercy on me!'

The lashes stopped, and Jerome made a solemn pledge:

'Lord, I abandon worldly books. As truly as I love You I shall reject my old ways!'

At this Jerome awoke – he had been delirious for a long time. His pulse had almost stopped, and his friends had already begun making arrangements for his funeral. They were amazed when he was suddenly entirely himself, and even more so when he shared his story. Tears flowed freely as he confessed his guilt, and for days he felt the pains of the lash in his flesh.

'From that day forth,' he wrote to a friend, 'I have read the Bible with more pleasure than I used to get from the pagan authors.'

For the next five years Jerome lived as a monk in the desert to the east of Antioch. He devoted himself to exploring Scripture and sought purity of spirit through the practice of asceticism. He found, however, that no extreme of self-affliction could make him proof against unwanted thoughts. The loneliest caves and valleys were no barrier to memories of the city (particularly the young Roman damsels), and in an effort to tame and occupy his roving mind he undertook the arduous task of learning Hebrew from a Jewish convert to Christianity. In this odd fashion he made an acquisition exceedingly rare in the church of his time.

Returning to Antioch in 379 Jerome was ordained presbyter, and afterwards spent time in Constantinople under the early ministry of Gregory Nazianzen. He was in Constantinople during the Second Ecumenical Council, before he finally returned to Rome in 382. Here he became acquainted with Bishop Damasus, to whom he shortly became an adviser on theological subjects. The Roman bishop was greatly impressed by Jerome's scholarship, particularly his fluency in Old Testament Hebrew. It seemed providence had sent Italy just the man she needed.

Hebrew is the original language of the Old Testament, while Greek is that of the New Testament. There had been a Greek translation of the OT, the Septuagint, since before Christ's birth, and thus the Greek church had always had access to the whole Scripture. This had been adequate at first, as the early converts to Christianity were mostly Greek speakers, but as the church reached out to more and more non-Greeks it became obvious that translation into other languages was essential.

Latin was the other main language of the Roman Empire – as a rule Greek was the language of the east, Latin of the west. Over the years the Bible had, book by book, been translated into Latin, but the result was far from satisfactory.

The translations were not all of a high standard, and later scribes had felt free to make corrections in their copies. Added to this was the perennial problem of misprint in ancient handmade books, so by the late fourth century we find the manuscripts of the Latin Bible hopelessly confused. From one town to the next there could be thousands of differences in the copies of Scripture in use.

Bishop Damasus urged Jerome to employ his skills in a careful revision of the old Latin version, to prepare a new standard text by comparing the best Latin manuscripts with the Greek, and to make whatever corrections were necessary. Jerome embraced the charge, and in the course of two years produced revisions first of the Gospels, then of the remainder of the New Testament, and later the Psalms.

With the death of Damasus in 384 Jerome departed for Bethlehem, and the work was abandoned. The scholarly monk, however, could not altogether banish the project from his mind. His partial revision had awakened many Latin speakers to the inadequacies of their Bible, and the pleas of friends eventually pushed him into embarking on a complete, and radical, revision of the whole Scripture.

Jerome's understanding of Scripture had matured greatly by the time he began his OT translation in 391. The original Latin Bible had been wholly translated from the Greek, as it was believed that the Septuagint was divinely inspired and that there was thus no need to consult the Hebrew original. In the preface to his revision of the Gospels Jerome expressed his agreement with this position, affirming the traditional view that all translation and revision should be made from the Greek. It was the received wisdom, and since there were few Christians skilled in Hebrew it was but rarely tested – few, even if so inclined, could compare the Hebrew and Greek.

With the passing of years, however, Jerome came to a new understanding of the relation of the Greek and Hebrew texts. His knowledge of Hebrew convinced him that some difficulties with the Septuagint text could best be explained as the result of poor translation from the Hebrew original, and he was forced to conclude that the Greek translation was not authoritative. Jewish tradition taught that the Septuagint (literally 'the Seventy') had been translated for the King of Egypt in the early third century BC. Seventy-two Jewish scholars had been sent to Alexandria for the purpose, and to test the accuracy of their work the king had housed each of the men separately and forbidden all intercourse between them. Rather than the 72 working together, each was to make a complete translation of his own. When the work was finished, so the story goes, the 72 copies were found to be absolutely identical. How could anyone doubt that the translation was divine, indeed infallible?

Jerome, forced by the inaccuracies he noted, now rejected this story as a myth. He perceived that translation was necessarily a flawed business, as the words of no two languages completely agree in meaning, and that there is always some blurring and loss of precision. He concluded that it was bad scholarship to make a translation from a translation, since to do so would necessarily increase the 'static' obscuring the original meanings. Earlier translations can be a guide, but they cannot be completely relied on.

Even more controversial was Jerome's devaluation of the books of the Apocrypha. These works, Jewish writings from the period between the two testaments, were included in the Greek Septuagint, but not in the Hebrew Bible. They had found acceptance amongst only a minority of Greek-speaking Jews, not the Jewish mainstream, and Jerome concluded that they were not to be treated as Scripture. They were instructive and useful, but not authoritative.

Jerome's first volume of OT translation was introduced by what he playfully called a 'helmeted preface', a defence against those who objected to any change in the traditional text and preferred the old and familiar to the accurate. Jerome urged those who objected to his translation to consult an expert in Hebrew, indeed any scholarly Jew, on the passages with which they disagreed.

By 405 Jerome's translation, the Vulgate, or 'book for the people', was complete. His skill in Hebrew and Greek, and his extreme lucidity and polish as a Latin author (an ability in some measure the product of his years of reading the best pagan authors – for even this now paid off in God's own time), ensured that his work eventually won over the whole Latin church, and in time replaced its inaccurate forbears. All things considered it would be hard to give the Vulgate any but the first rank in the long history of Bible translations; as we shall see, for more than a thousand years it was to be the scriptural nurture of most of the Christian world!

This longevity would have shocked Jerome himself, for like many others in his time he thought that the fall of Rome, fast approaching, heralded the end of the world itself. A world without Rome, a world ruled by the barbarians, was almost unthinkable, and Jerome's letters paint a grim picture of invasion, slaughter and chaos.

As the empire collapsed the conditions of life for its citizens became daily worse. Taxes had been heavy enough in earlier times, but now that a great deal of territory had been devastated or altogether lost those areas that survived were often forced to make up the difference. After the tax collectors had taken their portion there was little left to plunder! It was such conditions that spurred Jerome on in the other great work of his life, the spreading of monasticism. But while for the Vulgate he will ever be remembered with gratitude, his work here is much more open to criticism. It shows Jerome at his most energetic and passionate, but also at his most severe and hot-tempered. He could be a harsh man, and any who disagreed with him were in danger of a lashing from his pen.

While resident in Rome Jerome inspired many members of the greatest aristocratic families, the descendants of the generals and statesmen who had won the empire, to abandon their worldly wealth and pursue the monastic ideal of celibate, ascetic, holiness. In a grandly bizarre spectacle, some of the proudest Roman mansions were voluntarily stripped of their furniture and finery, and the halls which had once seen merriment and feasting on the largest scale now resounded at all hours with cries of praise. Most of the noble converts were ladies, often widows, and Jerome became spiritual mentor to their households. Some urged Jerome to teach them Hebrew that they too might sing the Psalms in the tongue of David, and this zealous school provided Jerome with critics and counsellors as he completed what might otherwise have been the lonely task of biblical revision and translation.

Not everyone looked favourably upon this burgeoning

movement. The pagan aristocrats of course viewed it with contempt, but there were not a few Christian ministers who viewed the ascetic extreme with more than a little wariness. Jerome responded to such critics with scorn, and he soon won himself many enemies.

When he left Rome after Damasus' death, several noble converts followed him to his monastic community in Bethlehem. His captivating writings were an open invitation, an exhortation, to the whole Roman world to embrace the same life. In his zeal for the cause Jerome was clearly guilty of neglecting the precept of the Apostle Paul – that marriage was for some and celibacy for others – as he began to treat with derision all who differed from his monastic view of holiness.

> Jerome's witty denunciations of certain unworthy Roman priests added to his unpopularity in some circles, though his barbs here were not unfounded. His letters paint a vivid picture of foppish young Roman ministers, dressed as finely as bridegrooms, sleeves soaked in perfume, begging their wealthy female parishioners for fine household items and spending long hours by the sickbeds of the rich, and with cunning speech securing themselves inheritances! By example and admonition Jerome worked to reform such evils, but he was usually more zealous than prudent, and his biting satire alienated many.

Such one-sided teaching could not go unquestioned (of particular concern was the new practice of vowing a daughter to perpetual virginity, and training her from infancy – regardless of her own inclinations – as a monastic). An Italian named Jovinian, himself a monk, became a vocal critic of the rage for monasticism. Ascetic celibacy, he urged, was not to be promoted as a superior state to charitable and chaste Christian family life.

'On account of the present troubles I myself have not married,' he said, 'but let no one jump from that to the assertion that there is therefore something intrinsically wrong with marriage. Let us not add man-made rules to the teaching of Christ.'

Many who had been inspired by Jerome to take up

monasticism were halted by Jovinian, and on due reconsideration returned to normal life. Such opposition made Jerome even more hard-headed, and he wrote a contemptuous work against Jovinian in which he so bluntly criticized marriage that even his dearest monkish friends could not agree with him.

A little more than a decade later (AD 406), a Gallic minister named Vigilantius wrote a work expressive of similar reservations on monasticism, after an extended stay with Jerome in Bethlehem. Jerome responded with *Against Vigilantius*, a highly personal, indeed scurrilous (Vigilantius' father had been an innkeeper – 'you seem to fear,' says Jerome, 'a drop in profits should sobriety and fasting take root in Gaul'), attack which made even his writings against Jovinian seem polite by comparison. Rightly or wrongly, Jerome saw himself as a man with a mission, a man with a vital message for his times, and his pen was a sword to any who stood in his way.

JEROME, WORKS

The First Sack of Rome

In the year 408 the fate of Italy was sealed. Stilicho, the last man who stood between Rome and disaster, was gone, and Olympius himself now openly controlled the weak Honorius.

The barbarian allies of Rome were dismayed at the assassination of their worthy leader. They knew that Stilicho had been unpopular with many Romans on account of his barbarian birth, and they felt his death as a personal insult to each of them. Revenge, however, was unthinkable, for many of them had wives and children lodged in the major cities of Italy, and they could not revolt without putting their families and property in danger. Some Romans, however, were determined to make revenge not only possible, but inevitable.

'Death to the barbarians!'

Shortly after the attack upon Stilicho's supporters the families of the barbarian allies became targets, and in an appalling act of treacherous murder Roman soldiers vented their hatred on these defenceless victims. Nothing could be more foolish, for in furious grief for their wives and children the barbarian allies abandoned the empire and joined the camp of Alaric, who with these timely reinforcements marched on Rome itself.

The Romans waited in vain for Honorius to come to their defence, and the Goths soon established a complete blockade of the city. Months dragged by, and food became very scarce in Rome. Some wealthy Christians became renowned for their care of the poor, but there was still not enough to go around. When winter came many citizens starved to death, and an embassy was sent to bargain with the Goths.

'What would you have from us?' they asked. 'Name your price for ending the siege, and dare not force the city of Rome, the city which has conquered the whole world, to fight for its freedom.'

Alaric laughed out loud at this threat from the powerless Romans.

'Here's my price! All your gold, all your silver, all your movable possessions and all your slaves!'

'What then will be left to us?' asked the startled ambassadors.

'Your lives!' said the grim barbarian.

News of the failure filled the city with despair. There was nothing to be done except to send a new embassy and hope to flatter the king into easier terms.

The second embassy had more success. Alaric was impatient to get his hands on Rome's riches, and the ancient city's defences were proving a frustrating obstacle. He finally agreed to a ransom of five thousand pounds of gold, thirty thousand of silver, and great weights of fine cloth and spices.

The siege was over, and Rome breathed easy for the moment. But it was not to last, for Honorius and his advisers continued to insult and infuriate these powerful strangers on Italian soil, and in 409 Alaric again threatened Rome, before he finally moved in for the kill in the summer of 410.

The Romans barely had a chance to defend themselves. When the Goths began a third siege the slaves of the Roman aristocrats abandoned their masters, and in the dead of night they attacked the guards of one of the city's major gates. The Goths were invited in, and Rome awoke to the sound of barbarian trumpets in her streets.

The scene of devastation and plunder that followed was unimaginable. For more than seven centuries Rome had not been captured by an enemy, and in those centuries she had conquered the world and stored the wealth of nations within her walls. Now, in a mere three days, she was stripped of her worldly goods, and thousands of her citizens perished. A great calamity to be sure – and yet there was something different, something altogether new, about this war.

The rules of war had stood unshaken for thousands of years, and Rome herself had always followed them in her spreading conquests. They were as simple as this: no conquered enemy is safe.

Alaric, however, and most of his soldiers, were converts to Christianity. Many had simply followed their leaders and knew little of the new beliefs, indeed most called themselves Arians, but however that might be Alaric knew enough of the gospel to perform an act for which he will ever be remembered – an act which changed the rules of war as they had stood throughout time.

'We must preserve the right of Sanctuary,' he ordered. 'The conquered city is yours to plunder. Kill those who stand in your way, but all who seek safety in the churches must be spared. Do not dare draw your swords against the houses of God!'

And so it was. Even gold and silver cups and plates which belonged to the churches were considered sacred, and the churches were filled to bursting with Christians and pagans alike, all seeking shelter under the power of the new faith. Rome might well fall, but the conversion of the barbarians would soften that fall. Can a scene more richly symbolic be imagined than that of these Roman pagans staring from the safety of the cathedral on the ruin of the world outside!

Jerome had been partly vindicated, and his call to the desert had preserved many Romans from this scene of ruin. Those who had once scoffed at the converts to monasticism, who had abused them and thought them fools, now lost their property to the barbarians, and many lost their lives as well. In poverty many now took the advice of the monks, and without a penny to their names they escaped the ruined city to seek out the communities of Jerome and others like him. Numberless aristocrats wandered the length and breadth of the empire in rags, desperately trying to find a new life for themselves.

The fame of a nun named Melania began to spread at this time. She had been born into a leading Roman aristocratic family, but widowed at the age of twenty-two she had abandoned the great city. Putting her two sons into the care of others, she had travelled to Jerusalem to begin a monastery. There she had embraced a ministry of caring for the sick and tending to the needs of prisoners, until 37 years later she felt a pull on her heart and returned to Rome to visit her family once more.

Melania first looked up her niece Avita, whom she found joined in marriage to a pagan named Apronianus. She then proceeded to search out her sons and grandchildren, and gathering the whole family together she made an impassioned plea, begging one and all to abandon their worldly goods and seek Christ alone. When word of her return spread, however, Melania received bitter abuse from the city's upper class.

'You're not going to listen to your cranky old mother are you?' they scoffed, and at first her relatives were quite ashamed of her.

But Melania was not to be put off. Through her preaching Apronianus was converted to the gospel, and this proved a decisive step.

'Little children,' said Melania, 'it was written four hundred years ago that the last hour was come (1 John 2:18). Why do you still cling to the falling world? The days of antichrist might surprise you, and you will lose in an instant all that you cling to now.'

Over several months, like a hen gathering chicks, Melania convinced all of her family to embrace monasticism and follow her back to Jerusalem. With this accomplished, only 40 days after their arrival in the holy city, the old woman died.

Now the wealthy Romans looked back in anguish upon these recent events. The warnings of Melania had proved true, but her family alone had listened and been saved by them.

ZOSIMUS, *HISTORY* 5.35 – 6.13; OROSIUS, *SEVEN BOOKS AGAINST THE PAGANS* 7.39; PALLADIUS, *LAUSIAC* 46, 54

Just Deserts

For a moment we take leave of the troubled west.

The Macedonians were a heretical sect of the eastern empire, one of several spawned during the Arian troubles. They have been called semi-Arians, since they believed that the Son was eternal but that the Spirit was not, while Arians held neither Son nor Spirit to be eternal. In Synada, a city of Phrygia in Asia Minor, a bishop named Agapetus led a sizeable Macedonian congregation.

Theodosius was bishop of the mainstream church in Synada. Unfortunately for his city, he was a far worse man than his Macedonian rival.

A greedy and hard-hearted man, Theodosius constantly stirred up trouble for the Macedonians, and in the words of the contemporary church historian Socrates Scholasticus: 'he did so not from any precedent in the church, nor through any desire of converting them, but rather because he was enslaved by the love of gold and was ever on the look out for means of extorting money'.

Theodosius used the courts to harass his opponents – Agapetus in particular – but finding by experiment that the law did not support the sort of persecution he longed for, the vicious shepherd visited Constantinople to petition for special authority to deal with heresy. In his absence Agapetus called an emergency assembly of his people. His address was far from what might have been expected.

'We are clinging to dead beliefs,' he began. 'The Arian fight is over, the Arians are defeated, and we alone are holding onto this idea that the Spirit is not equal to the Father and the Son. I feel that we are being punished for our stubbornness. I think we have gravely erred in our teaching.'

'No!' someone argued. 'This trouble is not from God, it is the godless Theodosius who is behind our sorrows. Don't give in to him!'

Agapetus shook his head firmly.

'I am not giving in to him,' he said. 'No doubt Theodosius is wicked, but in my heart I feel that God is using him to teach us a lesson. He is not innocent, but neither are we.'

There was a small murmur, of agreement, and Agapetus continued.

'Here is my opinion. I will lay it down as bluntly as I can, and I want you to give me your verdict.' Tears filled the bishop's eyes as he continued, 'I say we rejoin the mainstream church immediately.'

A long debate followed. Agapetus had carefully studied the questions involved before making this bold move, and he was able to point out the arguments of Scripture against the Macedonian belief. A few hours later, none was as surprised as Agapetus himself to find that the whole assembly had been brought into agreement.

'Then my friends,' he declared, 'there is no time to waste!'

Agapetus immediately led his followers to Theodosius' church, where the orthodox congregation was already gathered for prayer. Silence reigned as these strange visitors entered.

'What do you want of us?'

'I'm sure that I need not introduce myself,' Agapetus began, 'for we all know what has been happening lately. I will cut a long story short. My friends and I are here to beg your forgiveness. As bishop of the Macedonians I beg you to receive myself and my people into your congregation. Let there be no more bitterness between us.'

For a moment there was stunned silence, followed by a great roar of approval. The Macedonians were embraced by their new brothers and sisters, and there was joy in the whole assembly.

'We need your forgiveness also,' some said. 'None of us has been happy with Theodosius' proceedings.'

Soon there was a murmur passing amongst the original congregation.

'What about Agapetus?'

'A true man of peace.'

'And Theodosius is away!'

Within moments Agapetus was seated in the bishop's chair.

'You must be bishop of the reunited congregation!'

Theodosius meanwhile had enjoyed a resounding success in Constantinople, and armed with authority to punish the Macedonians he now returned to the city. Entering his church and lodgings, however, he was astounded to find Agapetus already in residence, and unanimously ejected he fled back to the capital in confusion.

'You would not believe it!' he told Atticus, Bishop of Constantinople. 'In my absence the church has united with the Macedonians, and Agapetus has been instated in my place!'

Atticus was shrewd enough to guess for himself what had happened. He had had his doubts about Theodosius, and this amazing revolution only confirmed them.

'Sorry, my friend!' he said. 'There is little I can do. I think you will have to get used to retirement – if that is your people's wish you should heed it.'

Atticus promptly wrote to Agapetus:

'I concur in the decision of the people to install you as bishop, and pray that God may bless your labours. Be under no fear of Theodosius. I have bid him retire gracefully. Rest assured that he will not bother you again.'

SOCRATES, *CH* 7.3

Augustine

After his dramatic conversion and the death of his mother, Augustine returned to his North African homeland. There he was ordained a presbyter, and in 395 he became bishop of the city of Hippo. It was a time of great trouble in the North African church, and no position could be more daunting than that of bishop in such a place.

One problem was the continuing growth of Manichaeism,

which Augustine himself had followed in his youth. Its tangle of false philosophy appealed to educated young minds, and there was a crying need for experienced and informed Christians to tackle the heresy head-on. Few were better fitted for such a task than Augustine himself, who knew the heretical beliefs more thoroughly than most Manichaeans. Having once given his life to them and discovered their emptiness and deceit in the hardest possible way, Augustine was well able to encourage and guide others trapped in Mani's web.

As a theologian and philosopher Augustine was a formidable opponent of Manichaeism, but in the work of God there is something more important than bookish wisdom. God's servants need an ear for His Spirit, and in this the new bishop particularly excelled. One evening Augustine was seated at dinner with friends.

'Did you notice,' he said, 'that I suddenly switched topics in my sermon today, and didn't at all finish what I had begun.'

'We couldn't fail to notice,' said one. 'In fact I was most surprised, for it didn't seem at all up to your usual standard.'

'Quite true,' said the bishop, 'but I believe that it must have been the Lord's doing. My life and ministry are in His hands, and I feel that there was someone present for whom God had a special message. I was preaching happily enough on the topic I had planned, but I became confused halfway and ended up wandering off into an argument against Manichaeism. I hadn't planned to mention anything of the sort!'

The next day Augustine was with these same friends when a merchant named Firmus approached and introduced himself. He fell on his knees before the bishop and began to weep.

'Pray to the Lord for me!'

Firmus explained that he had been a Manichaean for many years, but when he arrived in town the previous day he had wandered into Augustine's church on the spur of the moment.

'My heart melted at your words,' he said. 'Suddenly you began speaking as though your message was for me alone!'

The bishop's friends were silent as they reflected on the strange sermon of the previous day.

'Would that I preached only nonsense,' said Augustine, 'if a soul was saved every time!'

But Manichaeism was only the beginning. The other major problem of North Africa was not so easily attended to.

The church in North Africa had actually been split in two since the time of Constantine. It was then that the Donatists had appeared – a group that argued that the church needed to be stricter, and less willing to forgive Christians guilty of sin. The early Donatists had appealed to the emperor, hoping he would force the church to adopt their ideas, but when their appeal backfired, and they saw their proposals rejected by Constantine and Christians throughout the empire, they broke away from the mainstream church and asserted that they were the only true Christians.

> Heresy and schism are the two types of 'split' that can occur in the church. Put simply, a heretic opposes basic Christian beliefs, while a schismatic differs from the mainstream on a less vital issue.
>
> Arianism, for example, was a heresy, as Arius attacked fundamental Christian beliefs, and in such a case we can call the two sides Christians and Arians. In the case of a schism such as Donatism, however, it would be unfair to call the two sides Christians and Donatists. That would imply that Donatists were not Christians, which is not necessarily the case. Donatists held to most Christian beliefs, but differed in that they were stricter than the mainstream church. We should rather call it trouble between the mainstream church (or 'Catholic Church') and the Donatists.
>
> Words like catholic and orthodox, since they are in the names of some modern denominations, are often misunderstood. Catholic means 'universal', and originally only indicated that one agreed with the universal church – that is, that one was in communion with church leaders throughout the empire rather than a breakaway local group. Orthodox means 'right belief', or someone not guilty of heresy.

Constantine's first reaction was to outlaw the schismatics, but confronted with stubborn resistance he retreated to a policy of toleration. His son Constans repeated the attempt to forcibly end the schism, but succeeded only in exacerbating the contention. Imperial oppression gave rise to the Circumcellions, a group of Donatist extremists who dedicated themselves to terrorism and violence, and who were frequently responsible for the kidnap and torture or murder of Catholic ministers. A favourite barbarity was to ambush their foes and spray a blinding potion of lime and vinegar in their eyes.

Few had angered the Circumcellions as Augustine did. The great bishop was constantly ministering to the Donatists, and his words led many back to the church. Some Donatists living in and around Hippo took copies of his sermons and other writings to their own bishops, and when they saw that their leaders were unable to counter Augustine's criticisms they left the sect. Confronted with this, some Donatist ministers began to preach sheer malice:

'To defend the flock, the wolf must die! The man who should perform such a noble work could be assured of forgiveness for all sins!'

As even the Circumcellions began slipping back into the mainstream church, the remaining terrorists were spurred to even greater violence. When Augustine himself went on a preaching tour of some smaller towns, the Circumcellions laid an ambush on the highway.

'He is ours!'

On the fateful day Augustine employed a local guide to conduct him. This poor fellow, though he knew the road well, managed to become quite lost on the way, and after many winding detours brought the bishop and his companions into town on a little used track.

'I'm sorry we are here so late,' the blushing guide apologized. 'I swear it has never happened before. I don't know how I got lost, I walk this path every few weeks!'

But the truth of the situation came to light the next morning. A young man who had walked into town on the *right* road had seen the Circumcellion ambush.

'If you had taken the highway they would have had you for sure!'

Maximian, another North African bishop, was not so fortunate as his colleague. The Circumcellions attacked him in his own church, smashed the altar, and beat him ferociously

with its broken timber. He was dragged unconscious to the top
of a church tower and thrown down in full view of his people.

'Praise to God!' the Circumcellions cried.

A Christian farmer and his wife rescued the bishop's body
before the savages could do anything else to it, and were already
preparing it for burial when they realized that the poor man was
still breathing! The couple tended to his wounds, and some
months later the scarred bishop was able to make the voyage to
Italy. There he laid his complaints before the emperor, and
urged him to crack down on the Donatists.

Augustine also came to believe that the government should
move against the Donatists. In the early years of his ministry he
had taught that government should stay out of spiritual matters,
but the rising violence had forced him to reconsider.

'A religion which preaches senseless violence, and whose
followers walk the streets carrying clubs, must be stopped.'

From the emperor's hand came new laws that greatly
weakened the sect, but even after this defeat a smaller group of
Donatists lived on. It was to be another two centuries before the
schism completely disappeared.

Such was Donatism. Later in Augustine's life new problems
arose, and each called responses from his pen. The first was
Pelagianism. Pelagius was a British monk, teacher of a new
heresy.

'Man does not need the grace of God to be holy. God has
commanded us to be holy – why would He command something
that we cannot of ourselves achieve? We become holy through
sheer hard work.'

Augustine knew from experience the impossibility of holiness
without grace. He and his Manichaean friends had fruitlessly
chased sanctity for years, remaining slaves to sin until Jesus
entered their lives and changed their hearts. Pelagius' ideas,
however, were pleasing to many monks. If holiness was not a
gift from God, but something one worked hard to achieve, it
was something of which to be proud. According to Pelagius a
holy person (and who was holier than a monk?) had great
reason to commend himself.

Not so, said Augustine, for even the Apostle Paul had called himself the chief of sinners. He had been well aware that it was God who changed the heart and helped people to live according to the divine plan. No one should claim to have reformed him or herself – the praise is God's alone.

Some of Pelagius' ideas were convincing on first hearing – on the surface at least they seemed an incentive to godliness, and a rebuke to those who excused their sins with 'I can't help it, I'm only human'. But as the overall tendency of his thinking became clearer, alarm bells rang across the empire. Added to his insistence that man could be holy without grace were other equally unbiblical notions. Pelagius flatly denied any notion of original sin, and taught that children did not inherit a fallen nature from their parents. Adam had been created mortal, and would have died whether he sinned or not. The human race, he said, was not fallen in Adam, and the world was not in need of a Saviour. He added that it was possible to live entirely without sin, and that there had been many perfect and sinless saints.

Pelagius, and his disciple Celestius, travelled widely, and their teachings created contention in several cities. When Pelagius visited Palestine, Jerome's pen attacked his teaching with its customary vigour, and the heretic's followers responded by burning down the old man's (he was well over seventy, and only three years from his death) monastery, and beating its inhabitants.

Wherever it gained ground Pelagianism led to the calling of synods, and depending on the quality of the local opposition, and the rank of those who favoured Pelagius, the victory swayed between the parties. Africa was against him, Palestine for him, Rome wavered, but it was ultimately the influence of Augustine that put the matter to rest. When questioned in synod Pelagius and Celestius were guilty of great duplicity, and were prepared to mislead the bishops for the benefit of their system, but Augustine discovered their inconsistencies and equivocations with an unerring eye, and his writings on the subject exposed the fatal flaws of their teaching. Not content with the mere negative task of exposing Pelagianism, however, Augustine was the first theologian to explore at length the ideas of grace, election, original sin and free will, and to construct a system taking all of these into account – a majestic theological assessment of the state of humankind. Not all of his ideas have been embraced by the church at large, but his anti-Pelagian writings (indeed all of his writings) contain countless profound insights which have fired other Christian thinkers for more than one and a half millennia.

> The influence of Augustine's writings is such that the North African bishop can probably claim the very highest place among theologians, and no author outside the pages of Scripture has been so widely respected and quoted. His significance is due both to his personal genius and to the fact that the main problems of his era are among the most important the church has faced. It is hard to conceive more vital issues than Manichaeism, Donatism and Pelagianism – denials of creation, forgiveness, and grace respectively.

The other great problem of Augustine's later years was quite different – the gradual barbarian conquest of the Roman world. In the wake of Alaric's sack of Rome many pagans began pointing the finger at the church.

'None of this would have happened if Rome still bowed to her ancestral gods!'

The *City of God*, widely considered the greatest writing of the early church, is Augustine's response to this charge – it has justly been called a grand funeral oration upon the old Roman world, the triumphant last word in the warfare of Christianity and Roman paganism. The massive work of 22 books begins with a review of Roman history, showing that the city had been no stranger to calamities throughout its pagan past, and proving that none of the pagan religious systems has been capable of guaranteeing either happiness in this world, or salvation for the world to come. He puts the spotlight on the absurdities and corruptions of pagan belief, and shows that Rome's sin and wickedness are the direct result of her corrupt worship, and the direct cause of her plight. Such is the argument of the first ten books, but moving on from there Augustine proceeds to develop a message of hope – a message still relevant today.

'We should not expect any earthly city or empire to last forever, to give us that eternal peace and rest which our souls long for. There is only one city that endures, and that is the City of God. In this world it is an invisible city of the soul – a life near to God in the midst of turmoil. From the beginning it has been that way. Abel was a citizen of God's city, but Cain of the city of the world. Today we everywhere find Cain mixed in with Abel, and only at the end of the age shall the two cities separate. One will be named Heaven, the other Hell.'

Augustine was one of the few Christians of his time to look beyond the troubles of falling Rome to a brighter light ahead.

'Why should I care if Rome falls? If the barbarians who conquer are, or become, Christians, all the better. May they not make a new Christian world, one which honours God more than does Rome today?'

Amidst such varied writings and labours, little so strikes us as Augustine's tolerant humility and intellectual honesty. Even in the midst of his bitterest battles with the Pelagians he remained calm and respectful, in this very unlike Jerome. Remembering the words of Christ, that 'men will give an account on judgement day for every careless word' (Mt. 12:36), he spent his last few years painstakingly examining his own writings to ensure he did not leave behind him anything which he could now see was untrue. The two books of his *Retractions* are a confession of his earlier errors.

As to his personal life, in a time when many monks went to extremes with fasting and self-denial, Augustine was respected for wisdom and moderation. His clothing was neither expensive nor plain. It was a saying of his that it is as easy to sin with poor as with rich food: 'Everything must be done in the right spirit. Esau lost his birthright for a bowl of lentils!'

A verse that stood above Augustine's table, a verse which the bishop meant wholeheartedly, expresses well his temper:

Whoever slanders an absent friend
Shall not as guest at this table attend.

The last year of Augustine's life saw North Africa itself overrun by the Vandals, a barbarian tribe who had crossed over from Europe, and in 430, when Augustine was seventy-five, the conquerors reached the walls of Hippo.

'Lord, either free us from the Vandals, strengthen us to endure their victory, or take us from here to be with You!'

God chose the latter course for His bishop. Augustine came down with a fever, and being confined to his bed he spent his days in prayer. He had the seven penitential psalms (Pss. 6, 32, 38, 51, 102, 130, 143) written out and stuck to the wall, and he read them at length and with many tears. But even now the old man's labours were not at an end.

'Bishop Augustine, someone wants to see you.'

A young man was introduced, supporting on his arm a sick relative.

'Bishop, please lay your hands upon my cousin, that he might be healed.'

'If I had such a power,' Augustine replied, 'do you not think I would use it upon myself?'

'Please sir, I had a vision as I slept, and a voice bid me come to you.'

At this Augustine acceded to the request, and the man was immediately restored to health. And so the bishop left this life, even in his last hours doing the works to which he had been called. Nor did they stop then. Through his writings, Augustine guides the church to this day.

POSSIDIUS, *LIFE OF AUGUSTINE*; AUGUSTINE, *WORKS*

Patrick of Ireland

The barbarian invasions caused suffering and chaos throughout the empire, but nowhere was worse affected than the province of Britain.

Britain was doubly open to invasion, with the barbarian Picts of the north making frequent attacks by land from Scotland, and Irish pirates seizing every opportunity to plunder the coastal towns. It was in one such raid that a British teenager named Patrick was captured and enslaved by an Irish sailor. Once again, God was moving in mysterious ways!

Patrick was the son of a Christian family. His father and grandfather were both ministers of the church, but Patrick, in his autobiography, reveals that he was not at all spiritual as a young man:

'I was nearly sixteen when taken captive, but at that time I did not know God. The people of Britain were sinful, we were not obedient to our priests, and because of this God's wrath was upon us. We were attacked and enslaved, scattered among the nations, and I myself became a slave to Miliac, an Irishman. I was sent to tend his flocks in the fields.

'But the Lord took pity on my youth. He opened my heart so that I began to love Him, though previously I had always ignored Him. Every day the fear and love of God grew within my soul, and as I worked in the fields prayer was never far from my lips. By day I would say a hundred prayers, and again by night the same number. When I spent nights on the mountains or in the forests, in the snow, frost and rain, the cold would be forgotten as I stood in the silence alone with my God. His Spirit was a constantly burning fire within me.'

Six years passed as the young man, without Bible or church, without Christian friends or ministers, grew in the knowledge of God through the fellowship of the Spirit alone. Finally the Spirit's gentle breath became a definite call. As Patrick slept in the fields a dream voice comforted him.

'Your fasting has been pleasing to God. Soon you will return to your home.'

Later another dream came, this one even clearer. Patrick saw a ship in a harbour.

'Your ship awaits you,' said the voice. 'You must travel two hundred miles to find it.'

Patrick awoke suddenly, absolutely sure of what to do next.

'That was no dream. It was the voice of God!'

Trusting in the Lord Patrick fled his master, directing his steps to the distant shore. When he finally arrived at the Irish harbour Patrick was not surprised to find the scene, and most importantly the ship, just as he had pictured.

'Might I have a place on board your ship?'

The captain, a gruff old man, turned on Patrick with a scowl.

'I've no place for useless hands,' he said. 'Even less for runaway slaves.'

A guilty tremor passed through Patrick's body, and with heart pounding he turned his back on the harbour.

'Lord,' he murmured, 'why have You brought me here?'

He had already walked a fair distance, his mind a confusion of prayer and disappointment, when a voice boomed out behind him.

'Come back!' It was one of the men from the ship.

'What do you want?'

'The captain wants you. He says he's thought of something you can do. Lucky for you!'

And so it was that Patrick left the land of his slavery.

The ship had a quiet three-day voyage, but upon arrival in Gaul a scene of complete devastation greeted the Irish traders. The townsfolk had fled to the hills during a recent barbarian invasion, and not a soul was to be seen. The crew, determined to deliver their cargo, trekked the province's virtually empty roads for almost a month, but when their food supply finally ran out the captain turned upon the young runaway in despair.

'You have told us that you worship a great God. If that is so pray for us, otherwise we shall all perish.'

'Turn to my God in faith,' Patrick replied. 'He has abundance everywhere, and can satisfy our needs.'

'Show us what to do.'

Patrick began to lead the crew in prayer, and even as he spoke a herd of pigs came crashing out of the woods onto the road in front of him. With a cheer the hungry men rose and chased them, and several large swine were caught and roasted. Soon afterwards one of the men found a supply of wild honey, so for the moment their needs were satisfied.

That night Patrick dreamed again. He felt that Satan rolled a huge rock onto his chest, and overwhelmed with pain he lay paralyzed.

'Elias, Elias!' he cried in his horror.

'I do not know why I used that word,' he later said, 'but when I did, I instantly felt the sun shining upon me, and the stone was gone. It was the Lord who removed the weight from me, and His Spirit who cried out for me.'

It is thought that Patrick's cry has something to do with Christ's cry on the cross: 'Eli, Eli, lama sabachthani' (Mk. 15:34).

Patrick, rejoicing in these proofs of God's care, longed to devote himself wholly to the Lord's service, and once his party had made its way back to civilization his first concern was to commit himself to the instruction of some mature believers. After six years without the Scriptures his hunger for knowledge about God was enormous.

It was a few years later that Patrick finally made it back to his homeland. He enjoyed a brief reunion with his family, but destiny would not allow him to remain in Britain. A new series of dreams began soon after his return.

The mists of sleep parted one night to reveal a man, carrying a great bundle of letters in his hands. Patrick took one, and read the first words aloud:

'The voice of the Irish.'

As he spoke, a great wail rose up. A thick forest lay before him, and from its depths he heard a confusion of Irish tongues:

'Holy youth,' came the cry, 'we pray that you will come and walk amongst us!'

Unable to read further Patrick awoke. Dream followed dream in the nights ahead. Words that the young man could not understand filled his sleeping mind, only to end with the clear statement as he awoke:

'He who gave His life for you, is the One who speaks within you.'

In one dream he saw his own body. It became strangely transparent as he gazed upon it, and within he could see another man, much smaller, who knelt and prayed with mighty groans. When the groans ceased the inner man's appearance changed, until he appeared to be dressed as a bishop. Patrick awoke with the words of Paul ringing in his ears:

'The Spirit helps us in our weakness. We do not know what to pray for, but the Spirit Himself prays for us with groanings which words cannot express' (Rom. 8:26).

Patrick did not return to Ireland at once. He felt within himself that the time was not yet ripe, and from his parents' home he returned to Gaul to study under the leading monks of the time. After a period in Gaul he learned that certain ministers were already organizing a mission to Ireland. Surely the Lord's time for him had come?

'I have spent several years in Ireland,' he told those in charge of the new mission. 'I know the Irish speech, and have travelled a great deal of the island on foot. I know that this is my calling.'

But the mission organizers ignored the suggestion.

'We are looking for men with a high level of education,' they said. 'A mission such as this is not to be entrusted to a rustic.'

This was a crushing blow. What, Patrick asked himself, was God doing with him? A bishop was appointed for Ireland, and the mission party soon departed. In his despair there was only One to whom Patrick could turn.

'Why, Lord?' he asked. 'Have I come all this way to be rejected by You?'

There was no answer for some weeks, until finally a messenger arrived at the sorrowing Patrick's door.

'Bishop Germanus is holding a conference,' he said. 'You must attend.'

Unsure of what this might mean Patrick followed him to the bishop's residence.

'I have been rethinking the decision on your request to go to Ireland,' Germanus, one of the mission organizers, began, 'and I have decided that your local knowledge might indeed be of some benefit to Bishop Palladius. If it is still your wish you may depart for Ireland immediately.'

Patrick had no sooner received this joyous news than he was hastening for the coast, but on the road he met two travellers coming with equal speed in the opposite direction. He recognized them as two of Palladius' assistants.

'The bishop is dead!'

Again his hopes of a speedy departure were dashed, and he returned to Bishop Germanus with the messengers. What did this new problem mean? Was this the end of his own hopes of taking part in the mission?

Far from it. Germanus received the sad news in thoughtful silence.

'You, Patrick,' he finally said, 'you will be the bishop of the Irish.'

And so it was, in the fullness of God's time, that the great mission to the Irish began. Accompanied by the messengers and other assistants, Patrick set sail for the land that had so long been his desire.

The party's first landing on Irish soil was inauspicious. The local villagers gave the missionaries a violent reception, and they were forced to return to their ship and sail further down the coast.

'Pirates!'

A lone shepherd was the first to see Patrick's second landing, and he ran to warn the local chief, Dichu, of the danger.

'Pirates you say? We will see about that.'

Dichu armed himself and gathered his supporters, and he soon caught up with the small and unarmed band of foreigners.

'What do you want here?'

'We come in peace. We have been sent to you by the God of Heaven.'

'Well then,' said Dichu, looking at his supporters in surprise. 'I guess that you may as well stay under my roof.'

The missionaries were treated well, and over the course of a few days they shared the Christian gospel with Dichu and his whole family.

'I too wish to follow your Jesus, and make Him my own,' said Dichu. 'Please give me this baptism of which you speak.'

The foundation was laid! Dichu gave Patrick his barn, and it was here that services were held. More and more families joined the fledgling congregation as Patrick's ministry extended through the region, and the humble barn was eventually converted into Ireland's first regular church.

When nearly a year had passed and the first Easter in Ireland approached, Patrick heard that the leading men of the land gathered at this time for a festival of their own, and he determined to visit their meeting place. He instructed his brethren as to how they should observe Easter, and wishing Dichu and his family farewell he set out for the town of Tara. One prayer burned in his heart beyond all others – that he might have an opportunity to share the gospel with the Irish leaders.

Rather than going right into Tara, Patrick decided to spend Easter in his tent on the nearby plain. He knew that the pagan priests of the Irish, the Druids, would be gathered at Tara, and that he would not be a welcome guest to them.

'Lord, I am here,' he prayed. 'Provide an opportunity to speak with these men!'

With that Patrick lit his fire and knelt beside it. He intended to spend the night awake in prayer. Little did he know what danger this simple action could bring.

'A fire!' cried King Loegaire, the greatest man among the many chiefs, priests, princes and kings gathered at Tara. 'Who has disobeyed me, and held our traditions in contempt?'

The king was seated in his banqueting hall, gazing out into the night. In the distance he could see the small fire in the middle of the plain.

'King Loegaire!' the chief Druid menaced. 'If that fire is not extinguished tonight, it shall burn until doomsday. Unless we stop him immediately the man who has kindled that fire will overthrow all the rulers of this land!'

Poor Patrick did not know that the Tara festival was dedicated to the power of the sun, and that every fire in the kingdom was extinguished by royal command throughout the sacred season. A great bonfire was lit in the idol temple on Tara hill on the main day of the festival, a symbol of approaching summer, and only after its kindling were the pagans again allowed to light their household fires. King Loegaire was terrified by the words of the Druid.

'That shall never happen!' he cried. 'This night shall be our enemy's last!'

The king mounted his chariot, and along with his servants and two Druid priests he swept across the plain towards the unsuspecting bishop.

'King Loegaire,' the chief Druid advised, 'show this man who is master. Don't go to him, but stop at a distance and have him brought before you.'

Loegaire followed the suggestion and commanded his servants to show the lawbreaker no respect.

'Do not even rise when he salutes us.'

The startled Patrick was soon dragged from his devotions and taken before the king. As he approached, a young man named Erc forgot the king's orders and stood to welcome the newcomer. Patrick smiled meekly in his direction. Neither guessed that Erc would later become a Christian bishop.

'Who are you?' the king growled.

'I am Patrick. I come from Britain.'

'Why have you attempted to destroy our festival?'

'I am sorry, but I do not know what you mean. I did not mean to destroy anything.'

The king snorted loudly. 'Why have you come to Ireland?'

'I have been sent here from the great God of Heaven to give a message to the Irish people.'

'Is the message long or short?'

Patrick grinned. 'That depends on whether you want to listen or not.'

King Loegaire looked helplessly towards his Druids, who were scowling angrily at Patrick.

'We shall hear this message,' he decided. 'Begin.'

With a glance upwards, and a silent prayer of thanks, Patrick began to explain the teachings of the Scriptures. He spoke of the coming of Christ, and of His sacrifice and resurrection.

'It was in fact at this time of Easter that these events took place.'

The Druids began to argue with Patrick and tried to find some way to disprove the Christian teachings.

'How is this God of yours both three and one?' they asked. 'That is impossible!'

'What is that under your foot?' was Patrick's reply.

The chief Druid jumped and looked startled. Fearing that Patrick may have used magic to put something beneath his shoe, he stared at the ground for a moment, and then stood up reassured.

'There is nothing there at all!' he said. 'Only some white clover.'

'Precisely,' said Patrick, 'please pluck one for me.'

The chief Druid bent down and plucked a three-leafed clover. Even before he was standing up again he had guessed Patrick's meaning.

'The clover,' Patrick asked, 'is it one or three? If you look at the plant it is one. The same if you look at the Godhead. But if you look at the leaves you see three. It is just the same with the three Persons of the one Godhead.'

Because of this explanation of Patrick's the white clover, or shamrock, remains to this day the national symbol of Ireland.

When the conversation was over King Loegaire was quite unsure of himself. He did not have the courage to anger his Druids, but neither could he ignore the power of Patrick's words.

'Go your way, Patrick,' he said. 'Cause no trouble, and we shall cause none for you.'

Patrick's prayers had been answered, and his missionary work began to expand at an even greater rate. Even some of the Irish leaders were converted, King Loegaire's brother among them. The island's chief bard, Dubthach, was a particularly important convert, for he composed Christian poems which were a valuable aid to Patrick and his fellow missionaries in teaching the Irish.

Once, as Patrick and his fellow ministers were crossing the country on foot, they stopped at a well to say their early morning prayers. Two young ladies called Etna and Fedelm, daughters of King Loegaire, came down to use the well. They were cautious but inquisitive at the sight of the chanting strangers.

'Who do you suppose they are?' whispered Etna.

'I'm not sure,' her sister replied, 'but I think they might be spirits!'

Gathering courage from the peaceful appearance of Patrick and his men, the two girls came up and questioned them.

'Who are you, and where are you from?'

Patrick was delighted by the intrusion.

'It would be better if you asked about our God instead of ourselves,' he answered.

'Well then,' said Etna, shrugging her shoulders. 'Who is your God?'

'He is the God of all men, of Heaven and earth, and all things in them.'

At that the sisters began to ply him with questions.

'Where does God live? Is He in Heaven, the earth, or the sea? Does He have children? Does He have silver and gold? How can He be found? Is He young or old? Will He live forever? Is He beautiful?'

Patrick answered all their questions, even the bizarre ones, and the girls became ever more excited about this new God. Finally their questions dried up, and with great enthusiasm the girls demanded baptism.

'Please give us communion also,' they asked, 'so that as you have said, we might be with the Saviour in His suffering for us.'

After this success in the household of the king himself Patrick continued his mission in the western parts of Loegaire's realm. Thousands received baptism from his hand, a great number of the native Irish were ordained as ministers, and small monasteries soon dotted the countryside. Sure in the knowledge that the church was firmly established in the north, Patrick finally directed his steps to the south.

The great southern potentate, the King of Munster, listened with interest to the Christian teachings, but he did not embrace them. His son Angus did believe, however, and upon his father's death he asked to be baptized.

Patrick performed the ceremony himself. Bishops carried a staff on formal occasions (signifying their 'shepherding' or 'pastoring' of their people), but when Patrick raised his hands to bless Angus before baptism his staff accidentally fell from his hand, and its pointed end drew blood from the king's bare foot. Patrick was totally unaware of this, and Angus also remained quite silent. He gritted his teeth and went through the rest of the ceremony without a murmur. Afterwards, when Patrick was at dinner with the king and his guests, Angus asked an unexpected question.

'Before the baptism you told me what the water meant, that it symbolized cleansing, and dying along with Christ. You also told me that the white robe shows the purity that Christ has given me. I don't believe you explained what wounding my foot meant. I've been trying to understand it for myself and am not sure that I can find the reason.'

Patrick soon discovered how this strange misunderstanding had arisen, and he apologized profusely.

'Oh, that's all right,' said Angus, 'today I died to be with Christ. A gash in my foot is nothing.'

Patrick remained seven years in Munster, and in spite of troubles with the Druids and pagan chiefs his preaching enjoyed great success. There were now Christians all over the island, and Patrick felt the need to find a suitable location for what would become the island's main church, a base from which he and future bishops could overlook the work of the church throughout Ireland. His wanderings brought him to a hill near Armagh, the perfect spot. The hill was owned by one Daire, and Patrick spoke to him to request the site for the building of his church.

'I'm sorry, but you cannot have it,' said Daire. 'If you like I will give you a spot in the plain instead.'

Patrick was not at all happy with the area offered, and the next day Daire brought a gift that he hoped would soften the old bishop's disappointment.

'Here is a fine and valuable cauldron,' he said. 'It is a gift for you.'

'Gratias agam,' said Patrick. Absentmindedly he had used his native Latin for 'Thank you', instead of the Irish. Daire looked confused, and then he stalked out of the bishop's tent in a foul mood.

'That was a jolly good cauldron,' he mumbled to his servants. 'I've wasted it on a fellow who can't even say thank you. "Gratzacham" he says. Well what do you think that means?'

Daire reached home in a dark mood, and spitting angrily he sent his servants back to the bishop.

'Get my cauldron back for me,' he said. 'I'll show him what I think of such rudeness!'

The servants returned to Patrick and told him of their master's decision.

Patrick nodded quietly. 'Thank you,' he said, again in Latin. 'Take it.'

When the servants returned, their master hastened to greet them.

'What did he say?'

'He said the same thing as before. "Gratzacham."'

'Gratzacham when I give, and Gratzacham when I take away!' Daire said in astonishment. 'Well, I'll tell you, he's a patient fellow! For those Gratzachams I think I might just give the cauldron back. Come on!'

Daire and his men promptly returned to the bishop's tent.

'You may keep the cauldron, for I see you are a steady fellow, neither excited by possessions nor upset by their loss,' said Daire. 'I like your attitude. You can have the hill you asked for as well!'

And so it was that the hill in Armagh became the bishop's official residence.

Patrick was now well up in years, and his long journeys across the island had to cease. But there was great consolation for the bishop in his last years. He had come to an island where a bare handful of men knew the true God, and now the name of the Lord Jesus Christ was revered throughout the island, and Ireland was full of devout ministers and monks. When Patrick departed this life late in the fifth century none knew just how great a work he had accomplished. The light of the gospel that he had brought to Ireland was set to be a blessing far beyond that island itself.

PATRICK, *CONFESSION*; ANONYMOUS, *THE TRIPARTITE LIFE OF PATRICK*

Pictures, Saints and Relics

Back in the declining empire meanwhile, the greatest theological battle of the age was being fought. Its subject was the Incarnation. Before we explore this great debate, however, we must glance at other developments in this period. One was the use of pictures in churches.

The earliest churches had been simple buildings, and it was not until after Constantine, as the churches became richer, that it became common for them to be beautified with painting and sculpture. Such a change was bound to draw criticism, and some church leaders attacked the custom as likely to cause a despiritualizing of worship. Their complaints, however, had little influence – though as we shall see they were to make a dramatic reappearance centuries later.

Certain beliefs about prayer also created a stir at this time.

Christians have always prayed for each other. Many people are especially gifted with powers of prayer, and they dedicate much time to intercessory prayer – prayer for others. The question arises – why should we think that this intercessory prayer stops when a Christian dies? Death to a Christian is the perfection of life, not the end of life. Surely Christians keep up their prayers for their friends, and for the whole church, when they are before Christ's throne just as they did while on earth?

The thought of angels and departed friends and family watching over us, and praying for us, is very beautiful. God is very real, and heaven seems very near, to those who know they belong to a church that is partly on earth, partly already in heaven. In the early church many Christians would begin their prayers by calling upon their deceased friends to join them in prayer. It was like asking a friend still living to pray with you. Beautiful it may be, but the practice could lead to problems.

Long after the persecutions had ceased, many new converts looked back at the Christians of former times with great awe. The martyrs had suffered so much, whereas the new converts had it easy.

'It was these saints who pleased God, not the likes of us!'

They could no longer speak to the early martyrs as to fellow believers. To them the saints were heroes, not friends, and God, who had expected so much of them, seemed rather daunting. They would ask the saints to pray for them in the belief that the prayers of saints were of more worth than their own in the sight of God, and that without such aid they would be overlooked. The thought of departed friends living in the presence of God had originally made heaven seem very near – the thought of mighty saints of days gone by could make God seem further away than ever.

The tombs of the martyrs also became objects of great interest.

The pagan Greeks generally cremated their dead, while, like the Jews, the Christians buried theirs. The tombs had always been places to congregate for prayer, a place with a special sanctity, where one felt closer to the deceased. The belief in the resurrection especially, so new to the Greeks and Romans, gave the tombs a certain mystique, and the knowledge that the dead body would one day leap forth fresh from the grave inspired a great reverence for the remains, or relics, of the saints.

In superstitious minds these feelings could be easily perverted. We have already seen that Antony, the first monk, criticized the Egyptians for preserving the bodies of holy men without burial. Vigilantius also, the opponent of Jerome, condemned both prayer to the saints and the reverence shown to the remains of the departed. He described with revulsion the practice of kissing vessels containing relics and labelled those who do so 'ash-gatherers and idolaters'. Respect for the dead, he perceived, was being carried to the point of profanity. We shall later see what a wealth of superstitions grew up around these ideas.

The Incarnation

But we return to the great question of the age. It was rather simple. Jesus Christ is both human and divine. He is man and God. The question is, how?

The question of the Incarnation had caused controversy in the past.

Cerinthus, a heretic in the time of the apostles, was one of the first to teach falsehood on the subject. Cerinthus believed that Jesus Christ was a mere man, but that at his baptism the Word of God had entered his body. To him the Incarnation only meant that Jesus was a man 'possessed' by God. He even went so far as to say that Jesus' cry on the cross, 'My God, why have You forsaken Me?', indicated that the Word had departed from the body of the dying Christ!

The Apostle John himself opposed Cerinthus. His writings contain clear statements such as John 1:14, stressing that 'the Word became flesh', something Cerinthus denied. As John said, the Word did not *possess* a man, He *became* a man.

In April 428 an Antiochian minister named Nestorius became Patriarch of Constantinople. Nestorius was a renowned preacher, and many hoped he might prove himself another Chrysostom. The reality was to be far different.

Theophilus, Chrysostom's great rival, had died many years earlier, and Cyril, Theophilus' nephew, now occupied his place. Cyril was a better man than Theophilus, but he often displayed signs of a violent temper similar to that which had disgraced his uncle. Times were difficult in his city, and Cyril was the type of character to deal with problems head-on. Several violent scenes disturbed the first years of his reign as Patriarch of Alexandria.

Cyril, a bitter enemy of heresy, began his reign with an action few could excuse. With no provocation, he ordered the closure of a heretical church and the confiscation of its property. To be fair this was a rare occasion, and Cyril was not usually harsh without provocation, but in Alexandria, the empire's most violent city, Cyril wanted to show from the start that he was a strong man, a leader to be feared and respected. Soon afterwards a real test of his determination developed.

The Jews had been a powerful group in Alexandria for centuries, and their bitterness against the church had greatly increased now that the emperors themselves were believers. For centuries the Jews had delighted to see the Christians suffer at the hands of the pagans, but now that the church had won, and to the horror of her enemies had assumed the rule over Jews and pagans alike, hatred for the followers of Jesus was boiling as never before.

Trouble flared in an unusual fashion. The Jews were accustomed to spend the Sabbath watching theatrical displays and dancers, and the associated festivities habitually led to drunken disorder in the streets. An edict was posted in the theatre to curb the licence of such public amusements in future, and a number of Christians attended to learn the details of the new legislation. A friend of Cyril named Hierax was among them, and he expressed his approval of the restrictions in no uncertain terms. The Jews, already upset on account of the new regulations, immediately exploded. They insisted that Hierax had come only to abuse them and egg them into rebellion. The city governor, Orestes, acceded to their bloody requests and arrested Hierax and put him to the torture right there in the theatre. Cyril was enraged, and he summoned the Jewish elders and gave them a piece of his mind.

'If you ever again make such an attack you will suffer the direst consequences.'

The pride of the Jewish leaders was deeply wounded by Cyril's threat, and a bloody revenge was soon prepared. An armed ambush was planted in the city streets, and as Alexandria slept the Jews raised a terrible cry:

'The church of Alexander is on fire!'

The lie achieved its purpose of dragging the Christians out of their beds and onto the streets, and as the drowsy crowd rushed to the church the Jews rose from ambush.

'Death to the Christians!'

The confusion and panic that followed were terrible, and many were killed. At daybreak the outraged Christians gathered for revenge.

'To the synagogues!' Cyril commanded.

The mob moved quickly, and by afternoon all the synagogues were closed, and the whole Jewish community, guilty and innocent alike, was in exile. Governor Orestes was infuriated with the bishop.

'The law,' he shouted, 'is my responsibility! How dare you take it into your own hands to punish anyone?'

Cyril explained the terrible provocation that the Jews had given the church.

'Blame the Jews, for the mob would have attacked them with or without me. It is rather a wonder that it was done without bloodshed!'

Orestes refused to accept the explanation. Law and order were his responsibility, and here was a bishop exiling a large number of citizens without even telling him! Orestes, who had never liked the patriarch, now began to criticize him harshly both in public and private. Repeated messages of peace from Cyril were in vain.

The feud caused a lot of trouble. Most of the citizens supported Cyril, and the obstinate Orestes was held in contempt. Rumours even began to spread that Orestes was a secret devotee of the idols, and the sad affair reached its lowest point when a more precise story circulated.

'Orestes' friend Hypatia has caused this problem. In her scheming against the church she has sought to turn the governor's mind against the bishop, and she will not allow the two to be reconciled.'

Hypatia was the best-known pagan in the city. Her father was a pagan philosopher, and she had followed in his footsteps and become a teacher. Her school was one of the last remains of paganism, and she was one of the few who clung to the belief that the old ways might again revive. She was already very unpopular, and this new rumour threw fuel on the fire.

'If Hypatia were gone,' said a minor church official named Peter, 'the pagan school would disappear, and Orestes would stop insulting our bishop.'

Some extremists were inspired by such words to form a conspiracy against the poor woman, and soon after she was attacked in the street and brutally murdered. Her death, of course, only made the feud worse. It was a disgrace to the whole church of Alexandria, and although Cyril had no part in it, it reflected poorly on him as bishop.

The crime against Hypatia, however repugnant to the spirit of the gospel, must, for a moment, be viewed through Alexandrian eyes. The Egyptian Christians had endured terrible persecution for centuries, worse in fact than anywhere else in the empire, and the pagans had always seized every opportunity to do them injury. That some failed to turn the other cheek, and even returned violence for violence, is sad, but perhaps understandable. Nor should it be forgotten that much of the old pagan mob had now, nominally at least, slipped within the church's walls – the name 'Christian' no longer necessarily implied the high degree of faith that had been usual in the days of tribulation.

Such, at any rate, were the troubles of the first three years of Cyril's career, and if that were his whole story his name would by now be forgotten. His rival patriarch, however, Nestorius of Constantinople, has ensured that Cyril's name should remain famous to this day. In 428 Nestorius mounted the pulpit of Constantinople for the first time.

'What is the new bishop like?' was the question on all lips. People always listened carefully to the first sermon of a new minister, and from it would make a guess as to the preacher's character. Nestorius began his sermon by turning to the emperor.

'Give me, my prince, the earth cleansed of heretics, and I will give you heaven in return. Assist me in destroying heretics, and I will assist you in vanquishing the enemies of the empire.'

His words were indeed an indication of things to come. Cyril's troubles were nothing compared with those that Nestorius hoped to stir up!

Nestorius' early reign was a flurry of violent activity. Only five days after his ordination he ordered the demolition of the Arians' chapel in the city, and in feeble protest against his severity one of the heretics set the building alight with his own hands. The blaze spread on all sides, and many adjacent buildings were reduced to ashes. Nestorius, undeterred, continued his policy of confiscating heretical churches, and he quickly received the nickname, from heretics and Christians alike, of 'the Arsonist'. The blaze, however, did not last long. The headstrong minister soon blundered into a problem that would prove his undoing; the persecutor was himself to become a heretic.

Without doubt Nestorius believed that Jesus Christ was truly man and truly God, indeed he wanted to destroy those who thought otherwise, but for all that he had no deep understanding of the Incarnation. A skilful preacher he might have been, but in theological knowledge he was seriously lacking. His ignorance, and arrogance, led him into grave errors.

'Mary did not give birth to God,' he declared in a sermon. 'She only gave birth to the temple in which God dwelled.'

What on earth did that mean? Was Nestorius teaching the old heresy, that Jesus was just a holy man 'possessed' by God?

Nestorius insisted that he was teaching no such thing. Jesus, he said, was truly God, but when questioned more deeply he revealed his own confusion on the Incarnation in these fateful words:

'I cannot believe that a two- or three-month-old baby was really God!'

The whole empire was inflamed by news of the patriarch's opinions, and in 431 a council was held at Ephesus to address the issue. If Nestorius was guilty as charged he must be deposed immediately; the church could not allow a minister who denied the Incarnation, the foundation of Christian belief, to keep his place. The problem was so grave that this was only the third Ecumenical Council ever held.

Cyril led the proceedings at Ephesus, and it is for his resistance to Nestorius that his name is still renowned. He had previously tried to set Nestorius straight with letters discussing the theological issues, but they had gotten him nowhere. In council, however, he clearly exposed the heresy of Nestorius, and the patriarch was deposed, excommunicated and sent into exile. For his last 20 years Nestorius felt for himself what it was like to be on the receiving end of persecution. Sadly, his exile was far from being the end of the matter.

THE ACTS OF EPHESUS; SOCRATES, CH 7.7–34

The Council of Robbers

New strife began with the death of Cyril a little more than a decade later. Dioscorus succeeded him as patriarch, and he showed his 'gratitude' to the deceased by confiscating his estate and deposing several members of his family from the Christian ministry. The new patriarch seemed determined to make Nestorius himself seem like a gentle shepherd!

Dioscorus was not satisfied with the result of Ephesus. He hated Nestorius' beliefs with such a passion that he actually fell into error in the opposite direction, and he refused to speak of Christ as possessing two natures, divine and human. He lent support to Eutyches, a monk from Constantinople who took this extreme anti-Nestorianism to its logical conclusion. Eutyches claimed that, though the Incarnation had been a genuine meeting of human and divine, once the fusion of the two elements was effected the human factor was so overwhelmed by the divine that Christ was no longer truly human. His body, consequently, was not of the same kind as that of mortal men. Eutyches was opposed and convicted of heresy by Patriarch Flavian of Constantinople, but the patriarch himself was soon overpowered by a powerful conspiracy which formed against him.

Chrysaphius was a corrupt eunuch with a great deal of power in the court of Theodosius II. He was Eutyches' godchild, and already nursed grudges of his own against Flavian. On the patriarch's first day in office the greedy eunuch had addressed him bluntly.

'The wealth of the church is now yours. Do not forget that one word from me in the emperor's ear could have raised another to this position. Show your gratitude, and soon.'

'The wealth of the church is not mine but God's,' Flavian replied. 'The only riches I can offer anyone are the riches of communion with our Lord.'

His offer of consecrated bread was greeted with a sneer of disgust.

'Fill my pocket, not my belly.'

How is Jesus fully human and fully divine? No form of words can plumb the depths of the mystery of the Incarnation, but Scripture provides many pointers on the road to truth, and following their lead we can avoid the errors that lie on either side of orthodox Christology.

The second person of the Trinity, the Son or Word, entered the womb of Mary. In doing so He did not lose His divine nature, but emptying Himself of glory and withholding His hand from the exercise of His inherent powers He took on the limitations of a man. He grew in the womb as we do, and as a child grew in wisdom and stature. Throughout His life He was tempted and tried as we are, but at the age of thirty, with the beginning of His ministry, the reality of His divine nature began to be revealed through acts, such as the forgiving of sins and the working of mighty signs, which are possible only to God.

Jesus was like us in feeling hunger and thirst, tiredness, and the other pains of life, but He was unlike us in never committing sin of any kind. We sin because we fail to look to God's wishes for us, and instead concentrate on our own selfish wishes – whereas Jesus, because of His divine nature, had no sinful desires. Obedience to His own deepest desires meant obedience to the divine will, as they were one and the same.

Jesus is a man today and forevermore, but since His ascension to the Father He has cast away human limitations. He still has the physical body in which He walked the earth, though in its glorified state it is no longer subject to the conditions of mortal life. Jesus is one of us now and forever, and strikingly enough, even on judgement day we are thus promised a peer-trial. None will be able to accuse God of injustice if their sins condemn them to hell. 'How can we justly be judged,' someone might ask, 'by one who knows nothing of human limitations?' Jesus, by becoming a man, has left wicked men with neither quibble nor excuse.

The gravity of Christological error should be apparent. If, as Nestorius said, it is not possible to speak of the infant Christ as God, how is it any easier to speak of the adult Christ as God? The distance between child and man is nothing compared to the distance between man and God! If, as Eutyches said, Christ was not truly human, how can He be our representative and example? How can He be the last Adam if He was not the true son of His mother's flesh?

'I am sorry, but the church's gold is not mine to give.'

Chrysaphius teamed with Dioscorus and Eutyches, and the three called upon the emperor to summon a council to deal further with the question of the Incarnation. All hoped for the destruction of Flavian and the triumph of heresy.

The council again met in Ephesus, and Dioscorus, supported

by a band of soldiers, took charge of the proceedings. Chrysaphius had supplied the soldiers to ensure that all went 'smoothly'. Dioscorus' opponents scarcely dared open their mouths.

Leo, Bishop of Rome, was not present. He was the greatest Christian leader of the time, and he had sent representatives bearing a letter to the council. His letter clearly and beautifully explained the true Christology, and his messengers were the first to address the council.

'Bishop Leo could not be here, but he has sent us with this exposition of the faith.'

'Very well,' said Dioscorus, taking the letter and putting it away unread.

'Aren't you going to read it?' the Romans asked in surprise.

'First things first,' Dioscorus snarled, before summoning Eutyches to stand before the assembly. He was going to ensure that Leo's voice was never heard. Dioscorus and his cronies promptly overturned Flavian's sentence against Eutyches.

'Eutyches is no heretic,' Dioscorus announced. 'Flavian is the heretic!'

'Flavian says that Christ has two natures!' one of Dioscorus' supporters cried. 'Let him who would cut Christ in two himself be cut in two!'

Dioscorus now commanded the council to depose and excommunicate Flavian.

'Have you not won enough already!' his startled opponents pleaded. 'We have not opposed your will over Eutyches. Is that not enough?'

Dioscorus stood upon his footstool, and pounded his fists in the air.

'Condemn Flavian, or you will have to deal with me. If my tongue were cut from my body it would still cry "Depose Flavian!" Do you hear me you rebels? Where are the soldiers!'

These last words he cried at the top of his lungs. Chrysaphius' soldiers burst into the room, and Flavian was seized and beaten senseless. Dioscorus himself attacked his fellow patriarch, kicking and punching him like a wild ass. Flavian was sentenced to exile, but he died of his wounds only three days later.

When Bishop Leo learned of the proceedings at Ephesus he gave the false council a name which has stuck to this day, the Latrocinium, or 'Council of Robbers'. Robbers or not, in the bloodshed and confusion, Dioscorus and his cronies had triumphed.

ACTS OF THE COUNCILS; LEO, *LETTERS*

Chalcedon

But not for long. It had only been through the support of Chrysaphius that such a terrible scene had been possible, and the eunuch's days were numbered.

Theodosius II fell from his horse and died soon after the council, and his sister Pulcheria took his throne. Chrysaphius had often insulted this spirited woman, and she now took action against him and the other corrupt ministers of her brother's court. Chrysaphius was executed, and a new council was called to right the wrongs of the 'Latrocinium'.

At this fourth Ecumenical Council, the Council of Chalcedon, the question of the Incarnation was finally settled. Dioscorus was condemned and exiled, and all of the decisions of the Latrocinium were reversed. Flavian's innocence was proclaimed, and the deceased bishop was pronounced a second Abel, murdered by his jealous 'brother' patriarch. The extreme teachings of both Nestorius and Eutyches were condemned, and the middle ground was established for all time to come. Jesus Christ is one person but of two natures, human and divine. Surely there could now be peace?

Unfortunately not. The years of debate between patriarchs of Constantinople and Alexandria had opened a rift between the two great cities, and after Chalcedon that rift continued to grow until it eventually split the empire in two. The division, indeed, has not been healed to this day, and the reality is that it is only superficially a matter of Christology.

Following the defeat of Dioscorus at Chalcedon the

Alexandrians abandoned the teachings of Eutyches. Both sides agreed that he was a heretic.

But the Alexandrians picked faults with the words that the council used to describe the Incarnation. The council said that Jesus was one person with two natures. The Alexandrians insisted that this was wrong.

'Jesus is one person,' they said, 'but with one nature, which is a mysterious combination of the fullness of the human and divine natures.'

Surely such fussiness over words was not a sufficient warrant for more strife?

The argument about words, however, was a sign of much deeper problems. Dioscorus was the first Alexandrian bishop to be convicted of heresy. The Alexandrians usually left councils as victors. Now their pride was dented by defeat, and by the fact that Constantinople had imposed a new bishop on them. But their biggest grudge was to do with politics, not religion.

The Greek city of Constantinople was the home of the eastern emperor. For many years the non-Greek easterners, especially the Egyptians, had been turning against this rule from afar. They particularly resented the heavy taxes imposed on them by Constantinople. The volatility of the Alexandrian mob was in part attributable to this growing desire for self-rule.

The Alexandrians hated their governors because they were appointed by the emperor. Their bishops were their last source of pride, their only truly local leaders, and to have their new bishop appointed by the Greeks was just too much. The rebellious Alexandrians appointed their own bishop, and from that fateful day to the present their city has almost always been divided between rival bishops, one ruling a small number who stayed in the orthodox church, the other guiding the mass of the people who call themselves the Coptic ('native Egyptian') church. Political disaffection became a fuel that kept the theological quarrel burning long past its time.

Similar desires for independence created similar schisms in other areas. Many Syrians followed in the footsteps of the Egyptians. They shared the Copts' political disquiet and suspicion of the Greek patriarch, but the Council of Chalcedon had given them even greater cause for frustration. For centuries the bishop of Antioch – a city which was capital of Syria, birthplace of the mission to the Gentiles, and where the believers in Jesus had first been called Christians – had been the highest figure of the Asian church. Just as the Egyptians were proud of their tradition of leadership in Ecumenical Councils (Athanasius and Cyril for example), the Syrians prided themselves on being the most ancient Gentile church, and the only patriarchate in Asia. The Council of Chalcedon, however, against the wishes of Antioch, established Jerusalem, also in Asia, as a fifth patriarchate. Jerusalem's bishop became the chief authority over Palestine, territory previously under Antioch, and rightly or wrongly the Syrians felt this as an insult. What rights, they asked, will the Greeks take from us next?

The decades after Chalcedon saw many attempts to heal these divisions, but even the greatest concessions proved unable to effect a reconciliation. In 482 Emperor Zeno released the *Henoticon*, or 'Formula of Union', which was an attempt to please both sides by virtually returning the debate to pre-Chalcedonian days – in effect ignoring Chalcedon, and permitting freedom of belief on the point of contention. The *Henoticon* condemned both Nestorius and Eutyches, but it refrained from any mention of the one or two natures, referring more vaguely to Christ's full humanity and divinity. It added the striking denouncement of any who taught otherwise, 'whether at Chalcedon or anywhere else'. In the long run, neither side was happy with Zeno's fence-sitting. The supporters of Chalcedon took grave offence at the veiled slur, while many Copts and Syrians refused to be satisfied with anything less than an explicit condemnation of Chalcedon. The *Henoticon* fell by the wayside, and the strife continued.

Nestorius was now dead, but his name had not been forgotten. Through a complex chain of events it happened that a section of the church in Persia still remembered him fondly.

These Persians had been strongly opposed to the anti-Nestorianism of Eutyches and Dioscorus. Rebelling against the heretical Latrocinium they took sides with the exiled Nestorius, and by the end of the fifth century nearly the whole Persian church had joined them. The reason was again political.

The Persian kings had always feared and disliked the church within their realm. How could they be sure that these people would not betray them, and support the Christian emperors of Rome, if war broke out between the two nations?

When the Persian king realized that the supporters of Nestorius disagreed with the faith of the Roman emperor he eagerly gave them his support. This was too good an offer for most Persian Christians to refuse, and they joined in droves the sect that was at peace with the government. The Christians of Persia called themselves the Assyrian church; their opponents back in the empire labelled them 'Nestorians'.

But how heretical were they? Did they share Nestorius' confusion on the Incarnation?

Curiously, the answer is no. Their statements of belief on the Incarnation are actually very similar to those of other churches. Although the battle of the Incarnation began as a religious dispute, the schisms it caused must be viewed as mainly political problems.

THE ACTS OF CHALCEDON; EVAGRIUS, *CH* 2.4–5

Simeon of the Pillar

Finally we say farewell to the bitter battles of the Incarnation – but before leaving the east we must look at a couple of interesting contemporary Christian characters. One of the most original and unusual figures of church history lived in the desert near Antioch at this time. He was Simeon Stylites, 'Simeon of the pillar'.

Simeon joined a monastery as a young man, and he became famous for both brilliance as a student and excessive asceticism. He was accustomed to severe fasting, giving nearly all of his own food allowance to the poor as he strove to reach a state in which he could virtually forget about his body, and totally ignore pain and discomfort. He once went to the bizarre length of tying a rope (hidden by his clothes) tightly around his whole torso. It cut deeply into his skin, and he did not remove it until forced to do so by his brethren, who had noticed that he was leaving a trail of blood!

That Simeon was not quite normal was soon obvious to his fellow monks. He became unpopular, and the leader of his community eventually forced him to leave. None could understand this strange young fellow, and little wonder!

Simeon found a lonely retreat near Telanassus in which to practise his eccentricities in private. At Lent he visited a nearby priest and revealed his latest plan.

'I want to fast completely for forty days, but fear that I lack the strength of will to persevere. I would appreciate it if you would lock me into my hut for that period, and release me on Easter Sunday?'

The priest was dumbfounded. 'Don't be absurd. Suicide is no virtue but the most heinous of crimes!'

'I shall not die,' Simeon insisted. 'I will keep ten loaves of bread and plenty of water in my hut and use them in case of necessity.'

On these conditions the priest agreed to Simeon's request. He sealed the fanatical monk in, and forty days later arrived early to see the result.

'Simeon!'

The monk was almost unconscious on the floor, unable to speak or move. On the table, untouched, were the bread and water.

Simeon recovered quickly, and each year thereafter repeated the dreadful experience. It was not long before the fame of such bizarre austerities spread widely, and crowds of curious visitors, Christian and pagan alike, came to look at this almost superhuman monk for themselves. Simeon did not relish being a tourist attraction, but he made the most of his opportunities, and many curious pagans heard their first sermon from his lips.

Soon finding that he had lost all quiet, and annoyed by the constant crush of visitors in his narrow cell, Simeon thought of fleeing deeper into the desert – but he was restrained by the knowledge that he would then be unable to share the gospel with others. His solution was one of the most peculiar ideas in church history.

Simeon built himself a pillar two days' journey from Antioch. It was nine feet high, and upon the summit Simeon took up permanent residence. Day and night, whatever the weather, Simeon had no shelter but the hood of his cape. His small supply of food and water was passed up to him once a week. Now the crowds could come as thick as they pleased!

Come the crowds did. Visitors to this bizarre scene were far more numerous than before, and Simeon was especially pleased to see that the wild pagan Arabs of the desert came in their thousands to see this new wonder of the world, and from his vantage point he addressed the crowds with sermons every day of the year. The sick came to ask his prayers, and Simeon became famous as a judge, settling disputes between the wondering onlookers.

> In Simeon's time a most frightful scene took place in Inmestar, a town near Antioch.
>
> Shortly after Cyril chased the Jews out of Alexandria, the Jews of Inmestar were celebrating a day of feasting. They got themselves drunk and started to curse Christ and His church, and some of them kidnapped a Christian child and bound him to a makeshift cross. They mocked and insulted the child, and later pulled him down and gave him such a severe flogging that he died under their hands. The culprits were soon discovered and punished, but nothing could heal the ill feelings created by yet another grim chapter in the four-century-old hatred of the Jews for the church.

As the years passed the crowds became ever larger, and Simeon made several additions to his aerial pulpit. He spent nearly forty years up above the Syrian desert, and by the time he had finished making additions his pillar was 60 feet high! He could be seen from miles away, hands raised in prayer, as he addressed the crowds.

Many Christians, understandably, criticized Simeon's eccentric behaviour, but the pillar preacher had his defenders as well. The wild Saracens had never before been reached with the gospel, and now they were for the first time shocked into listening to the Christian message by Simeon's unusual antics. In their thousands the wild desert men received baptism, converted by the words which they would have ignored had they come from anywhere else but the top of a 60-foot pillar!

Simeon's supporters insisted that, strange though the monk's behaviour might be, it could not be condemned as contrary to the gospel. They also pointed out the biblical prophets who had done strange things to get the attention of the nation.

'If Ezekiel can lie on his side for more than a year (Ez. 4), and if Isaiah can go about stripped and barefoot for three years (Is. 20), why can't Simeon stand on a pillar and preach to the nations? Who are you to judge another man's servant?'

The local church leaders determined to test Simeon. They wanted to know whether he was puffed up with pride on account of his fame, and they sent him an order in the name of the local bishops.

'The bishops command you to come down. You must live on your pillar no longer.'

No sooner was the message spoken than Simeon began to climb down. 'No good would come to me if I were to disobey the ministers of the church,' he declared.

At this proof of humility and obedience the bishops' messenger immediately stopped the monk's descent. 'Stay right there,' he said. 'You have adequately proved your obedience. You may stay on your pillar as long as the Spirit moves you!'

Simeon's death, at the age of seventy, was the end of an era. Imitators have been few and far between!

Gelasios was a more conventional but no less respected monk of the same period. He was the leader, or 'abbot', of the monastery of Nicopolis in Palestine. 'Abbot' comes from the Aramaic *abba*, 'father'.

Gelasios owned a beautiful leather Bible, worth 18 pieces of silver. It was particularly valuable because it contained the whole Scripture, which was very unusual for a single volume in those times. Gelasios left it permanently in the local church for the use of the whole community.

A stranger who visited the church was filled with greed at the sight of the beautiful Bible. He stayed in the church pretending to be at his prayers until everyone was gone, and then he snatched up the Bible and rushed from the church with all speed. Gelasios saw his flight and correctly guessed what had happened. He sighed, but resisted the temptation to follow. The thief took the Bible to a trader in a nearby town.

'I will take 13 pieces of silver for it.'

'Lend it to me first,' said the trader, 'I will examine it and judge whether your price is fair.'

The trader could not decide how much the Bible was worth, so he took it to Gelasios' monastery.

'Abbot Gelasios,' he said, 'could you please give me your opinion. A man wants 13 silver pieces for this Bible.'

Gelasios touched his familiar Bible, and smiled sadly. 'Buy it,' he said. 'It is beautiful, and well worth the price.'

Later the thief visited the trader again.

'I have shown it to Abbot Gelasios,' said the trader. 'He thought your price too high.'

The thief visibly jumped, and his heart began to race. 'Did Gelasios say nothing else?'

'No.'

Snatching up the Bible, the thief dashed from the store.

'I no longer wish to sell it!' he cried over his shoulder. Reaching the monastery at speed he threw himself at Gelasios' feet. 'Forgive me!' he cried. 'Here is your book!'

Gelasios shook his head. 'Keep it.'

'Father Gelasios,' the thief cried, 'if I take it I will never have another day's peace so long as I live!'

'If that is the case,' the monk said indifferently, 'I will take it.'

Amazed and inspired by the patient calmness of the abbot, the thief became a member of the monastery that very day.

Gelasios could also be firm when occasion demanded. A monk who lived near Nicopolis had died and left his property to Gelasios' monastery. Knowing Gelasios' easy temper, a local peasant farmer named Batacos claimed an ancient right to the plot and demanded it be handed over to him. He was surprised to meet resistance.

'The land is the monastery's,' said Gelasios, 'it is holy land. It has been dedicated to God, and is not mine to give away.'

Batacos was a hot-headed man at the best of times, and this opposition infuriated him. Determined to break the abbot's will he began to steal whatever grew on the land, and even to beat those who worked it. When Gelasios and his fellow monks were unmoved Batacos took his complaints to court. He loved litigation, and had several other cases pending, so with a roll of papers under his arm he headed off to Constantinople on foot. Lawsuits had been a favourite pastime of pagan society, and the passion for them still ran high in many people.

Passing Antioch on the way to the capital, Batacos went to see the famous local ascetic for himself. Wandering amongst the crowds at the foot of the pillar, he was shocked to find that Simeon immediately singled him out.

'Where do you come from, and where are you going?'

'I come from Palestine,' said Batacos, 'on my way to Constantinople.'

'Wherefore?'

'For many reasons,' he replied, a guilty flush spreading across his cheek. 'With your prayers, holy Simeon, I hope to return successful and bow before you.'

'Wretch,' Simeon cried, 'you hide the fact that your actions are directed against a man of God! The path before you is blocked with thorns, and you will not see your house again. Flee this place and seek your enemy. Who knows? He may pardon you before you drop into the grave!'

Batacos was immediately seized with a fever, and taking the first carriage he hastened back to Palestine. On the way home he stopped in Beirut, and there he died.

Gelasios also played a role in the major events of his time, and in the months following the Council of Chalcedon he was often in mortal danger. Egypt to the south, and some of the Syrians to the north, had set up their new 'revolutionary' churches, and Palestine looked as though it might follow suit. It was a supporter of Dioscorus named Theodosius who first stirred up trouble.

Theodosius returned to Palestine from Chalcedon with great speed, and arrived ahead of Bishop Juvenal of Jerusalem. He went first to Gelasios at Nicopolis, knowing that if he could sway the leading abbots the people would be his.

'The Council of Chalcedon has approved the teachings of Nestorius,' he told the abbot. 'Heresy has won the day, and Bishop Juvenal has betrayed us!'

Gelasios, suspicious, questioned the deceiver closely. With the Spirit's guidance he exposed Theodosius' lies, and he sent the traitor away with a firm reprimand.

The thwarted Theodosius hastened from the monastery to Jerusalem, and there he enjoyed much greater success. Most of the city fell for his lies, and he attacked those who disagreed with a heavy hand. His supporters proclaimed him bishop, and Juvenal returned home to find his city locked against him.

Juvenal himself was well pleased with the result of Chalcedon. He had been made a patriarch, and was in no mood for rebellion, but finding it impossible to gain a hearing in Palestine he was forced to leave the province. The triumphant Theodosius now sent for Gelasios.

'Juvenal has lost!' he said. 'Curse him, and acknowledge me instead.'

'I cannot,' the abbot replied. 'Juvenal is my bishop, as he is yours.'

In fury Theodosius ordered Gelasios to be thrown out of his church. The abbot was dragged outside, and then bound to a stake. Theodosius' supporters piled sticks around him, but before the fateful fire could be lit the ruffians began one by one to fall back from their task. All alike were dumbfounded by Gelasios' calm demeanour. He stood unflinching in the midst of the pile, his face as peaceful as if he had been out for a stroll. Who would cast the first spark?

A crowd began to gather, and the supporters of Theodosius altogether lost their nerve. Gelasios was well loved, and it would not do for them to make his opposition to their leader too conspicuous. They unbound him, and he walked free.

Theodosius' tyranny did not long survive this scene. Leo of Rome, Empress Pulcheria and her new husband, Emperor Marcian, all wrote letters to the monks and other spiritual leaders of Palestine, explaining to them the results of the council. The deceit of Theodosius was thus exposed, and in July 453 Juvenal returned to his flock and the usurper was arrested by the authorities. Gelasios won great praise for his firmness, and the old abbot ended his days in peace.

THEODORET, *HISTORY OF THE MONKS* 26; 'GELASIOS', *THE SAYINGS OF THE DESERT FATHERS*

Attila the Hun

Over in the west, meanwhile, the empire was collapsing around the ears of its startled rulers.

King Alaric of the Visigoths breathed his last soon after the sack of Rome, but his death brought little relief. The Gothic army under his successor Adolphus soon left plundered Italy behind and marched into the province of Gaul. Here they eventually established their own kingdom, permanently severing much of Gaul from the empire.

North Africa fell to the Vandals in the 430s, and Rome could only watch as areas of Spain, Britain and Belgium were seized by other barbarian tribes. The emperor was powerless to defend his realm, and all the wild northerners knew it. But the worst was yet to come. The greatest barbarian tribe of them all was just now thundering across the Roman frontiers.

The name of the Huns struck terror into civilized Romans and northern barbarians alike. Before confronting Rome the Huns had already established their rule over most of the other barbarian tribes, and they held an empire that straddled northern Europe. It seemed to be their fate to complete the destruction of Rome which others had begun.

The Huns had indirectly caused huge damage to the empire

even before setting foot on Roman soil. The Goths and Vandals themselves had invaded the empire in the hope of escaping the Huns, who were pressing on them from behind. It was easier to snatch a province from Rome than to resist these bloodthirsty foes!

Attila was the Huns' greatest king. He began his reign as joint ruler with his brother Bleda, but in 445, in typical Hunnish fashion, Attila decided that one head was better than two, and Bleda lost his.

The Huns were a warrior race, and their chief object of worship was a god of war. Attila was a shrewd man, and he used the pagan superstitions of his people to his advantage. When a very ancient sword was accidentally discovered in some long grass by one of his followers, Attila declared that it had been dropped from heaven by the war god as a gift to him and his nation:

'With the war god's sword, our army is invincible!'

The 'invincible' Huns marched where they pleased in Roman territory. Whole armies perished by their swords, and great tracts of land were handed over to them. Only the payment of huge ransoms preserved the Romans from complete destruction, and it was not until 450, when Attila invaded Gaul, that an alliance between the Romans and Visigoths finally challenged the supremacy of the Huns.

Attila was bent on defeating Theodoric, king of the Visigoths, and on plundering the new Gothic kingdom in Gaul. The Visigoths would have stood little chance against him had not Attila stirred up the Romans to join them. The western empire was now ruled by Valentinian III, yet another weak ruler. His sister was Honoria, a spirited but somewhat foolish woman who despised the weakness of her brother and her nation.

'As Attila's bride,' the young woman mused, 'the world would be mine. A union of Rome and the Huns would be unstoppable!'

With this wild dream in her head Honoria sent Attila her ring.

'I am yours,' she wrote. 'This ring is a pledge of my love. Valentinian is a coward. Do not let him stand in your way!'

The barbarian was delighted with the proposal. Even as he marched on Theodoric and the Visigoths he sent messengers to the Roman court:

'I demand Honoria as my bride. As a dowry, I shall expect half of the empire to become mine. Obey, or perish.'

Such a request was too much even for the weak Valentinian. Aetius, the leading Roman general, was sent into Gaul at the head of the Roman troops, and there he joined forces with the mighty Visigoths. The Romans and Goths, so recently bitter enemies, now prepared for war with the common foe.

Attila was engaged in an attack on the city of Orleans when the allies first challenged him. The city was almost his, but the king of the Huns was forced to raise the siege and retreat to a better position. He knew the importance of the coming battle, and he chose the Catalaunian plains as the site for the greatest test which his invincible sword would receive.

The pagan king was nervous at the prospect of the battle ahead. The union of his two enemies had disturbed his plans, and he dared not fight without a message from the gods. He called for soothsayers, and these pagan prophets slaughtered animals and examined their bowels. In the blood, bones and guts of the dead animals, they claimed to read the mind of their gods.

'It does not look good for us,' they reported. 'But one of the enemy leaders will die today.'

Attila was heartened by the ambiguous news.

'Surely Aetius will be the man who falls,' he thought, 'and with him gone, the empire will be ours.'

The Huns now prepared for battle, and before the trumpet sounded Attila gave a speech to his myriad troops.

'Remember our glorious past, all our mighty victories,' he cried. 'Stand firm today, and you will see the greatest victory yet! The Romans are cowardly and weak. Forget them! It is the Visigoths alone who stand against us, and they are but one nation! They cannot defeat our countless hordes. The day is ours!'

Attila immediately led his troops to the fight. He himself was stationed in the centre of the front line, wielding his sword just like the tens of thousands who served under him. Attila's main force swiftly crashed through the centre line of the allies. This blow split the allies into two separate armies, and Attila concentrated his main attack on the Visigoths.

The battle of the Catalaunian plains was the greatest battle of its era, and one of the greatest of all time. For sheer numbers killed, and the barbarity of the Huns especially, it would be hard to imagine a more terrible event. Tens of thousands died in a single afternoon to satisfy the pride of the hideous Attila.

King Theodoric himself fell on that fateful day. As he rode amongst his troops, encouraging them to stand firm, he was struck by a javelin and fell from his horse. He was soon trampled and crushed, and Attila's troops closed in upon his disheartened Goths. Torismund, son of the fallen king, was at the head of a valiant band of horsemen. Anxious to avenge his father he rallied the troops, and his vigorous leadership put new heart into the Visigoths. After their early danger they managed to stand firm for the rest of the day, and when the armies separated at nightfall it was seen that the Huns had lost by far the most men. The following morning might see them crushed completely.

Aetius rejoiced in the victory, but he was alarmed at the prospect of the complete destruction of the foe. If the Visigoths exterminated the Huns, what was to ensure that they might not turn their arms against the weakened empire next? To his mind the world was safer with the Huns still around, to keep the other barbarians from getting out of line. He wanted to humble Attila, not to kill him. Torismund was eager for the following day's battle, for revenge and for glory over the most dreadful king of the age, but as the evening passed the cunning words of Aetius slowly turned the young prince's head.

'Your brothers, as soon as they hear of your father's death, will seek the kingship for themselves. The battle with Attila could be a long one, and there is no guarantee that tomorrow will be as successful as today. I suggest that you return to your land and receive the crown before you even contemplate further fighting.'

So the victorious Visigoths returned to their homeland, and Attila escaped alive from the scene of his first and only defeat.

Attila, who had falsely promised his men a great victory, knew that he must swiftly restore confidence in his leadership. With great speed he rebuilt his army, and within a year of his defeat the Huns were ready for a new campaign. The conquest of Italy, the heart of the west, was now the goal, and the helpless empire looked on in amazement as the Huns raged through the north of Italy in bloody revenge for their recent defeat. Great and ancient cities were reduced to rubble, innocent victims perished in their thousands, and it seemed that the empire's final hour had come.

But Attila's mind was uneasy. The city of Rome lay defenceless before him, but the conquest of the ancient capital was not as simple as it sounded. The name of Rome still had a magical power in the ears of the wild barbarian. From his youth he, and the whole world with him, had heard of the might of Rome. This one city had conquered the world, and its power had once seemed eternal. Even in its weakness Rome struck fear into his superstitious mind. Had not Alaric died within months of capturing the great city? Attila paused, and pondered.

The Romans themselves were terrified at his approach. Mighty as their name might sound they lacked any means to defend themselves. In their weakness they had no option but to send an embassy to the conqueror and beg for his mercy.

Bishop Leo was chosen as the representative of the Romans. The great minister marched out to meet the foe with a small band, and at the foot of Attila's throne he delivered one of the most important speeches of his life. His words proved more effective than weapons of war. The barbarian was awed by Leo's majestic appearance, and the bishop's words struck him with great force.

'I shall spare your city,' Attila pronounced. 'But my demand for Honoria's hand remains unchanged. Send her to me, or I shall return next year and destroy you.'

Fortunately for Rome, the next year was Attila's last. After leaving Italy the king of the Huns returned to his palace and celebrated his marriage to yet another concubine. The drunken wedding festival proved too much for the ageing barbarian, and he died in the night from a burst blood vessel.

The death of Attila was the death of his nation. Within weeks of his funeral his enormous empire was gone, as the hordes that had followed him turned on each other, each clan seeking to assert itself over its neighbours. The Huns were soon no more than a memory.

PRISCUS, HISTORY

The Fall of Rome

But Rome gained only a little breathing space from the death of her fearsome enemy. Only two years later it was the Vandals who appeared in full force before the ancient city's gates.

Aetius was now dead, murdered by the jealous and suspicious emperor's own hand. Vengeance did not long delay, and a conspiracy soon dispatched the unworthy emperor as well.

In the few provinces that remained to the western empire, many citizens no longer cared if they were ruled by Rome or the barbarians – indeed some looked with envy at the areas which had already been conquered. What evil could the barbarians do them that the Roman rulers were not doing already? Many had been reduced to poverty by rampant taxation, and they had nothing to lose from a change of masters.

In Rome itself the prophecies of the past became the hottest topic of gossip. An ancient story told that Romulus, the founder of Rome, had seen 12 vultures in flight as he began the work of building the city, and these vultures had been interpreted for hundreds of years as a prophecy that the city of Rome would survive for 12 centuries. Those 12 centuries were now coming to an end.

Even a Christian, Hippolytus, the great Roman theologian of the third century, had made a prediction about the fall of Rome. He had suggested from hints in Scripture that the Roman Empire would survive until about AD 474. Was there anything to these ancient beliefs?

When Gaiseric, king of the Vandals, led his troops to the gates of Rome in 455 the trembling Romans dared not oppose him. Again Bishop Leo was their only defence, and again the trustworthy minister pleaded successfully with the enemy. Rome was sacked, but the lives of the citizens were spared, and the buildings were saved from destruction. Forty-five years had passed since the capture by Alaric, and the years in between, however grim, had seen the capital well replenished with all that money can buy. All of this was now loaded onto the Vandal ships and carried to their new North African kingdom.

But Gaiseric left, and still Rome stood. For 20 years the shadow of the western empire dragged on its painful existence, and those troubled 20 years saw no less than eight emperors take the throne. In the end, western Rome disappeared with a fizzle instead of a bang. Late in 475 the last emperor of the west, Romulus Augustulus, came to the throne. He, like several of his predecessors, was no more than a puppet, and in the following year the great barbarian chief Odovacar tired of watching the show.

Curiously, the last emperor of Rome shared his name with the two great fathers of his nation. Romulus built the city of Rome, and Augustus (Augustulus is another form of Augustus) was Rome's first emperor.

'Forsake the purple,' Odovacar offered Romulus, 'and you will live.'

The offer was too good to refuse. The last of the emperors went into a peaceful retirement, and with little opposition Odovacar took the reins of government into his own hands. Italy now had a new king, and the empire of the west was gone.

A Light in the Darkness

In the last years of the empire, and in the dark days after its fall, God raised up many great men to guide his church. Society fell to the ground, law and order disappeared, but God never deserted his people. Of the great Christian leaders of the time, Severinus is perhaps the most striking. It was to his hands that God entrusted Noricum and the surrounding provinces (present-day Austria).

Attila's invasion had been hard on the people of Noricum, but harder still was the barbarian conqueror's death. For years there was war amongst the tribes who had once been united in Attila's empire, each seeking to establish a territory for itself or to plunder its neighbours, and the citizens of Noricum, and indeed of all central Europe, lived in perpetual fear. Countless barbarian clans roamed the shattered remains of the Roman provinces, and any day, and from any direction, a new invader might appear – robbing, murdering and enslaving.

Into this scene of devastation there came a stranger, alone, on foot. That a traveller from the east, a monk, should choose to visit their dying land was a great surprise to the people of Noricum.

'Who are you?'

The stranger smiled. 'My name is Severinus.'

'Your speech seems to be that of a North African.'

'Perhaps so. In fact I have seen many lands. None, however, is dearer to me than the eastern desert where the great monks live.'

'Are you running from something?'

Severinus laughed. 'If you think me a runaway slave,' he said, 'then prepare money to buy me back if my master calls for me!'

'But why have you come here, of all places?'

'I have come to obey, not to flee, my master's will.'

And that was as much as the citizens could extract from the enigmatic monk.

Severinus settled in a town called Asturis. Here he took a room from the local minister, and he lived a quiet life of prayer and meditation. Weeks passed, and the stranger was all but forgotten. Life went on as usual until one day, as the townspeople were gathered in church, the monk came bursting in upon the solemnities.

'Hear my words, minister of God,' he cried, 'and listen to me all you people. Destruction is coming upon your town, a great destruction that can only be averted by prayer and fasting, and a wholehearted commitment to the service of God. Every one of you must abandon his own evil desires and begin to show mercy and compassion. Will God look with mercy upon you if you fail to be merciful to your own fellow citizens? Hear the words of the Lord, and prove your faith by acting upon them.'

There was stunned silence, until the minister regained his composure.

'Who are you to burst into my church like this? Don't go getting an overblown view of your own holiness, my friend. You are out of line.'

Some of the people laughed.

'Are you worried by the German warriors prowling about? Forget about them. We have resisted them in the past, and shall do so in the future.'

Severinus was unmoved, and again he pleaded with the people to save themselves, both body and soul. This time the people shouted him down. They were confident of the strength of their town, and they thought the monk's words pure nonsense. They knew that German tribesmen were plundering the surrounding region, but this gave them little cause for worry. The barbarians had repeatedly failed to pierce the walls of Asturis.

'My duty to you is done,' Severinus cried over the congregation's jeers. 'I am leaving. But mark my words. God's sentence will be executed upon you before the week is through.'

Severinus left and moved on to Comagenis, a nearby town already controlled by barbarians. The conquerors had a stronghold in the centre of town, and from there could sally forth against the citizens at will. Again Severinus addressed the local church.

'If you desire to see God's hand at work for you,' he declared, 'then join me in three days of prayer and fasting. All must give freely to the poor, for they are suffering the most from this oppression. Have faith, and we shall see what God will do.'

While the people were listening to the monk's words an old man came running to the gates of the town.

'Asturis has fallen!'

'Asturis!' the men at the gate echoed in surprise. 'How?'

'We ignored the words of a servant of God!' the old man cried. 'The monk Severinus warned us of our fate, but we scoffed at him. Do you know where he has gone?'

'He is here in our town!' someone called out. 'He is probably in church right now.'

The old man ran off as fast as his legs would carry him. He was not surprised to find the monk addressing the local citizens.

'Holy Severinus!' he cried, throwing himself at his feet. 'I, almost alone amongst my people, believed your words in our congregation last week. I was prepared when the moment of our destruction came, and I fled before it was too late. Those who ignored you have been destroyed, and their wealth now belongs to the Germans!'

After this not a soul dared ignore the monk's words. The church was filled throughout the following days, and at all hours the fervent prayers of the congregation could be heard. The rich unsparingly opened their purses to the poor, and all awaited the revealing of the arm of the Lord with eager anticipation.

At nightfall on the third day, as the congregation celebrated communion, a powerful earthquake hit the town. The panicked barbarians rushed out of their stronghold and forced the citizens to open the gates for them. They wanted to be out in the fields, safe from falling objects, until the danger had passed.

As they hurried into the darkened fields two divisions of the barbarians happened to approach each other from opposite directions. Both sides presumed that they were faced with a hostile force, and in the black night a bloody battle began. The following morning, the slain littered the fields around about the walls, and the stunned citizens saw that their town was freed from its oppressors.

The fame of the monk spread throughout the region, and when famine struck the important city of Favianis, ambassadors were sent to beg Severinus to give the people the benefit of his preaching and prayers. Taking the pulpit in Favianis, Severinus wasted no time in uncovering the root of the people's sufferings.

'There is no scarcity in this city!' Severinus paused and allowed an angry murmur to pass around his audience. 'God has plentifully supplied your needs, and He will continue to do so.'

The people were exasperated by this apparent, and insulting, untruth.

'We didn't call you here to laugh at us,' they said. 'If there is no scarcity among us, why do our bellies growl?'

'Because your food is hoarded in the storerooms of the rich!' He paused. 'Procula, stand up!'

Everyone looked with surprise at Procula, a rich widow of the town. She rose, blushing deeply. Until this moment she had been a complete stranger to the monk.

'You are a noble woman, born of parents rich and free,' said Severinus. 'Why is it then that you have made yourself a slave, a slave to the most wicked master of all, avarice, which is idolatry? Give the food that you have hidden to Christ's poor, for if not you may as well feed it to the fish of the river, for you will make no profit from it. Do this, trust to the Lord, and He will do the rest.'

The famine came to an end that very afternoon, as the hidden stores of the deeply ashamed Procula, and some others like her, were opened to the poor. But this new supply soon ran out, and now all of the citizens, rich and poor alike, were reduced to the same extremity. 'Trust in the Lord,' was the only message that Severinus could give them.

So they trusted. When some ships unexpectedly appeared on the river Danube the whole city held its breath. The ships came into port.

'We set out at a bad time,' the new arrivals, food traders, told the ecstatic citizens, 'and got stuck in an ice jam upstream near Passau. It was terrible, we thought we would be iced in for ages, but there was a freakish heat wave and the ice melted away in no time.'

The people of Favianis thanked God for their deliverance, and the city's food stores were plentifully restored. In these troubled times, however, the end of one trouble was usually the beginning of another. War was the next evil to approach the city walls, with a lightning attack from the wild Germans. Much property was stolen, and a few citizens were kidnapped.

'We must give the barbarians something to think about,' Severinus told the local military commander. 'They act as though they can attack us with absolute freedom. We must make a show of force.'

'But what can I do with a handful of men who aren't even properly armed!'

'Trust to the Lord,' Severinus responded. 'He will fight for you. Only agree that you will not harm any prisoners you take, and that you will bring them straight to me.'

So the commander and his small band set out on the trail of the raiders. They found them at the second milestone from the city, all at ease and enjoying a drunken celebration for their success.

'The enemy!' the Germans cried. For a moment they scurried about in disorder, then fled into the forest, leaving prisoners, plunder and even their weapons and clothes behind them. A few were taken captive, and these were led back to Favianis by the bemused conquerors. Severinus ordered that they be untied. He treated them to a meal, and then let them go.

'Go,' he said, 'but warn your friends that if they return here the wrath of God will destroy them. You will not be so well treated next time.'

The name of Severinus now began to be repeated with awe even in the camps of the wildest pagans, and fear of the holy man filled many a fierce warrior's breast. Indeed the number of people coming for his advice became rather too much for the monk, and he left Favianis and found a secluded retreat in a dilapidated rural homestead named 'The Vineyards'. Here he returned to his accustomed life of prayer and meditation.

But not for long. God spoke to the monk in his lonely meditations, and Severinus could have no peace so long as he resisted the divine call.

'Return to my people,' came the voice of the Lord. 'This rest is but for a season. Greater labours still lie ahead.'

Severinus returned to Favianis and built a hut on a nearby
hill. He was now removed from the city's bustle, but near at
hand for the city's need – a need which was great indeed. A
constant stream came to the monk's door – for guidance, for
justice, for inspiration and for healing. Soon a crowd of disciples
inhabited the hill, each in his own hut imitating the life of the
master.

Severinus became a light to the barbarians as well. The
Rugians were a fierce tribe who dwelt on the northern shore of
the Danube, just across the river from Favianis. Their king,
Flaccitheus, thought highly of the Roman monk and often sought
his advice. His son and successor Feva did likewise, though he
was hindered in the friendship by the bitter temper of his wife.

Queen Gisa was an Arian, a cruel woman who wished to
force her orthodox subjects into obedience to her priests, and
fierce persecution would have been inevitable were it not for
Severinus' influence over Feva. When some citizens from a town
near Favianis were taken prisoner by the Rugians, Gisa
demanded they be rebaptized as Arians. Feva resisted her, so the
infuriated queen instead set them to work as the lowest of
slaves. Severinus sent a plea for mercy to the queen, but he
received a haughty response.

'Please, servant of God, hiding within your humble hut, we
are quite capable of dealing with our slaves without your expert
advice.'

Severinus was not at all disheartened by her words.

'The Lord will do what Gisa will not.'

Queen Gisa at this time had several goldsmiths employed in
fashioning jewellery for her. True to her nature, instead of
paying for their services, she had arrested the jewellers and put
them under close guard with their food as their only pay. On the
very day that Gisa refused Severinus' request her son Frederick,
a young boy, was at play in the courtyard outside the prisoners'
quarters. Curious to see what the jewellers were making, the
child dashed past the guards and into the workshop.

'Get out!' one of the men growled. 'Can't you see we are
busy!'

'I beg your pardon!' the proud lad cried. 'But I am Prince Frederick, son of King Feva and Queen Gisa!'

'Grab him!'

The jewellers seized the child by the scruff of his neck and held a knife to his chest. The guards came in to find their young prince in mortal danger.

'Too long we have slaved for that wretched woman!' the jewellers cried. 'Free us, or the child dies!'

This news shook the queen's guilty heart.

'Is Severinus avenged so soon? 'Shall his prayer spill the blood of my dear son?'

Instantly messengers were dispatched to ask the monk's forgiveness, and the captive Romans were sent back across the Danube. The goldsmiths were also promised freedom, and Frederick was released safe and sound.

In this time of bitter division it seemed that the whole region agreed in one thing only – Christians, Arians and pagans were united in admiration of the monk of Favianis. A Rugian man had spent 12 years with a crippling illness that gave him terrible pains and robbed him of the use of all his limbs. His mother, at her wit's end, put the young man in a cart and took him to the monk's door.

'Heal my son!' the woman cried, falling upon her knees.

'What can I do?' Severinus asked, raising the woman up. 'I have no power to heal just as I please! All I can do is share what I know of the way to obtain God's mercy. I suggest you begin by showing kindness to the poor.'

The desperate woman had nothing at hand to give away. She began to remove her clothes, and to offer them to the beggars.

'Woman, cease!' Severinus cried. 'I see how earnest you are, and I beg you to put your clothes back on! Carry out your desire to help the poor at a more appropriate time.'

Severinus began to pray, and in no time the young man was standing upon his withered legs. After a time of prayer and fasting the Rugian and his mother returned home. He had come in a cart; he went home pushing it.

Two brothers, wandering barbarians, once stopped to visit

the hut of the famous monk. They were Arians, on their way to Italy to seek their fortunes. Their names were Odovacar and Onulf. The mighty Odovacar had to stoop to enter the monk's hut, and once inside he could not rise to his full height.

'Go on,' Severinus said to him, 'go to Italy, dressed as you are in the skins of beasts. Today you are poor, but men will soon crowd your door seeking a gift.'

So Odovacar went on his way and, as we have heard, eventually became the first barbarian king of Italy. When that day came Odovacar remembered the monk's prophecy, and he sent messengers to Favianis.

'You need not crowd my door,' he wrote, 'but ask any gift, and it shall be given you.'

Severinus asked only that the new king forgive a certain Roman whom he had exiled.

With Odovacar's conquest of the western empire the troubles of central Europe only further increased. In the years that followed, the barbarians destroyed town after town, until the refugees of the whole region were crowded into the area around Favianis. The burden on Severinus was now enormous. He was forever employed in embassies, pleading for the release of captives. His hill had become a thriving monastery, and the oppressed Romans came in their thousands seeking comfort and assistance. Severinus supplied them with food and clothing, but it was a charity that could only be supported by continual tours of the region. In the areas least affected by war he would plead with the citizens to give a tithe of their produce for the support of those poorer than themselves. Severinus himself used next to nothing of these supplies. He fasted almost continuously, and even in the depth of winter, when the broad Danube was solid ice, he never wore a pair of shoes.

Even in the times of greatest distress Severinus never failed to insist upon the important truth that the service of God must come first.

'No matter the situation,' he said, 'our striving is for nothing if we fail to make God our first priority.'

This was strikingly proved in the experience of one local

farmer. During a plague of locusts Severinus called the people to a prayer meeting.

'Let us pray first to the Lord of the harvest,' he said. 'Without His blessing, locusts or not, our fields are good for nothing.'

One poor man did not attend the meeting. His crop was his last hope, and his mind could not rest a moment that he was away from his field. While everyone else was in church, he was driving the locusts away from his grain.

'I know how this fellow's prayer meetings go on. I could be there all day, and what would become of my field then!'

The following morning he rose to find that his whole crop had been devoured overnight, while the fields of his neighbours were virtually untouched.

Severinus was an old man by now. The decline of his ageing body seemed to proceed at the same pace as the decline of the province he had made his home. The Rugians and other barbarians were lording it over the whole region, and only the name of Severinus preserved Favianis itself from their cruel oppression. In the last months of his life Severinus frequently reminded the people of his approaching end.

'I am soon to leave you,' he said, 'but fear not, for God will deliver you from this wasteland. This land shall be a desert place, and you will find a better home elsewhere. The barbarians who scour this land will find no trace of the civilization they have destroyed. When you are gone they will even dig up the dead in the hope of finding hidden treasures from the past. When the Lord delivers you from this awful place I request of you only one thing, that you carry my bones with you as the Israelites carried Joseph up from Egypt.'

The dying monk paid a last visit to Feva and his queen. Touching the chest of the king, Severinus addressed the cruel Gisa.

'What, Gisa, do you love most? The soul in your husband's breast, or gold and silver?'

'My husband of course.'

'Then cease to oppress the innocent, or your crimes will be your husband's, and your own, undoing.'

A brother of Feva, Frederick, now had authority over Favianis itself and the area around it. Severinus summoned the barbarian to meet with him.

'I go to the Lord now,' he declared. 'While I lived, you dared not sate your appetite for plunder on this hill. You have spared only those under my protection. God's wrath will be upon you if you dare to go further once I am gone.'

The barbarian prince was indignant.

'What!' he cried. 'You accuse me of wishing to rob charity funds from a monk! I am a lawful prince, not a tyrant.'

'Mark my words,' said the old man, 'God is not mocked!'

It was the depth of winter. On the fifth of January Severinus developed a pain in one side, and for three days he suffered in silence. Just after midnight on the eighth, the old man summoned his disciples.

'Lament not,' he said, 'for the exodus which I have prophesied will surely come. I am about to pass on, and I repeat my request that my bones not be left behind.'

He kissed each of the brothers in turn, and then took Holy Communion for the last time.

'Do not weep for me!' he commanded. 'Sing me a psalm instead!'

But the weeping of his friends could not be halted so easily.

'Praise the Lord,' Severinus himself sang out, reciting Psalm 150. 'Let all that has breath praise the Lord!' And so saying he breathed his last.

The news of the monk's passing spread swiftly through the region. The barbarous Frederick wasted barely a breath.

'To the monastery!'

With the holy man gone Frederick's superstitious fears disappeared. His soldiers looted Severinus' hill, taking all of the garments that were stored for distribution to the poor. In his blind greed the barbarian even commanded his aide to seize the communion plate and goblet from the monk's chapel. The aide went quickly to obey the orders, but his heart filled with dread even before he laid his hand upon them. He sheepishly returned to his master.

'I cannot.'

Frederick was not to be stopped by one man's conscience, and a soldier was sent to do the dirty work instead. The soldier returned bearing the spoils of the chapel, but upon handing them to the prince he fell into a fit of trembling. In delirium he fled the scene of his sacrilege, and later, in a spirit of repentance, became a monastic hermit on a distant island.

But Frederick was still not satisfied. In vengeance for all of the years that the monk had forced him to restrain his rapacious desires he stripped every last object from the monastery, and then retired across the Danube to plot new mischief. Within a month he was dead, slain by his own nephew.

Some more years of decline and barbarian oppression followed, but the people never lost hope of the promised light ahead. Finally an army came from the south, led by King Odovacar of Italy, and the Rugians were overthrown and Feva and Gisa were carried to Italy in chains.

'Italy has been devastated by wars,' Odovacar told the impoverished citizens of Favianis. 'It needs new citizens to help in rebuilding. Why live in misery here, in this land so open to attack, when a broad and safe province beckons you?'

The citizens were quick to leave the scene of their sufferings behind, and true to their promise the coffin of their great leader accompanied them on the long march across the Alps to their new home. The people were distributed among the empty farms of Italy, and the remains of Severinus himself were given a final resting place in a mansion near Naples, the very mansion in which the deposed emperor, Romulus Augustulus, had spent his retirement. This resting place symbolized a new age. The emperors were gone, and the men of God had taken their place as guides of the nations.

EUGIPPIUS, *LIFE OF SEVERINUS*

The Conversion of the Franks

The fifth century, now coming to a close, was the most troubled time that the church had yet faced. Roman persecution had been terrible, but not nearly so terrible as the collapse of society itself. The great cities lay in ruins, the people were in poverty, and no one knew what the future might hold.

There might have been joy in the fact that many barbarians had abandoned idolatry, but the reality was not so simple. Most of the barbarians were Arians, and this, as we have seen, could mean trouble. Although most were peaceful towards the church, there was always a danger of religious persecution. The Vandals reminded the whole church of this. The church suffered a long and terrible persecution in their new North African kingdom. Gisa, and others like her, showed that the same might happen anywhere. Somehow, to gain lasting peace, the barbarians had to be reached with the true gospel. This was the church's great task in the sixth, and succeeding, centuries.

The Franks were an extremely savage tribe who ruled over northern Gaul. Unlike most of the other barbarian peoples they had not embraced any kind of Christianity and remained firmly entrenched in the old idolatry. Churches were frequently plundered by their raiding parties.

During one such raid an ornate ewer, finely made and very ancient, was carried off from a sacked church. The local bishop, greatly upset by its loss, sent messengers to Clovis king of the Franks.

'Even if you will not restore to us anything else you have stolen,' they said, 'our bishop begs you to return this one ewer.'

'Come to Soissons with me,' said Clovis, softened by the submissive entreaty. 'That is where we are to divide the booty. If the ewer is part of my share your bishop may have it.'

At Soissons the king addressed his men before the distribution began.

'Valiant freebooters,' he said, 'I ask of you all that this ewer be granted me in addition to my normal share.'

'Surely you shall have it!' the men cried. 'All we have is yours!'

But among them was one particularly avaricious and foul-tempered fellow. He raised his battle-axe and struck the ewer.

'You, king, shall have nothing but your fair share!'

The Franks were shocked by these words, but the king pretended to ignore them. He picked up the damaged ewer and handed it over to the Christians.

'Go in peace.'

Clovis' pride had been rattled by this occurrence, and he meditated revenge for many months. At the year's end a parade was held, and the king strode through the ranks of his men, inspecting the state of their weapons. When he came to his enemy he rebuked him sternly.

'No one else has equipment in such poor repair as yours. Your spear is a disgrace, and so are your axe and sword.'

With that Clovis snatched the man's axe and threw it to the ground. As the soldier angrily stooped to retrieve it Clovis swung his own axe and smashed his enemy's skull.

'Just as you did to my ewer at Soissons!'

The affair of the ewer, a mixture of generosity and brutality, was as close as Clovis came to the church in the early years of his reign. All of this was to change, however, when he took to himself a beautiful young wife.

Clotilda, a princess of the Burgundians, was one of the few orthodox Christian barbarians. Her childhood had been the scene of many misfortunes. She had witnessed the murder of both her parents at the hands of her brutal uncle Gundobad, and was herself only spared because of her youth. Her elder sister, Chroma, fled to the safety of a nunnery, but God had other plans for Clotilda.

Clovis was intrigued by reports of the beautiful and unfortunate young princess. Contact was established through his messengers, and a marriage proposal soon followed. Affairs were swiftly arranged to his satisfaction, for Gundobad dared not stand in the way of Clovis' wishes.

Clotilda herself had no choice in the matter, and we cannot know how she viewed her changing lot. Certainly she hated the wild pagan manners of her new household and laboured to change them by prayer and example. Indeed she did more than pray for her husband, and in private moments she was bold to witness to the fierce king.

'The gods you worship are no gods at all! They are made of wood and stone, and cannot help themselves, let alone anyone else. The legends about them are really only stories about famous kings of olden times. How could real gods fight wars against each other!

'You should worship the God who made heaven and earth out of nothing. At His command the sun began to shine, and the sky was covered with stars. God filled His world with fish, beasts and birds, and it is He who provides us the fruit of the tree and the vine in their seasons. You should be thankful to the One who made you!'

But her words fell on deaf ears.

'You are quite wrong,' Clovis insisted, 'for our gods made all those things you mentioned. We have a god of fruit and a god of water, a fish-god and a sun-god. I see no reason to worship your Christian God – there's simply no need for Him!'

Clotilda was not put off by her lack of success. She continued to pray, and to pester her husband. Finally, when the couple's first son was born, she had her first victory.

'Baptize him if you must!' Clovis blurted. 'Just stop nagging me about it!'

The delighted queen ordered that the church be richly ornamented for the baptism.

'We must make the church and the ceremony as beautiful as possible,' she told the bishop. 'Who knows, the solemnity of the service might succeed in interesting the king. It can't hurt. My arguments have certainly failed!'

So a new surprise was in store for King Clovis.

'You want me to go to the baptism as well! Is it not enough that I allow my son to be baptized?'

'You will not be required to stay for long,' said Clotilda meekly. 'It would mean a lot to your humble servant.'

The king gave in, the day of baptism came, and the ceremony was performed with all due solemnity. But before nightfall there was tragedy in the royal family.

'I should have known that something like this would happen,' cried Clovis. 'Had he been dedicated to my gods he would have lived. Baptism into the name of your God has struck him down within a day!'

So it seemed. Baby Ingomer was dead, and the king was furious.

'Why God has chosen to take our son I do not know,' Clotilda answered. 'But I do know that Ingomer now enjoys eternal life in heaven.'

Clovis was unmoved, and he continued unrepentant in his idol worship. Some time later Clotilda bore a second son, Chlodomer. Like Ingomer he was a sickly child, but the pleas of Clotilda once again worked on the king, and the boy was baptized. Things did not go smoothly this time either.

'You have done it to me again!' Clovis cried. 'No sooner is the boy baptized than he takes a turn for the worse. You should have been too ashamed to even ask for a second of my sons to be baptized. He will die because of your God, just as his brother did.'

Clotilda was devastated.

'Lord, what do You mean by this suffering?' she prayed. 'How will I ever be able to mention the gospel to my husband again! Spare my child, I beg you.'

The queen was soon rushing to Clovis' apartments.

'Your majesty! The Lord has restored Chlodomer!'

So He had. But the king was still unimpressed.

War later broke out between the Franks and the Alemanni. In a furious battle the Alemanni gained a decisive advantage, and Clovis watched in horror as his troops were slaughtered on all sides. Tears filled the warrior's eyes, and he looked to the sky in anger.

'Ye gods!' he cried. 'Is this your will for the mighty Franks? Where is your protection now? Do you wish to destroy us by the hand of the Alemanni?' The king groaned aloud. 'Why is my faith in you so much less than the faith of Clotilda in her God!'

His heart filling with remorse, Clovis raised his hands to heaven.

'Jesus Christ, You whom Clotilda calls the Son of God, You who help those who trust in You, I beg Your help. Show me the

miraculous power that others say they have experienced
through calling upon You, that I may believe and be baptized
into Your name. I have called upon my gods, but I see that they
have no intention of helping me. I want to believe in You, but I
must be saved from the foe!'

Even as the king spoke the battle began to turn. The king of
the Alemanni was struck down, and his men were immediately
thrown into disarray.

'King Clovis!' the enemy cried. 'Our king is dead, and the day
is yours. We shall submit to you!'

Following this great victory Clovis shared the story of his
conversion with his wife. Clotilda was overjoyed and
immediately summoned Remigius, Bishop of Rheims, to instruct
her husband in the duties of his new faith.

'Your words please me,' Clovis said to his instructor, 'but
there is a great problem ahead, for my men will not lightly
abandon their gods. I will, nevertheless, share with them what
you have shared with me.'

Clovis summoned a national assembly, but before he could
address his men a great cry exploded from the warrior throng.

'We shall abandon our mortal gods! We shall follow the
immortal God whom Remigius preaches!'

So without further ado preparations were made for a massive
national baptism! Obviously there had already been a desire for
change in many hearts, and the rumour of the king's intentions
was enough to set things rolling. The hand of God was leading
the Franks in quite unexpected ways.

Clovis was the first to go forward to the pool of baptism.
Bishop Remigius, mindful of the nation's violent past, addressed
him boldly.

'Bow your head in meekness, mighty man. Adore what you
have burned, and burn what you have adored.'

The year was 496. The closing years of the chaotic fifth
century had seen a sign of times to come. The conversion of the
Franks was a great turning point, and a promise of the church's
glorious future.

The conversion of the Franks provided an enormous

challenge for the ministers of the church, for they now had the difficult task of shepherding this wild and warlike band. Most of the Franks had indeed abandoned their old idolatry, but it was a lot longer before they started to show a real understanding of the gospel of Jesus in their daily lives. To teach the most warlike of nations the way of peace and love was a daunting task.

The conversion of the barbarian tribes was a very different thing to the conversion of the Roman Empire. Rome was slowly converted over centuries, while many of the tribes were converted in a very brief space of time. There are important reasons for this difference, which had important consequences.

Roman society was individualistic. In the great cities there were people of many nationalities, and of different religions and philosophies. To a great degree, people lived as they wished. There was no close feeling of brotherhood between the citizens of a city, and as a result conversion to Christianity was quite a personal process. A Roman felt free to choose his own faith, and in the case of Christianity not even persecution would stop him.

The barbarian tribes were different. Whole nations lived close together, and there were very strong ties between people. There were no strangers in your clan, and all followed the same code of conduct and worshipped the same gods.

Many barbarians had the spiritual courage to break these chains and converted to Christianity on their own. More common, however, was what is known as 'national' conversion. Put simply, instead of the church growing one by one, the whole nation slowly becomes more used to the Christian ideas, until many people are ready to convert at the same time. National conversion and being truly born again are usually quite different. A tribe might be convinced that Christianity is superior to its idols, and therefore convert, without having a deeper knowledge of God. It is often only after the 'national' conversion that true personal conversions begin.

But even before the conversion of Clovis, Christianity had been slowly softening the Franks' wild spirits. Genevieve was a nun of Paris, famous for her wisdom and piety. On one occasion Clovis' father, King Childeric, had made preparations to execute several prisoners outside the gates of Paris.

'Close the city gates,' he commanded. 'Lest we get Genevieve out here annoying us!'

The king was obeyed, but word of the execution spread quickly through the city and, true to form, Genevieve came racing to the scene. The gates sprang open at her touch, and the ageing woman threw herself at the pagan king's feet.

'I shall not leave you until you promise to spare your enemies!'

And so, unwillingly, the king did. The superstitious pagans had never before seen such sincerity and love, and they were very often overpowered by it.

All the same, Clovis' first prayer had been a warrior's prayer, and to his death he retained a warrior's heart. When Bishop Remigius first delivered a sermon on the sufferings of Jesus, and His brutal treatment at the hands of the Jews, the doughty king could not restrain himself.

'Had I been there with my trusty Franks,' he cried, leaping from his pew, 'those Jews would not have dared!'

It was no idle boast. Nothing more convinced Clovis and his Franks of the truth of the Christian faith than the success that they enjoyed after their conversion. Clovis' reign saw a great many battles, and the king returned victorious from them all. He conquered much of the surrounding territory from other barbarian tribes, and thus liberated the Christian citizens of what had once been Roman Gaul from their pagan and Arian masters.

In time he came to grips with the greatest conquerors in Gaul, the Arian Visigoths of the south, who were now ruled by Alaric II, namesake of the great conqueror of Rome. It was evident that the future of Gaul lay with one or the other of these tribes, and in 507 the Frank declared war on his powerful neighbours. In their march against the Visigoths, Clovis' army passed through the region of Tours.

'Tours,' Clovis warned his men, 'was the home of Martin, Gaul's greatest saint. Show your respect for him, and be on your best behaviour. Requisition nothing but fodder and water.'

One of his soldiers dared make light of the command. He saw a peasant carrying hay, and stole it by force.

'Well,' he said, 'it's fodder, isn't it?'

Clovis was told of this, and he struck the soldier down on the spot.

'We will get nowhere if we offend against God's saint!'

No one else dared commit a similar offence. Before moving on Clovis sent messengers to the local church, which was dedicated to Martin.

'See if you can bring me some good word from God's house,' he said, loading the messengers with gifts for the church. Anxiously he awaited their return, praying that God would make clear to him the outcome of the battle ahead. The messengers entered the church as the choir was singing Psalm 18:

'You have armed me with strength for the battle. You have subdued those who rose up against me. You have made my enemies turn in flight, and I have destroyed my foes' (Ps. 18:39–40).

The messengers took this occurrence as a sure sign, and the whole army was encouraged by their report.

Clovis now marched to the River Vienne, but he was unable to cross because of flooding from heavy rains. He spent the night in prayer that God would provide his army some means of crossing, and at first light a huge deer emerged from the woods and entered the stream, and in sight of the Franks bounded across with sure steps. Report soon spread through the camp.

'We have discovered a natural ford!'

The army crossed and came to Poitiers, and there they camped on the night before battle. In Poitiers was a church dedicated to Hilary (a fourth-century opponent of Arianism), and that evening the Franks saw what appeared to be a pillar of fire in the sky above it. They could only interpret it as a token of heaven's approval.

'Hilary conquered the Roman Arians,' they said, 'Clovis shall conquer the Gothic Arians!'

The two armies met at Vouille, ten miles beyond Poitiers, and the kings themselves took centre stage in battle. Clovis and Alaric fought hand to hand, and when the Gothic king fell his forces were soon overwhelmed. In the confusion of the Frankish triumph, however, Clovis himself was endangered. After striking down Alaric he found himself surrounded by Goths, two of whom lunged forward to avenge their king. Both men struck at the Frank with their spears, and Clovis received two wounds to the belly. Wheeling swiftly he dropped his head and hugged close to his horse's back, and through his stallion's speed made it to safety without further injury. A thick leather undergarment had narrowly saved his life.

Following the victory, the Franks were masters of most of Gaul. Of all the early barbarian conquests, theirs alone proved to be lasting. The name of Gaul was eventually forgotten, and the kingdom of Clovis' successors became known as France. Arian Vandals and Goths, pagan Huns – all of these mighty nations disappeared and left little behind them. The Franks alone survived to take a major place in the new Christian world which was coming to birth, and in which their conversion was a seminal moment.

GREGORY OF TOURS, HISTORY 2.27–37

Justinian and the Roman Revival

The Vandals, conquerors of North Africa, have left us only their name: their cruel and senselessly destructive ways have made them a proverb to this day. Throughout its brief history their kingdom was a nightmare of 'vandalism' and bloodshed.

Gaiseric, the king who led them in the conquest of North Africa, was a savage persecutor of the church. Ministers and laymen alike were tortured or killed at his command, and church buildings were confiscated. In the confusion and carnage of the barbarian's reign Carthage, the African capital, was without a bishop for more than twenty years.

Gaiseric's death in 477 brought some relief, and the early years of his son Hunneric's reign seemed to promise a brighter future. Hunneric allowed the orthodox Christians to elect a new bishop for Carthage, and Eugenius was chosen for the task.

Eugenius put new spirit into the Christians and won the hearts of many Vandals, but his work sparked bitter complaints from Hunneric's Arian ministers, who insisted that their teachings were in danger if the Christians continued to preach freely. The king followed their advice and forbade Eugenius to allow Vandals to enter his church.

'It is enough that you are allowed to teach. Do not attempt to convert the Arians, or there will be trouble.'

Eugenius was put in a terrible predicament by this order. He could not just forget about the souls of the Vandals in order to protect his own flock. The church has a mission from Christ to teach the whole world, and the commands of a king should not stop it. Eugenius ignored Hunneric's order.

The king's first move upon hearing of this disobedience was to place soldiers at the doors of all churches. Any Vandals caught entering the churches were arrested and put to the torture. Some were blinded, others killed. Many Vandal women had their hair twisted around sticks and pulled from their heads in clumps, scalp and all, before being led through the city, blood streaming from their wounds, as a warning to others.

Hunneric later resolved on even tougher measures. He began by calling a council, in which the Arian and Catholic ministers were to discuss their opposing views. He had no intention of making it a fair trial.

Prior to the council Hunneric arrested and executed several leading Christian theologians, but their colleagues refused to be cowed by the bloody warning. To the king's extreme displeasure they skilfully defended their beliefs in council, and Hunneric responded by formally condemning the Christians and forbidding the teaching of anything but Arianism. The Christian ministers, including Eugenius, were thrown out of the city, and all of their property was confiscated – even their clothes.

'Anyone who offers them shelter will be burned!'

The impoverished ministers, utterly dumbfounded, spent many days locked outside the gates of Carthage. When they saw Hunneric and his men ride forth from the city one morning they ran to the king to plead their case.

'What wrong have we done? We came to the council at your request, and now we perish from hunger and cold!'

'Ride them down!' cried the barbarian. He and his men knocked the ministers to the ground and trampled them beneath their hooves. The survivors were later split into two parties, one of which was sent into exile, while the others became slave labourers.

The next few decades witnessed a return to the darkest days of persecution, broken only by Hilderic, who reigned from 523–30. He favoured and protected the church but was deposed and thrown into a dungeon by his cousin Gellimer, a brutal Arian, who took the throne after him.

The eastern empire could not look on these happenings with indifference. The natives of North Africa were not just fellow Christians – until recently they had been fellow citizens.

> Hunneric punished a large group of Christians by cutting their right hands off and tearing their tongues out. Thus mutilated they fled to Constantinople, and there they amazed the entire city with the most striking miracle – all could still speak clearly, and did so until their deaths. Here was a great act of God, and one that a whole city watched for years. Many authors record the extraordinary occurrence (including a leading philosopher, Aeneas of Gaza: 'I saw them myself and heard their speech, and diligently enquiring by what means such an articulate voice could be formed without any organ of speech I examined their mouths. I found that their tongues had been wholly torn away by the roots, an operation which the physicians generally suppose to be lethal!'), and even the bitterest enemies of Christianity have been grudgingly forced to admit that something *unusual* did occur here.

For years Constantinople had been too engrossed in its own battle for survival to spend its energies on foreign affairs. But now times had changed. Justinian had recently come to the throne, a ruler determined to restore the ancient glory of Rome.

In response to the usurpation of Gellimer, Justinian mounted a massive invasion of the Vandal kingdom. Belisarius, one of the greatest generals of Roman history, was put in charge of the difficult undertaking and in June 533 set sail for Carthage at the head of a mighty Roman fleet. After a two-month voyage the Roman troops pitched their first camp in Vandal territory. A source of fresh water was located, and on the following morning some of the soldiers went out to collect vegetables from the surrounding gardens. 'Requisitioning' food supplies was normal practice for invading armies, but Belisarius was not impressed.

'I forbid you to take anything but water without payment,' he said. 'It is not our numbers or strength which will win this province for us, but the hatred which the local people feel for their Vandal masters. If you plunder the peasants they will rightly turn against you and unite with the Vandals to defeat us.'

The soldiers saw the wisdom of the general's words, and they maintained good order on their march to the capital. Instead of the local farmers fleeing from the invaders, they joyfully welcomed the Romans as liberators and held markets at every stage of their route to supply their needs. Town after town opened its gates, and within a fortnight the Romans were marching on Carthage itself.

Gellimer felt that his only chance was to overwhelm his enemy in one decisive battle. He split the Vandal forces into three parts, took charge of the main body himself, and placed the other two divisions under his brother Ammatas and nephew Gibamond.

'When the Romans approach Carthage Ammatas will attack them head-on, and just as they engage, Gibamond, at the head of two thousand cavalry, will charge in from the left. While they are still reeling I will rise from ambush and challenge their rear, and in the confusion of the moment they will be ours!'

But even so the barbarian was not completely confident. In secret he ordered that the imprisoned Hilderic be executed if the Romans should triumph.

'He'll not get his hands on the kingdom again!'

When the day of battle came his fears proved well founded. Ammatas, instead of waiting for the appointed hour of battle, decided to win glory for himself by a sudden and unaided assault. He rushed at the head of his troops into the thick of the fight, and after striking down about a dozen Romans he received a mortal wound. With their general dead, his army fled in terror.

Gibamond arrived at the appointed time but was too late to

be of any use. A division of only six hundred Romans disposed of his two thousand horsemen in short order, and when Gellimer himself arrived the Romans were already gone, and only corpses lay to mark the scene of battle. In desperation the king threw himself at the Romans, now outside the gates of the capital itself, and after a bloody encounter his forces were crushed and Gellimer himself was forced to flee to the desert. There he spent the following weeks in reorganizing the scattered and disheartened Vandal troops. In this brief exile only one pleasing piece of news reached the fallen king – Hilderic was dead, just as ordered.

The Romans were invited with celebrations into the capital. The remaining Vandals fled to the churches for Sanctuary, and North Africa again became part of the Roman Empire. After one further battle, against the regrouped forces of Gellimer, the Vandals were completely destroyed. The treacherous king himself was spared and sent into a peaceful exile.

Justinian was delighted at Belisarius' success, and even greater ambitions began to agitate his heart. His gaze now focused on the city of Rome itself.

Italy was ruled by the Ostrogoths. This barbarian tribe had invaded in 489, and after several battles had taken control of much of Odovacar's realm. In 493, King Theodoric of the Ostrogoths treacherously murdered Odovacar with his own hand and became king of all Italy.

The Ostrogoths were mainly Arian, but Theodoric's reign caused few complaints amongst the orthodox. He was generally just and mild, though in the last years of his reign he did exercise some severity towards the church. He left no son, and was succeeded by his daughter Amalasontha. Amalasontha ruled with justice and wisdom, but she was murdered in 535 by her cousin Theodatus, who took the throne after her. Seizing the opportunity, Justinian dispatched Belisarius to avenge Amalasontha, and ultimately to restore Italy to the empire.

The great general landed in the extreme south of Italy. He marched along the coast to Naples, which was speedily captured, and then assaulted and took Rome itself. Belisarius' troops were rather bemused by their too-easy success. Where was the Gothic king?

Theodatus, in fact, was already dead. His people had quickly tired of his criminal and cowardly character, Witiges had been elected as his successor, and by the time the Ostrogoths were prepared to defend themselves it was already too late to save Rome. Rather than being besieged by the invaders they found themselves in the strange position of having to besiege the invaders inside Rome itself!

Belisarius' army suffered a difficult siege at the hands of Witiges, but the skill of the Roman general eventually prevailed, and the Gothic army was crushed and its king captured. In the hour of victory, however, fearful that the triumphant general might attempt to establish himself on the vacant western throne, Justinian ordered Belisarius' immediate return.

Belisarius returned to Constantinople with Witiges, and the defence of Italy was handed to lesser generals. The Goths, inspired by the departure of their formidable foe, were swiftly reorganized. Under the leadership of a new king, Totila, they began to win back the territory they had lost.

The loss of Belisarius was much more than the loss of a great general. Under him the soldiers had been well disciplined, and he had prevented cruelty and injustice towards the locals. Under the weak generals who succeeded him, and the voracious Roman tax collectors, it was not long before the people began to long for a return to the Goths!

The savage but brilliant Totila, with an army only five thousand strong, won a resounding victory over a far superior Roman force at Faenza. Proceeding from there to Naples, he happened to pass Monte Cassino.

'I have heard of a famous monastery in this place,' he told his followers, 'and of a great man of God named Benedict who lives here. I wish to meet him.'

Messengers were sent, and the meeting agreed to. Having heard that Benedict was blessed by God with prophetic insight Totila dressed Riggio, his sword-bearer, in royal robes, and sent him to the monastery in his place.

'We shall see whether the rumours about him have any substance.'

Riggio, surrounded by the royal attendants, found Benedict sitting in the monastery courtyard.

'Son,' the monk said with a smile, 'lay aside the clothes which are not your own.'

Riggio stepped back, and then fell down upon his face.

'Forgive me holy father,' he cried. 'I meant no harm by this trick!' With no further ado he returned to the king.

'What you have heard is true!'

King Totila himself now proceeded to the monastery. When he caught sight of the old monk he also fell prostrate and refused to rise at Benedict's repeated request. Finally Benedict raised him from the ground with his own hands.

'You, King Totila, are father of many evils. The Lord commands you to put an end to your brutality.' Totila trembled silently, and the monk continued. 'You will enter Rome; you will triumph across the sea. You will reign nine years, and in the tenth you will die.'

This meeting was a turning point for the Ostrogothic king. He was from that day a different man – indeed he became known as a gentle and considerate ruler – and as a result enjoyed even greater success than before. When he attacked Naples the citizens begged a one-month truce that they might await reinforcements, and Totila not only agreed but offered them three months instead. Like Belisarius he protected the property of the farmers and won the affections of the people in the process. He even stamped out one of the most common evils of ancient war – the theft of the enemy's wives. In Totila's camp, rape was punished with death.

The Romans were powerless against the rejuvenated Gothic army, and Justinian finally bowed to necessity and sent Belisarius back to Italy. The general returned to find his good work ruined. No longer able to rely on the goodwill of the people, and with badly depleted troops, his genius was his only resource. Totila captured Rome in 546, only to see Belisarius win it back two months later. Belisarius put the little he had to brilliant use, and the scales of war swayed one way and another, until the jealous emperor again intervened and recalled his general. Immediately Totila recaptured Rome and then crossed the sea to seize the island of Sicily from the Romans. To Justinian he now offered the olive branch.

'Let this war be at an end, that lasting peace and close friendship may be established between our nations.'

Justinian was deaf to repeated offers of a peaceful settlement, and in 552 a new expedition was launched. The fate of Italy was decided by a single mighty battle, in the tenth year after the meeting of Benedict and Totila. The Gothic king fell, his forces were scattered, and a Roman general named Narses completed the conquest of Italy.

Though he never led his own armies Justinian is remembered as one of history's great conquerors, and his reign marks a new age in Roman history. His conquests added new strength and life to an ancient empire, which until his accession had been slowly dying. The eastern empire again became a major force in Europe, Asia and Africa, and with its new-found strength actually lived on to outlast most of the new barbarian kingdoms, surviving in all another nine centuries.

From this time onwards the eastern empire is commonly called the 'Byzantine Empire', Byzantium being the name of the town which was replaced by Constantinople. The Byzantines usually called themselves simply *the* Roman Empire, as their western rival was now gone. The western and eastern empires are often called the Latin and Greek empires respectively.

Foreign conquests were only one side of the restoration under Justinian – indeed the emperor's most renowned achievements are not those of the battlefield, but of the law court. Justinian inherited a legal system in hopeless confusion and resolved upon its repair.

The centuries of Roman history had produced an utterly intimidating quantity of legislation and legal interpretation. The most respected ancient law books had been supplemented by innumerable imperial edicts, particularly under Christian emperors keen to bring the legal system into conformity with Christian ideas. And so the courts were now smothered, and the execution of justice impeded, by an unwieldy mass of ill connected documents. Contending parties could produce conflicting legislation in court, and it was often unclear which was valid.

Justinian appointed a team of lawyers to bring order to the chaos, and over the course of several years a series of volumes was issued setting forth the law in concise and final form. All earlier tomes were superseded (in fact appeal to other authorities was banned – and to keep things simple it was made an offence to write commentaries on the revised code), and the myriad laws were carefully distributed into categories. Christianity was now acknowledged as the foundation of the state, and whereas heretofore Christian legislation had been virtually an afterthought, an appendage to Roman law, Justinian's Code begins with the creed, and with the legislation specifically relevant to the church. Justinian's legal reform is to this day the basis of the civil law of most of Europe.

Above war and lawmaking, however, Justinian's most passionate interest appears to have been theology. Just as he wished to reconquer the lands lost to the barbarians, and to restore the legal system, Justinian wished to unite his subjects in their religious opinions as well.

The Copts and Syrians were still opposing the Greek church on the question of the Incarnation. We need not go into the details of these arguments again, but need only point out that the rebel groups which denied the Council of Chalcedon were by now known as Monophysites ('one-naturists'). Justinian was determined to bring these troubles to an end, and in 553 he summoned the Fifth Ecumenical Council. The new council, held in Constantinople, returned to the arguments of a hundred years before, and although it did some interesting work it completely failed to convince the Copts and Syrians. No council was going to heal the old divisions.

Unfortunately for the Monophysites, the emperor could do more than just call councils. In his eagerness to unite his empire

Justinian did the very thing most likely to divide it – he began to persecute his opponents. Leading Monophysites were imprisoned or exiled, and the entire movement might have been destroyed had an opponent worthy of the battle not confronted Justinian's measures. The man who proved Justinian's undoing was nicknamed, even by his friends, 'the mule's saddle'. Into his story we shall venture shortly.

VICTOR OF VITA, HISTORY OF THE VANDAL PERSECUTION

Benedict

But first we return briefly to Italy, to see more of the great monk Benedict.

Benedict, a son of one of the best Italian families, left the 'world' behind at the age of only fourteen. Sickened in spirit by the greed and immorality of the Italian cities, the teenage monk abandoned his worldly prospects to seek a hideaway of prayer and devotion. For some time he wandered the country in search of a suitable location, eventually coming to Subiaco, a remote and mountainous area. While following a rugged trail through the hills he met a monk named Romanus, who asked him where he was going.

'I seek a cave in which I might live as a hermit.'

Impressed by Benedict's passion and sincerity Romanus offered his help.

'If you can find such a cave nearby,' he said, 'I will bring you food whenever I can. Be assured that I won't reveal your location to another soul.'

Benedict embraced this offer, and he found a suitable cave and spent about three years in almost complete solitude, broken only by the occasional visits of his new friend.

Some shepherds eventually discovered Benedict's cave. They were more than a little surprised by the young cave dweller, but they left their first meeting with a deep impression of Benedict's calm piety. Word of their find spread, and local villagers began to visit the wild location. They brought bodily food to the monk and received spiritual food in return.

One morning Benedict was sitting alone outside his cave. He had come out to pray, but his mind began to wander as he breathed in the silence.

A blackbird came up close and began to flutter about the monk's head. Benedict watched the little bird's dance and was quite mesmerized as it wheeled about in smooth circles. The bird came so close that the monk could have caught it in his hand.

Benedict fell into a daydream, and the beautiful face of a woman he had once known appeared before his eyes. Suddenly the young man's mind felt as though it was no longer his own, and he was filled with a great longing to flee his retreat. Passionate overwhelming desire to abandon this hard life, to go to the city and find a wife, surged within him, until in a flash the daydream disappeared. Benedict sobbed out loud, and groaning in mixed dismay and rage he jumped to his feet, and in a fit of frustration flung himself into a patch of nettles and prickle bushes that lay close by. Thorns and stinging nettles tore his flesh, but for the moment he didn't care. When he stood up his whole body was scratched and bleeding, but he felt that a great victory had been won. Never again did thoughts of abandoning his chosen life occur to him.

> The place where Benedict rolled in the thorns can still be seen today. Francis of Assisi visited the site seven hundred years after Benedict and planted two rose bushes beside the briers. The roses thrived and spread until the weeds were gone. This has always been seen as a great symbol. The hard life of the monk has been exceedingly fruitful, just as every beautiful rose is hedged by thorns.

Benedict inspired a number of followers to settle in the area around his cave, and when the abbot of a local monastery died Benedict was invited to replace him. The offer, however, was turned down immediately.

'My life is not like that which I hear you lead,' he said. 'I fear that I will be far too strict for you.'

'Come all the same,' the monks insisted. 'If we displease you as we are, then reform us as you will.'

The men of this monastery had been accustomed to a fairly easy life, and in spite of their protestations of willingness to change Benedict's efforts at reform caused much friction. Benedict put great emphasis on the spiritual duties of prayer and Scripture study, required all to engage in physical work, and showed himself exceedingly vigilant in the suppression of misbehaviour. It was only a few months before a group of dissolute monks formed a conspiracy against the young abbot.

'We can't get away with anything around here. Benedict goes, or we do!'

The cabal took extreme measures and found some poisonous herbs to mix into their abbot's wine. Unsuspecting, Benedict sat down to his evening meal and said a prayer and made the sign of the cross over his food. As he did so, his cup split in two and his wine spilled over the table. He looked at the monks around him in amazement, and the guilty looks on several faces silently told their own story.

'How could you have thought of something so wicked?' he asked in horror. Shaking his head he gazed at the dark herbs the wine had left behind as it ran to the floor. 'Why did you not simply ask me to leave? Go and find yourselves an abbot to your own liking. May God forgive you.'

Benedict returned to Subiaco, and he remained there until he was nearly fifty years old. His fame spread far beyond the local region, and Italians and Goths alike came to his retreat. More and more monks placed themselves under his guidance, and in time there were 12 monasteries dotted over the hillside, each with its own abbot, but all following the rule of life of Benedict.

Fame eventually brought new sorrows. Florentius, a priest in the neighbourhood of Subiaco, burned day and night with jealousy. He longed to be thought of as somebody great, but even his own congregation paid him little attention. Whenever they needed spiritual advice it was not their own minister they sought, but the great abbot who lived so nearby.

Envy choked Florentius for years, until finally snapping he began to take revenge. He started malicious rumours about Benedict and repeatedly exhorted his congregation to avoid

Subiaco. His attempts proved vain, and failure drove him to utterly crazy measures.

'Get out of my region or I will ruin your monks.'

Florentius gathered seven prostitutes and paid them to visit Benedict's main monastery. The women went to Benedict's garden, and there tried to entice the monks to sin with them. None fell for the devilish trap, but Benedict admitted defeat on the spot.

'The man who will do this will stop at nothing,' he said. 'I must leave, or something terrible will come of it.'

With sorrow Benedict moved on, taking only a small group of monks with him. He gave firm instructions to those who stayed behind, and prayed that God would protect them from Florentius' envy. Only a few hours after his departure a messenger arrived at Subiaco.

'Florentius is dead! His balcony collapsed and crushed him.'

Maurus, a leading disciple, received the news with joy.

'Quickly! Follow the abbot and tell him to return. It is time for celebration!'

Benedict was resting about ten miles from Subiaco when the messenger caught him. The monk's reaction was far from what had been expected.

'My enemy is dead,' he said with a tear. 'Is his condemnation any cause for rejoicing? Tell Maurus that I shall not return, for I feel that this move is God's will. Tell him also that I am disappointed in him – that he should show such pleasure at another's death.'

Benedict now directed his steps to Cassino, a town by the foot of rugged Monte Cassino, one of the wildest areas left in Italy. An ancient pagan temple atop the mountain witnessed that the local peasants were still addicted to the worship of idols, but the preaching of the monks soon saw the idols and their altars destroyed, and the temple itself converted to a church. The monks built a monastery beside it, and in this new home the abbot lived out his last 14 years.

When a famine struck the region, the impoverished locals began coming to Benedict's monastery in great numbers. The monks could not refuse these people their charity, and it was not long before the monastery itself was out of grain. The day finally came that the monks sat down to a meal and found that only five loaves of bread remained to them. No one grumbled, but downcast faces said more than words.

'Are you so upset over a little bread?' Benedict asked. 'What matter if today we lack? Tomorrow is a new day. Wait for the Lord.'

The next morning the monastery arose to the prospect of a day without food, but when the gate was opened a number of sacks were found just outside.

'Someone has left about two hundred measures of flour for us!'

Thus it was that the monastery made it through its first food shortage – and the monks never did discover the identity of their benefactor.

A servant named Exhilaratus was once sent to the monastery by his master with a gift of two wooden flasks of wine. On his way, however, Exhilaratus hid one of the flasks beside the track so that he could enjoy it himself on the way back.

'No one will know.'

Upon his arrival at Monte Cassino he presented the flask to Benedict, who thanked him warmly, and the servant turned to go.

'I would watch out if I was you, however,' Benedict added. 'Have a good look before you drink.'

Exhilaratus stood speechless. Embarrassed and confused, he waited for the monk to say something more, but when the abbot turned to other business the confounded servant left without another word. When he found his flask he followed the monk's instructions, and tilted it over before picking it up.

'AH!'

Exhilaratus leapt backwards as a snake darted out of the stolen flask. In terror he confessed his sin, and it was just such stories that spread the fame of the great abbot even further. It was during these years that King Totila visited the abbot, as related earlier. It was also here that an infamous Goth named Zalla visited him.

Zalla was the cruellest of the Arians, and the most rapacious of the Gothic chieftains. Rich and poor alike suffered from his brutality, and he frequently kidnapped people and put them to torture in the hope of extracting confessions of hidden money. Some did reveal hidden gold; others, who had nothing to confess, died under the tortures.

Zalla once captured a poor farmer, and to throw the cruel barbarian off the track he falsely confessed to a secret treasure.

'You are right!' he cried. 'I have gold, but it is stored at Benedict's monastery!'

Little did he realize the extent of the Arian's greed.

'Good!' said Zalla, tying the farmer's hands together and mounting his horse. 'Lead me there.'

After a long journey, the pair reached Monte Cassino and found Benedict reading outside the monastery's gate.

'That's him,' said the shamefaced peasant.

Zalla shoved his prisoner out of the way. 'Get up! Do you hear me?' he cried. 'Give me this man's money.'

Benedict looked up from his book, and as he did so the rope which bound the peasant's hands fell to the ground. Zalla looked with shock from the abbot to the peasant and back again, and then dismounted.

'Man of God, forgive my harsh words. Pray to your God for me!'

Benedict summoned his fellow monks. 'Prepare a meal. We have two guests.'

After the meal Benedict delivered the Goth a stern warning. He lay before him the teachings and example of Christ, and in the name of God commanded him to abandon his ways. His words did not miss their mark, and Zalla left Monte Cassino suitably chastened.

Benedict's lasting fame, however, does not rest upon any of these striking occurrences. It is for the 'Benedictine Rule' that he is ranked among the great men of history.

In Benedict's time there were hundreds of monasteries throughout the Christian world, and depending upon the abbot, and the character of the monks, these monasteries could be very different places. Some were great temples of prayer and meditation, where the sick were tended and the hungry fed. Others were dark dens of sloth and greed.

Benedict composed a rule (i.e., a code of conduct) for the monks who lived under his guidance. It was not the first such monastic rule, but Benedict's was the greatest and most thorough yet seen. With wisdom and moderation it set forth clear responsibilities and standards of behaviour. It rapidly won a wide distribution and became a light and guide to countless wayward abbots and monks. Within a few generations it had superseded all earlier rules in the west, and its simple clarity established the pattern for a style of life which was to inspire Europe for centuries.

Benedict's Rule firmly establishes daily times for prayer, the singing of psalms and meditation, and for the study of Scripture and other religious writings. It also requires monks to work six or seven hours per day at gardening or some other manual labour, teaching or writing. Benedict well knew that 'idle hands do the devil's work', and his rule about daily work was very significant. After the fall of Rome, during the dark days of the early barbarian kingdoms, it was his hard-working monks who kept society together. They cared for the sick, educated children, protected the helpless, and with their unwearied copying preserved the literature and scientific knowledge of the ancient world.

Those wishing to become monks were severely tested before even being allowed within the monastery's walls. Benedict knew that the hard life of the monk was not for everyone, and he said that anyone who sought admittance to the monastery should, with no ceremony, have the door closed in his face! Only if they persisted in knocking and entreating for four or five days should they be allowed in, and even then they were to be given a room far from the other monks. For two months their character was examined, and they were repeatedly warned of the difficulties of monastic life. At the end of two months the Rule of Benedict was read to them, and they were asked if they wholeheartedly agreed to follow it. If so they went on to six months of probation, at the end of which the Rule was read to them again, and they were again free to accept it or leave. After four more months the Rule was read to them a third time, and they were invited to take a binding vow before God and man.

'If you wish to stay any longer, you must pledge to be a member of our community for the rest of your life. In the sight of God you will no longer be free to come and go as you please. Marriage is for life, and just so is the monk's vow. Dare not take it unless you have the strength to carry it through.'

Monks were to pledge poverty, chastity and obedience. Poverty meant that no monk had possessions of his own, and everything was shared between the brothers of the monastery. Obedience was to be wholehearted, and given first to God and then to the abbot. This insistence, however, did not grant an abbot tyrannical power. The Rule dictates that an abbot faced with a major decision on the monastery's future must assemble the whole community for debate – for in Benedict's own words, 'it is often to younger men that God reveals what is best'. It was illegal to publicly quarrel with the abbot, but differences of opinion could be respectfully raised in private.

Benedict's Rule encourages frugality and fasting but urges monks to avoid extremes. Importantly, the Rule was not intended to be stifling. Its regulations were not meant to stop the monks from experimenting and going further in the power of the Spirit, exploring new avenues of Christian experience. Its last chapter expressly states that the Rule is a bare minimum, a beginning and grounding for the monk's life, and it discourages those who follow it from resting content with its guidance alone.

'Search the Old and New Testaments, and explore the writings of the Fathers of the Church. In these you will find true riches, and a far greater "Rule" for life.'

Benedict himself had no idea of God's plans for his Rule – he was simply trying to do his best for the monks he lived with – but he was so successful in this that for six centuries his Rule was the rule of life for most European monks. Its influence was so great that some have called the period from 600-1100 the 'Benedictine Age'. The monks, with Benedict's guidance, were to be the greatest force in the history of the whole period. But back now to Benedict the man, and his last days on this earth.

Benedict had a sister named Scholastica, a pious woman who lived in a nunnery near Monte Cassino. Once a year the pair would meet, in a hut some way between the monastery and convent.

Now the time came that Scholastica was well advanced in years, and she felt that her next visit to her brother would be her last. The pair met at the appointed time, and spent a joyful day of prayer and conversation, but when evening came the elderly nun begged her brother to stay.

'Let us not waste this opportunity,' she said. 'It may be our last. I long to speak with you of the things of God until morning.'

'You know that is impossible,' Benedict apologized. 'I cannot spend the night away from the monastery.'

At this refusal Scholastica folded her hands upon the table and rested her head upon them. Silent tears filled her eyes as she sat in passionate prayer. A moment later she raised her head, and at that moment a thunderclap shook the building and a mighty downpour began. Benedict raced to the window and looked outside in amazement. He looked back to his sister, and shook his head in wonder.

'The sky was clear a moment ago. What have you done?'

'You would not hear my prayer,' she said, 'but God did. Go back to your monastery now, if you can.'

The storm was so violent that the abbot was left with no choice but to remain. The siblings spoke until daybreak, and then parted for the last time. Only three days later Benedict fell into a daze while standing at his window. He thought he saw his sister, and as he smiled at her he saw a dove burst from her body and fly into the heavens.

'Go to the convent,' he told his fellow monks. 'Bring the body of Scholastica here and place it in my tomb.'

The monks left immediately, and found that Scholastica had passed away just as Benedict had said. Amidst the sounds of worship and thanksgiving she was buried at Monte Cassino, in

the church which had once been a pagan temple. Only a little
more than a month later her beloved brother was laid to rest
beside her. Little as it was realized at the time, 21 March 543
saw the death of the most influential man of the sixth century.

GREGORY THE GREAT, *DIALOGUES* BK. 2

Jacob Baradaeus

From the father of a great monastic order we return briefly to
the east, to the father of an entire church!

Justinian, as we saw earlier, was determined to unite the
Christians of his realm. The Syrian and Coptic bishops who
opposed him were 'honourably' imprisoned in Constantinople,
and the emperor did all he could to force their congregations to
obey new leaders. But even in his own family this plan met with
a determined opponent. Justinian's wife Theodora, sympathetic
to the Monophysite bishops, found a way to ensure the survival
of their churches.

Jacob of Syria was born about AD 500, and because of a vow
of his parents was sent to live in a monastery as a child. He
thrived in that potentially harsh environment and became
renowned for sanctity, wisdom, and moral and physical
strength. During a visit to Constantinople in 542 he was
summoned to meet Empress Theodora.

'The churches of Syria and Egypt are in disarray,' she told
Jacob in a secret meeting. 'My husband's plans to crush them
will succeed unless new ministers are consecrated quickly.'

The problem was that new ministers had to be consecrated by
a bishop, and a new bishop could only be consecrated with the
agreement of three other bishops. These were old laws designed
so that only worthy men became ministers, but they were now
working in Justinian's favour, since if he removed the bishops
the people did not dare appoint new ministers for themselves.

'It would be against our law.'

As it happened, God soon provided for the patient people.

Jacob surreptitiously visited the imprisoned bishops, and was himself consecrated. He then returned to the east, and for more than thirty years lived a roving life, appointing new ministers for all of the churches. He was later given two fellow bishops, so that the three together could consecrate new bishops for the main cities.

Jacob never stayed long in one location, and he traversed the empire many times on foot. As a disguise he wore nothing but rags, dressing as a beggar in a patchwork coat made from mule's saddle-cloths! His nickname, Baradaeus, means 'the mule's saddle'. By the time of his death every city had its own Monophysite clergy, and the scheme of Justinian was in tatters. To this day the church of Syria is named the Jacobite church, in memory of its great defender.

JOHN OF EPHESUS, *LIFE OF BARADAEUS*

Cato and Cautinus

After the conversion of Clovis, the church in Gaul was blessed with many great ministers and monks. Among the most saintly was Gall, Bishop of Clermont, who passed away in 551. Following that bishop's death, however, his bishopric became the scene of a most bizarre battle.

Cato, a local priest, was nominated to succeed Gall. Puffed up with his success, Cato immediately snatched the reins of the church, and before his predecessor was laid to rest he had already dismissed several ministers whom he disliked. After Gall's funeral the local bishops came to Cato and offered to consecrate him.

'You are obviously the choice of the people. It is usual to await the king's approval, but as he is only a child we will install you now and support your case when it later comes up before the princes.'

But to their surprise Cato refused.

'You should know,' he said haughtily, 'indeed it is common knowledge, that I have always been a man of the greatest piety and holiness. I have stood all night in psalm singing, I love the poor, and I have done my time in the lower ranks like any future bishop must. Your ordination can give me nothing that I don't already possess. In my own good time I will ask the king to confirm my position, and you, if you please, may as well return to your own bishoprics.'

The bishops left, marvelling at the upstart's pride, and with their departure Cato began to lord it over his ministers as never before. Cautinus was the archdeacon of Clermont, and for him Cato showed a particular hatred. He threatened to dismiss him, to disgrace him, and finally even to kill him. Cautinus did all he could to soothe his 'bishop's' wrath.

'Bishop Cato,' he said, 'let me prove my obedience to you. I will be your ambassador to the royal court and seek ratification of your appointment.'

Cato snorted contemptuously. 'What sort of fool do you think I am,' he mumbled.

The archdeacon soon tired of this treatment, and feigning illness he withdrew from his duties and secretly left Clermont. He went straight to the royal court, which as yet was not even aware of Gall's death, and a council of bishops soon showed its disapproval of the situation in Clermont by consecrating Cautinus himself as bishop. Now the fun really began!

Cautinus' appointment sparked a bitter feud. Cato had raised many of his friends to power, and these men made no secret of their opposition to Cautinus. The bishop was forced to dismiss most of them, a move that all but split the local church in two, and when the bishop of Tours died Cautinus saw that his best hope of restoring peace would be to recommend Cato for the position. Affairs were arranged as he wished, and an embassy came to invite Cato to fill the vacancy.

'I'll think about it,' was the arrogant priest's only answer.

Days passed, the party from Tours tired of waiting, and an immediate decision was demanded. Cato arranged a meeting with the embassy, but he first assembled a mob of beggars and gave them clear instructions. While Cato was involved in discussion with the embassy the beggars began pounding on his door.

'How can you leave us, good father, you who have always cared for us? Who will provide our daily food if you do not? Don't desert us!'

The cocky priest turned to his guests with a look of profound sympathy.

'Well, dear brothers, there is the decision made for us. Just see how the poor folk love me! I am afraid that I cannot come and help you.'

Cato, in fact, was still hanging out in the hope of finding some way to overthrow Cautinus. He went so far as to pay a woman to pretend to be demon-possessed.

'Cato, I know you!' she screamed in church. 'Don't punish me you holy saint of God! When will the people see their folly and put you in the place of Cautinus! Cato is a great saint, Cautinus the blackest of sinners!'

No one fell for such tricks, but it happened that the people soon saw that the woman's words about Cautinus were not entirely untrue.

Cautinus was incapable of handling the pressure of his new position, especially under the attacks of Cato, and he began to soothe his sorrows with strong wine. He was often in such a state after dinner that four men were required to wrestle him off to bed, and he repeatedly appeared drunk in public. His alcoholism greatly damaged his health, and he became prone to epileptic fits.

Drunkenness, however, paled into insignificance beside the avarice that he began to display. Several wealthy people had properties bordering on his land, and he demanded that they sign the ownership over to him. He spread malicious rumours about those who resisted, and attacked them in the courts. He simply evicted a number of poor folk by force.

A priest named Anastasius had a property that Cautinus desired, and the bishop summoned his victim to a meeting. First he used flattery, then threats when that failed, and finally he had his opponent locked away and denied even bread and water. Anastasius, however, was made of stern stuff.

'I will starve rather than leave my children in poverty!'

When Cautinus saw that the priest was as good as his word he had him secretly taken to the crypt of a nearby church. One of the tombs was opened, Anastasius was thrown inside, and the heavy marble slab was replaced on top of him. Cautinus' henchmen left the crypt and guarded the door.

'No point sitting here all night on alert,' one of them said. 'He'd be dead already. That slab would have crushed him.'

With that the guards made a fire and brought out some wine. It was wintertime, and with the warmth of both fire and wine the two were soon asleep.

Anastasius, however, was not dead. Like Jonah he had almost gone down to the grave alive, and also like the prophet, every moment in the tomb was filled with trembling prayer. He was almost crushed, lying flat upon the dead man's bones. For the rest of his life he would tell the story of his terrifying ordeal, and especially of the dreadful stench of the corpse. He could stuff his cloak into his nostrils and refuse to breathe for a time, but afterwards would be forced to take in huge gulps of the thick miasma to escape suffocation. He could not roll over, but he could stretch out his hands on both sides, and after what seemed an age he felt that there was something hard projecting beneath the marble slab – the crowbar!

Cautinus' cronies had used the crowbar to raise and lower the lid, and they had left it sticking out of the tomb. With a prayer Anastasius tried to move it, and after protracted effort felt the slab above him shift slightly. He kept tugging on the crowbar until there was a big enough gap to poke his head through, and he finished the task and emerged just as the last light of day disappeared. He saw where the guards were stationed and crept to another door. This door was secured with huge nails and large locks, but there were small gaps between the planks of which it was made. Anastasius knelt for a while, staring out through one of these. In the dark he saw a man passing, a peasant woodcutter.

'Friend!' Anastasius rasped in a low voice. The man heard and came closer.

'Who's there?' he asked, his whole body shaking as he addressed the crypt!

'Presbyter Anastasius,' came the reply. 'An enemy has locked me in here. Can you see a way to let me out?'

'Surely I can,' the relieved woodcutter cried, and with a few blows from his axe the door was swinging wide open.

'Don't tell a soul,' said Anastasius as he took to his heels. 'I recommend that you get away quickly as well.'

Anastasius rushed home, collected his title-papers, and headed straight for the king's palace. His story amazed the whole court.

'Not Herod, not Nero himself ever did such a thing!'

Cautinus was summoned, but when he arrived and saw that it was Anastasius appearing to accuse him he was dumbfounded and immediately fled back to Clermont. This was evidence enough for the king, and he gave Anastasius new title deeds that confirmed his possession and prevented anyone taking the land in question.

Cautinus, however, retained his authority and continued to disgrace the church until a plague, perhaps the worst the region had seen, struck Clermont. The first symptom of illness was an open sore like a snake bite in the armpit or groin, inevitably followed by death within three days. In an effort to escape infection Cautinus abandoned his duties and fled from town to town, but in vain.

The final note of this bizarre story, however, is a high one. Cato remained in Clermont during the plague, and again led the church in the bishop's absence. His pride and deceitfulness in earlier times were well known, but in the memory of the people all was soon forgiven. He buried the dead, tended the sick, and finally died of the illness himself.

'Whatever he may have been before,' the grateful people said, 'he has now washed it away with his true concern and compassion!'

GREGORY OF TOURS, *HISTORY* 4.5–31

The Wild Barbarian World

The world of the early Franks was indeed a wild one. Imagine yourself among them for a moment.

It is the evening of a major religious festival, and the early Frankish Christians are sitting quietly in church. Suddenly the doors fly open, a crowd of the demon-possessed bursts in, and racing through the church, leaping and dancing, they start screaming that they are being tortured by the prayers of the faithful. Some jump through the air and smash lanterns lighting the evening service, but as the oil from the lights runs down on them they drop to the ground and are immediately returned to their right minds. Indeed this was so familiar an occurrence that the Christians would count the broken lamps the following morning, and be sure that just so many demoniacs had been healed the night before!

Other evils were not so easily healed. Some of the early Frankish rulers were among the cruellest villains ever to afflict humankind.

Duke Rauching was a man of almost unbelievable greed and cruelty, and it seemed that torture was his chief pleasure. When he dined a servant would be forced to stand before him holding a candle between his shins, and as the light burned down to the stub the poor fellow was not even allowed to cry out in pain.

'Kill him if he makes a sound.'

The duke would be convulsed with laughter as the servant squirmed and wept, and as soon as the ordeal was over a second candle would be put in place and the gruesome torture repeated until the drunken monster shuffled off to bed.

The power of the church was all that stood against fiends like Rauching. When two of the duke's servants fell in love they dared not ask their master's permission to marry, and after waiting two years they escaped to a church and begged the priest to help them. The minister promptly married them and offered temporary Sanctuary.

'I will not let you have them back,' he told Rauching, 'unless you promise to allow them to live as man and wife, which is their God-given right. You must also promise not to punish them.'

The barbarian stood silent for some time, and then grasping the altar he swore an oath.

'I shall never separate them. Indeed I shall go further, and ensure that they remain forever united!'

The priest, a simple man, did not see the cunning in the duke's words. He sent the couple back to their master, who promptly buried them alive.

'Never to part!'

Word of the atrocity reached the priest within an hour, and he ran to the scene as fast as his legs would carry him. With his own hands he dug up the unfortunate couple, but found that the girl had already suffocated. Her husband, at least, survived, and the priest ensured his safety. If such a tale can have a remotely happy ending it is that the duke eventually met the end he deserved, and after being discovered in a plot against the king his skull was smashed, and his body thrown naked from a palace window. His wife escaped punishment only through flight to the Sanctuary of a church.

Unfortunately for the Franks, Duke Rauching was not unlike many other rulers of his time. King Chilperic was little better than the duke, and his queen, Fredegund, was perhaps the greatest fiend of them all.

Chilperic actually had a number of wives, one of whom was a noble woman named Galswinth. Indeed Galswinth was too noble for the king's liking, and when she dared complain of the ways of the court Chilperic had her strangled.

Merovech was a son of Chilperic by another wife, but when the prince came of age his suspicious father put him in custody for fear that he might join the conspiracies afoot against him. When Merovech fled to Tours and took Sanctuary in the church of St Martin his father threatened Gregory, Bishop of Tours, with the destruction of the whole region unless his son was immediately expelled. But Gregory stood his ground.

'To deny Sanctuary is a crime at which even heretics quail.'

Merovech, however, was too impatient to long remain in safety, and when he ventured beyond the church he was murdered.

Chilperic was a bizarre character, a curious blend of barbarity and vanity. He treated subjects of all ranks with brutality, cruelly persecuted the Jews (many of whom he forcibly baptized), and delighted in torture and extortion – but at the same time he considered himself an artistic and philosophical genius of the highest order! He wrote poetry and hymns for the church(!), but when his work met scant approval, as though to avenge himself on the language itself, he proceeded to meddle with the alphabet, adding four new letters and compelling all school masters to use them in their lessons! He even dared to dabble in theology and published an edict enforcing on his people the ancient heresy of Sabellius – which denied that Father, Son and Holy Spirit were distinct persons, and called them simply 'masks' of the one God. He summoned Bishop Gregory and read him the new law.

'From now on this is what you must teach.'

'My king,' said the bishop, 'you must abandon this evil thinking. Follow the teaching of the apostles and the Fathers of the Church rather than your own whims.'

Chilperic was infuriated.

'It seems I must summon wiser men than yourself! They will agree with me!'

'Anyone who accepts your law will be not a wise man, but a fool.'

Bishop Salvius of Albi came some time later, and the king read the proposal to him.

'Allow me, my king,' he said boldly, 'to tear that paper to shreds!'

Thankfully the king abandoned his theological scheme. At his assassination in 584 all his other curious 'contributions' died with him.

Chilperic was not the king of all Gaul. The custom of the Franks was to divide kingdoms between the sons of a deceased king, and Chilperic had reigned alongside his three stepbrothers, each over a different province. Now that Chilperic was dead, with no adult son to succeed him, his wife Fredegund called upon Chilperic's stepbrother Guntram to defend her realm while her son grew to manhood.

King Guntram was the best of the kings of the time, and

probably the only one with a truly Christian character. His charity and love for his people earned him the nickname of the 'bishop-king'. Unfortunately for his reputation, however, Guntram now became the protector of Fredegund, one of the cruellest women in Europe's history. The widowed queen had developed a taste for blood under her husband's barbarous rule, and for the rest of her life continued to plot and scheme behind the scenes. It was soon after Chilperic's death that she sent a servant to the household of Brunhild, one of her sisters-in-law.

'Tell her that you have fled from me, and that you now seek her protection. Once you have won her confidence you should find it easy to dispose of her.'

Fortunately for Brunhild, the jealous queen's plot was uncovered at the last moment. The servant was severely flogged, and confessing the whole scheme was granted his life and returned to Fredegund. His mistress greeted the failure with her usual kindness, and had his hands and feet cut off.

At about this time Fredegund tried to win the heart of a vicious Frankish chief named Eberulf, but finding her addresses scorned she sought revenge by telling Guntram that she had discovered the man behind her husband Chilperic's murder.

'Eberulf!'

Guntram knew Eberulf's evil character, and he was easily led to swallow the lie. He ordered the chief's execution, and the wanted man fled to the Sanctuary of St Martin's.

Eberulf soon made life miserable for the whole congregation. He would roam about the church blind drunk, and he once beat a priest senseless for refusing to get him more wine. Several friends and servants attended him, and together they would clamber over the tombs in the church crypt and raucously insult the priests during services. One night Bishop Gregory had a strange dream, and he described it to Eberulf the following day.

'I was ministering here,' he said, 'when King Guntram burst in and demanded that you be driven from God's altar. I told you to grasp the altar cloth, but saw that you took hold only feebly. I blocked the king's approach, for a moment we stood breast to breast, and I commanded him not to despise God's church. You briefly came up behind me, I was filled with anger towards you, but then you returned to the altar and again held it feebly while I wrestled the king away. Suddenly I awoke in fear, not knowing what the vision meant.'

'It is a true vision,' the barbarian said defiantly. 'You now know my intentions.'

'How so?'

'If the king comes for me,' Eberulf replied, 'I shall hold the altar with one hand, draw my sword with the other, strike you dead immediately, then slay all the priests I can get my hands on. Death will be sweeter with my hands drenched in your blood!'

But, threats or no, the bishop persevered in protecting his enemy.

Fredegund and Guntram eventually sent a cunning rogue named Claudius to hunt Eberulf down. Claudius visited Eberulf in the church, and swearing that he wished to help him regain the king's favour he enticed Eberulf to dine with him in the evening. When he got Eberulf alone, one of his servants grabbed the victim from behind while Claudius attacked him with a knife. Eberulf managed to draw his own dagger, and as Claudius struck him in the chest he replied with a stab to the assassin's armpit, and with another swipe severed Claudius' thumb. Eberulf collapsed dead, and Claudius, fearing that Eberulf's friends would quickly return, fled to the local abbot.

'Save me!'

Even as he spoke Eberulf's men arrived on the scene and struck the wounded man down. They then looted the church and fled, leaving the abbot himself half-dead upon the floor.

Fredegund next attempted to assassinate one of the kings, Childebert II, but her scheming was again uncovered. She then murdered a bishop who displeased her, and afterwards poisoned a Frankish chief who dared to reproach her for the crime. She even turned her evil eye on Guntram, her protector, and sent a crony to assassinate him while he walked to an early morning church service, but the murderer got drunk the night before his mission and fell asleep just outside the church. He was arrested for his unusual behaviour and confessed his intentions.

Fredegund's daughter Rigunth was almost as fiendish as her mother. Rigunth lived like a whore, and her mother despised her. The pair would fight like wildcats, slapping and punching each other.

'I am the daughter of a queen!' Rigunth would cry. 'You began as a mere serving girl! I should be the mistress, and you the servant!'

Fredegund once tried to 'appease' her daughter.

'Why should we fight any longer, my dear?' she said. 'As a peace offering, I am willing to give you whatever possessions of your father's are still in my keeping. Would you like that?'

Rigunth surely would! She followed her mother into a strong room, where a chest filled with jewels and ornaments was opened to her view. One by one Fredegund took out the treasures and handed them to the girl.

'I'm tired of this,' Fredegund sighed. 'Take the rest for yourself.'

Rigunth swooped to the task, but while she was reaching down to take more her mother slammed the chest's heavy wooden lid on her throat. She pressed down with all her might, and Rigunth's eyes were soon standing out of her head.

'Help!' a maid screamed. 'Mistress Rigunth is being killed by her mother!'

Servants burst in, and the younger woman was saved from certain death. One can imagine how much worse the family feuds were following this!

Fredegund later stuck her nose into another family's feud. The feud had been started by a young Frank's complaints that his sister was neglected by her husband, a brute who wasted his days with prostitutes. When the husband refused to mend his ways he was killed in a bloody brawl, his family avenged his blood on the young woman's brother, and the quarrel looked sure to continue.

The old queen repeatedly warned the feuding parties to stop disturbing the peace, but finding her complaints ignored she invited both sides to a party. There she got them completely drunk, and – what? Made them kiss and make up? No! She had them beheaded of course, and then fled lest the king punish her. It seemed she simply couldn't help herself when an excuse for cruelty offered.

Hopefully this catalogue of crimes has given some idea of the difficulties facing a Christian, especially a minister, in these barbarian nations. A great historian once compared the church of this period to Noah's Ark. All that was good and worthwhile was within, while outside was nothing but a raging storm, despair and death.

The church could awe even the vile Fredegund, and when her son Lothar became ill she made the bishops a gift of a vast sum of money. It was no doubt nothing but attempted bribery (of God!), but it at least shows that even the worst savages knew something of the power amongst them.

The right of Sanctuary was a great power for good, and even the most depraved barbarian rarely dared drag someone from the altar. King Childebert's men once got around the right of Sanctuary in an inventive manner. Not daring to attack their enemy *in* church, they made a hole in the roof and dropped a stone from above. On the opposite extreme was King Guntram, who did not dare execute an assassin who attacked him in church!

This respect for the church could be a dangerous thing if abused. Two notoriously criminal bishops, Salonius and Sagittarius, were deposed for a list of crimes which is almost hard to believe. They robbed, bashed and murdered their congregations, fought as soldiers whenever opportunity arose, and committed countless adulteries. King Guntram had them deposed and shut up in separate monasteries, but when his eldest son fell ill soon afterwards the disgraced bishop's cronies had a word in the king's ear.

'Your son is ill because you have allowed the exile of innocent bishops!'

Guntram ordered their return, and the two bishops returned home with a great show of penitence. It lasted about a week. Soon they were back to their old tricks, feasting endlessly in a drunken stupor surrounded by a company of prostitutes, and it was a good thing that Guntram's fear of the church did not save them a second time! Both were imprisoned, but later escaped to become wandering beggars.

It is not surprising that false prophets and teachers should proliferate in such times. In 580 a stranger arrived at St Martin's late one evening. He carried a large cross, from which dangled several phials of 'holy oil'.

'Summon Bishop Gregory immediately.'

The message was delivered, but as the hour was late Gregory promised to see the visitor on the following day. When morning came the stranger burst into the bishop's room in a fury.

'You should have hastened to me!' he cried. 'The king will hear of it, and you will regret this affront!'

The stranger moved on to Paris, and there gathered a crowd of simple followers. He met the local bishop, Ragnemod, in the street, and after heaping abuse on him was arrested and imprisoned. His travelling bag was searched, and an assortment of exotic roots, some moles' teeth, mice bones, and the fat and claws of a bear were found inside – the standard equipment of a wizard. His cross was confiscated, his magic ingredients cast into the river, and at Ragnemod's request he was expelled from the region. Upon release, however, the stranger made up a new cross and returned to his old practices. He was soon gaoled for a second time.

Bishop Gregory, visiting Paris at this time, entered church for midnight prayers one night to find the wizard unconscious on the floor. He had escaped from his cell a few hours earlier, but now so stank of filth and alcohol that the bishop could not bear to approach him. It was impossible to wake him from his stupor, so some of the younger priests carried him into a corner, while others mopped up the mess he had left behind. The church floor was strewn with sweet smelling herbs to remove the smell. The following day Gregory called a meeting to decide what should be done with the wizard. The problem was quickly solved, for a man at the meeting recognized him as his own runaway servant and put him back to work without further ado.

Some years later an even weirder 'miracle-worker' appeared

in Tours. Desiderius wore a tunic of goat's hair, and in public pretended to be on an almost permanent fast. Those who saw him in private, however, knew that he ate with such speed that it was difficult to put the plates before him swiftly enough!

Desiderius claimed to be an equal of the apostles and said that angels constantly went back and forth between himself and the Apostles Peter and Paul in heaven. Many paralyzed people came to him hoping for a cure, and Desiderius ordered his followers to forcibly stretch their withered limbs. Some were twisted and tormented until their sinews nearly snapped, and were sent away half-dead. Several died under Desiderius' 'healing' ministry.

In spite of this many were enthralled, as Desiderius did appear to have genuine supernatural powers. He often told people what they had said about him in secret, and this filled them with fear lest he expose their secret thoughts. When the local ministers became fully aware of the danger, and urged on their flock that the supposedly miraculous powers were demonic, not divine, the people themselves chased Desiderius from the city and he was not heard of again.

Not many years later the worst impostor of them all appeared in Bourges. This was a simple man who had been attacked by a swarm of insects while chopping wood in the forest, and as a result of a sickness caused by their stings had become quite mad. He began to wander the country dressed in animal skins and claimed to be a healer and prophet. He later acquired a female sidekick, and the pair named themselves Christ and Mary.

Gullible crowds flocked to them, bringing their sick for the impostor to lay his hands upon. The 'healer' would lie upon the ground shouting prayer after prayer, and would then rise and command all present to bow and worship him. Many claimed to have been healed, and the simple folk were even more impressed by his accurate predictions of future events. Within months he had three thousand followers.

His followers showered him with gold and other presents, and the deceiver won even greater popularity by giving this booty to the poor. He soon felt powerful enough to resist the authorities, and he began to rob those he met on the road. He finally moved to Le Puy and encamped his followers in battle lines around the church, then sent messengers to announce 'Christ's' arrival to the local bishop. His ambassadors were his most crazed followers – a group of men who danced naked across the fields as they went to deliver their message!

The bishop, more than a little disturbed, asked several sturdy servants to visit the 'enemy' camp and see what was going on. The servants found the Antichrist unguarded, and they approached as though about to worship at his feet. One bowed to kiss his knees, but with a quick move tackled him to the ground and ran him through with a sword. In the shock of the moment the impostor's followers were scattered, and 'Mary' herself was arrested and taken to the authorities. She was put under torture by the local duke and confessed that her master was a magician, aided in his work by demons and skilled in causing hallucinations. Not all of the followers of the false Christ were saved by this confession. Some lapsed into insanity and never recovered, while others continued to believe that their Christ was the true God, and that Mary herself, now imprisoned, was also divine.

It is hard to conceive the strength of character and stamina the ministers and missionaries of the period required in order to stand against such a wild society. We can thank them, and the Lord who inspired them, that so much has changed.

The work of an abbot or bishop was especially difficult, and only the toughest were fit for the task. Defending the weak from dukes and kings, exposing heretics and false prophets, disciplining the licentious, and tending to the needs of thousands during plague and war were not jobs for the faint-hearted!

This is well illustrated in the case of an abbot named Sunniulf. He was a good and holy man, but he was so humble that he always tried to control his monks through gentle pleas. He would never dream of commanding obedience.

One night, however, Sunniulf had a vivid dream. He saw a river of fire, into which a great number of men were diving feet first. Many could be seen actually in the flaming river, some up to the waist, others to the armpits, still others to the chin. A thin bridge stretched over the river, and at its far end was a large white house.

'From this bridge,' a voice resounded, 'shall all those be cast who fail to properly use their authority over those in their care. Those who keep good discipline shall cross safely to the mansion on the other side.'

Sunniulf awoke, and from that day was much stricter with his monks.

There are many beautiful and instructive stories of the work of the church in this period. We have already heard about some of the church leaders of the time, among whom none stood higher than Bishop Gregory of Tours. Besides his labours as a minister, Gregory was the author of several historical works. His writings on the Frankish kingdom and church provide the best information we have about the early days of any of the barbarian kingdoms, and with two more stories, both from Gregory, we shall bid the early Franks farewell.

A woman accused of adultery was given the traditional barbarian punishment: a stone was tied to her neck, and she was thrown into a river. But, in Gregory's own words:

'The Lord, the friend of the innocent and helpless, provided a stake which none could see. This stake caught the rope and stopped the woman from sinking to the bottom, though she was entirely below water. At evening her relatives received permission to search for the body, that they might bury the poor unfortunate, and going to the river they soon spotted her suspended from the stake. They hooked the woman and dragged her out of the water, but to their amazement found that she was not dead, and once restored to the air quickly came to herself. Fearing that her cruel husband might repeat the punishment they took her to the church, and then they quizzed her on how she had survived.

'"That I don't know," she said. "It seemed like a dream. I never felt the water but for the moment when I sank, and then again when you pulled me out."'

And, finally, the beautiful story of a Frankish mother:
This woman had but one son, who was sent in his youth to be

educated in a monastery. The boy was bright and made good progress in the study of Scripture. He also showed talent as a singer, and it was his mother's delight to hear his strong young voice ringing out in the church choir. But tragedy struck with a lightning hand and, as was not uncommon in those times, the youth contracted a fever and died very suddenly.

His mother was inconsolable. A river of tears at the lad's funeral was not enough to extinguish her grief, and each new day found the poor woman mourning hopelessly by the tomb of her child. This sad state continued for weeks, until one night a strange dream broke her lonely slumber.

'Why do you mourn?' asked a man in shining garments. 'Shall your sorrow never cease?'

'Not while life remains to me,' the woman cried. 'Only death can dry my eyes.'

'Have you no faith?' the man asked. 'Compose yourself. Believe that your son now lives with us, in the House of my Father and yours. To show your heart that this is so go to church tomorrow and listen carefully to the choir. It is fitter to rejoice than to mourn for those who have gone to be with God.'

With a sigh the woman awoke, and sleep was impossible for the rest of the night. At dawn she rushed to church in obedience to the dream.

'Thank you Lord,' she gasped, the channels of her tears suddenly transformed to rivers of joy – for amongst the many voices joined in spiritual song, her own son's unmistakable voice resounded loud and clear.

GREGORY OF TOURS, *WORKS*

Isle of Saints

Ireland was the great Christian land of the sixth and seventh centuries. Only a few generations after Patrick himself, Ireland was sending out its own missionaries. In fact, she often sent them back to the lands from which she had received the Christian faith.

These new missions were much needed now that barbarians

had conquered so much of the old Christian world. (Ireland had never been part of the Roman Empire, and hence she survived Rome's fall.) The many great Irish monasteries and missionaries won Ireland the nickname of 'Island of Saints' – but before we meet the first of these missionaries, we must glance at another fascinating side of the early Irish church.

The early Irish monks were great seafarers. They explored the North Atlantic Ocean for centuries, and they were the first Europeans to discover and colonize many northern islands. Their motivation for exploration was an interesting one.

An eastern monk who wished to find a quiet retreat had an easy task. The desert abounded with solitude and silence, and many hermits spent years secluded from the outside world in lonely caves. This was not so easy for an Irishman. Ireland had no desert, so the Irish monks had to discover one!

In their light boats, called curraghs, the monks would venture on the wild seas in search of barren and (usually) uninhabited islands. Upon wild sea girt rocks they would make their homes, and there be sustained on the simplest fare. Islands so barren and small that they had never been settled were now peopled with thriving monasteries, and the hard work of the Irish monks 'made the desert to bloom'.

Some of these wild islands were already peopled, or nearby ones were, and the monasteries then became mission bases for the conversion of these forgotten lands. By 579 the Irish were in the Orkneys, a generation later they were in the Shetlands, the Faeroes were next, and eventually Iceland as well. Many of these Irish communities lasted for hundreds of years, only to be chased away from their settlements by the savage pagan Vikings of later times. But that is the story of another century.

The greatest name amongst the Irish seafarers is that of Brendan. He was one of the first monks of the 'ocean desert' and lived in the sixth century, though exactly what he did is hard to discover, since after his death he became a favourite subject of the Irish storytellers. A fascinating legend was spun around him, and a layer of myth and fantasy obscured his real achievements. The story of Brendan's voyage as we have it is legend rather than history, but we cannot pass it by.

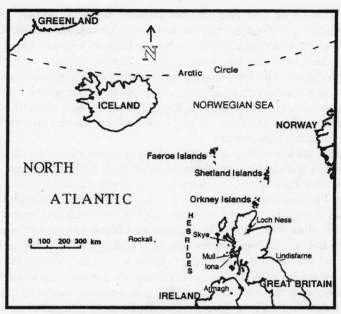

The British Isles and the Irish Desert

According to the story, Brendan and his crew set off from the Irish coast at about the summer solstice. After sailing for 40 days they sighted a high and rocky island. They went ashore and were met by a dog. The dog led them to a hall, where they discovered a splendid meal prepared for them.

'All this food!' the monks whispered. 'But where is everybody?'

The monks ate, and then spent the night in the empty building. The following morning they returned to their boat, and after the death of one of their number, divinely punished for stealing a necklace from the uninhabited hall, a young man met them with provisions for their voyage.

'Blessings for the journey ahead.'

That journey was to last seven years. They were not years of discovery as we would understand it, but rather a probationary period of divine testing, as the monks travelled back and forth between various small islands. Their journeys were punctuated

by the great festivals of the church, each of which was
celebrated, at the divine command, in a particular location. The
monks had embarked in the hope of finding a famed Land of
Promise beyond the ocean, but they sought it not by
exploration, but by prayerfully awaiting a revelation. This is
clearly a legend rich in allegory – the ocean of life with *the land*
beyond, reached not by striving but by the will of God, the
ocean itself given meaning and order by the annual rhythm of
the church's observances.

The wonders they encountered were many. One island was
covered with enormous sheep; another with birds which sang in
beautiful harmony, and one of whom told the monks that he
and his feathered friends were fallen angels who through the
Lord's mercy had been spared torments, and had become birds
rather than demons. A third island was home to a supernatural
monastery, inhabited by monks who had not aged a day in 80
years, and whose lamps were lit each evening by a flaming
arrow which came flying through one window, struck all of the
wicks, and then disappeared through another window. On a
fourth island was a poisoned spring, whose waters rendered
Brendan's monks unconscious for several days. A particularly
strange and barren island proved to be the back of a whale, as
the monks discovered to their peril while lighting a fire for
cooking, and after a harrowing encounter with a sea monster
they found another monastery on an island flat and treeless, but
covered with beautiful flowers.

After further wandering the monks encountered a huge
crystal column rising from the ocean. They rounded the strange
obstacle and made for land beyond, but here, even out at sea,
the noise of a blacksmith at work could be heard. As they
neared the shore a savage tribe of smiths came charging to the
beach, throwing lumps of molten metal at the uninvited guests.

'We have come to the gates of hell!'

A nearby mountain belched smoke and fire as the monks took
frantically to the oars.

Back in safer waters they found a small rock rising just above
the sea's surface, and upon the summit saw Judas Iscariot,

beaten over the head by each passing wave! On another rock was a hermit named Paul, who had lived there 90 years. For the first 30 years he had been fed by a friendly otter that brought him a fish every third day; for the last 60 years he had not eaten at all!

Finally, after seven years of wonder and nonsense, the great purpose of Brendan's mission was achieved. The monks sailed into a dark cloud, and emerging on the other side found a new island – an island covered with apple trees, and so vast that after walking for 40 days they still had not reached the other side. The monks came to the banks of a mighty river and were greeted by a young man.

'This is the land you have been seeking in all these years of your sea pilgrimage. Jesus did not permit you to find it sooner, for He wished first to show you His wonders in the deep. But this land is not for you, yet. Fill your ship with its treasures and return to your homeland, for you, Brendan, shall soon rest with your fathers. Your visit here is only a promise. When many years have passed your people shall return here and make it their home, at a time when Christians are suffering under the hand of their enemies. Here, Christ shall be their light.'

With that Brendan returns home and the legend ends.

Brendan's story is a very tall tale, but it does have a kernel of truth. Looking closely at the details we can recognize several islands and features of the Atlantic Ocean.

The island rich with sheep is probably one of the Faeroes. 'Faeroes' comes from the Danish word for sheep, and from the seventh century onwards the area has been renowned for them. The island of birds is perhaps Vagar, one of the Faeroes, which is a well-known bird haven. Other Atlantic islands are known to possess poisoned springs, the crystal column is clearly an iceberg, and the land beyond that must be Iceland. Brendan was not alone in considering Iceland an entrance to hell; the pagan Norsemen thought the same, and little wonder in view of Iceland's many active volcanoes. The smoking mountain must be a volcano, and the molten metal thrown by the smiths is probably a legendary description of a violent eruption. Many other possibilities could be pointed out, but these are enough to show that Brendan's story, however exaggerated, is based on the real world.

Brendan himself probably saw but few of these sights. Hundreds of monks followed in his footsteps over hundreds of years, and they travelled much further (collectively speaking) than Brendan could possibly have done. Most of these other monks, however, were forgotten over time, and all the stories of the incredible things they had seen in the ocean eventually came to be considered as the discoveries of one man. It is not unusual for legends to grow in such a fashion.

But the most impressive feature of Brendan's story is the startling fulfilment of its prophecy. The young man's speech at the end inspired Europe for hundreds of years. A new home had been promised, a land of wonder, to be settled by the Europeans in troubled times to come, and Christians were so sure that this land existed that they drew it on their maps as though it was just as real as any other land they had discovered. All of which would be rather uninteresting, except that there really was such a land on the far side of the Atlantic, an enormous land which was, in troubled times, settled by countless Europeans. That land is, of course, the Americas.

* * *

Putting our feet back on firmer ground, we introduce Ireland's first great missionary to the outside world.

Columba, born into Irish royalty, embraced monasticism as a young man. He is reported to have established several monasteries in Ireland before his fortieth year. He was an accomplished scribe with a great love of books, and while visiting an abbot who had an excellent copy of the Vulgate Psalter he made a copy for himself without seeking permission. Abbot Finnian was angered, and claiming that the new copy should be given to him he appealed to King Diormit, member of a rival royal clan to Columba's. Diormit decided for Finnian, Columba refused to obey, and the case ended up entangled in the broader political troubles of the day. When war broke out Columba felt a partial responsibility for the ensuing bloodshed (his own clan was victorious), and feeling the impossibility of a peaceful Christian life in his homeland he resolved upon voluntary exile. In 563, with 12 companions, he embarked on a search for an island desert.

Columba sailed to the west coast of Scotland and settled on the barren island of Iona – three miles long, a mile and a half wide, and completely uninhabited. In this rocky and windy desert the monks built themselves simple huts from the branches of a few straggly trees. Little could it have been imagined that these were the beginnings of one of the world's great monasteries. Iona was to be the main base for a massive missionary effort to nearby Scotland, and beyond.

The gospel had been preached in Scotland long before Columba's time. The greatest of the earlier missionaries to the north had been Ninian, a monk of the early fifth century, but by Columba's day the majority of the natives of Scotland were still pagan, and those touched by earlier missions were in great need of revitalization and sound leadership. The extensive travels of Columba and his followers by land and sea saw dozens of churches and monasteries spring up on the nearby islands and in mainland Scotland itself over the next few decades, and though there is no precise record of the course of events during the evangelization of Scotland, there is no shortage of stories which preserve some idea of Columba's life and ministry.

Many stories were told of the Irish monk's prophetic foresight. One journey took him to the Hebrides islands, and as he and his monks were walking along the coast of the famous Isle of Skye the abbot suddenly stopped and stabbed his staff into the ground.

'Let us break our journey here. One of the chiefs of the north shall soon visit this spot, and here he shall breathe his last.'

So the monks sat down to wait, and it was not much more than an hour later that they saw a boat approaching the beach. Two young men clambered out bearing the feeble body of an ancient Pict between them, and as they approached the monks the old chief was the first to speak.

'What is your reason for being here?'

Columba greeted the stranger warmly.

'You have found favour in the eyes of our Lord,' he said. 'Though you have never known Him, He has sent us to you.'

Columba himself could not speak the old man's language with any fluency, so one of his fellow monks interpreted as he preached the gospel. The words of life burned into the old man's heart, and along with his companions he was baptized immediately. Rising from the waters, he embraced the abbot.

'I thank you. You have opened to my view the place that the good God has prepared for me, and to that place I can depart with joy!'

So saying he gave up his spirit and was buried on the spot.

In the course of his journeys Columba is reported to have encountered one of Scotland's most famous 'daughters'.

'When Columba came to cross the River Ness he saw a man being taken for burial, and inquiring about his death learned that a savage water beast had attacked him in the river. This did not deter the monks, who needed to cross over, and Columba told one of his young companions to swim across and retrieve the ferry boat from the other bank. All looked on anxiously to see whether the beast would reappear. The man had reached mid-stream when their fears were realized, as the beast surfaced and surged towards the monk. Everyone quaked with fear, but Columba made the sign of the cross and rebuked the beast in the name of Christ: "Go no further." The beast stopped suddenly, and then moved swiftly backwards as though pulled by ropes. The swimmer then completed his mission, and returned in the boat.'

This account, written in the seventh century, is the first reference to a dangerous creature in the vicinity of Loch Ness, now the legendary home of 'Nessie', the Loch Ness Monster.

Travelling some time later by boat along the rivers that dissect Scotland, Columba and his crew spent the night in the open air by a stream, having left their craft in a small nearby village. Around the middle of the night Columba awoke suddenly, and after rousing his companions he sent some of the younger monks to retrieve their boat.

'Swiftly,' he insisted.

The monks returned with the boat and again lay down to rest, but Columba directed their gaze back to the village. Soon the sounds of battle could be heard, and many of the buildings went up in smoke before their eyes, including the place where their boat had been stored.

Columba himself met with people from all levels of society and forged many close friendships among the tribesmen. Colman was one such friend, a God-fearing man who delighted to offer the monks the use of his house whenever their missionary journeys took them his way. This Colman was much afflicted by Ian, a Pict of royal blood who had adopted a life of piracy and plunder. He had twice raided Colman's property, and not satisfied with that had returned a third time to empty the unfortunate man's house. This time, however, just as the pirates carried the booty to their ship, Columba and his monks appeared on the scene.

'You have no right to that property,' the old abbot thundered. 'Put it down.'

Ian scoffed at him and clambered into his boat without concern.

'Mind your own business, old nuisance.'

Columba followed the pirates as they pushed off, and clinging to the side of their boat waded out with them.

'O Lord Christ,' he prayed, 'show Your glory to these that scorn Your chosen ones!'

The pirates ignored him and were soon gone, and the disappointed abbot waded back. He sat on the shore for some time with his friends. When he finally spoke, it was in a dark voice.

'This despiser of Christ and His servants shall not reach his home.'

A squall soon rose up in the north and descended on the strait which the pirates were sailing. Ian and his crew were lost at sea that day.

The king of the Picts, Brude, was inclined to welcome neither the Irish monks nor their faith. His neighbours the Scots were of Irish descent, invaders who had overrun formerly Pictish land (in these times the people of Ireland were known as Scots – for simplicity I have called them Irish), and this made him distrustful of any Good News which these roving Irish missionaries might bring. When the abbot once came to speak with the king Brude ordered that the gates of the royal fort be locked against him.

The unwelcome group approached the royal gates regardless. They prayed, Columba made the sign of the cross upon the gates, knocked, and then pushed. The bolts drew back and the doors flew open, and the troop of monks boldly entered. Brude was startled, and he immediately welcomed the visitors. That day marked the beginning of a new relationship between the two men, and thereafter the king treated the missionaries with honour.

Columba's time was divided between missionary journeys and Iona, but his popularity in Scotland was such that even when he spent periods on the island he would receive a constant stream of visitors. Between the Scottish mainland and Iona lay the island of Mull; Mull was inhabited, and only a narrow strait separated it from Iona. Often the monks would hear a voice bellowing to them from the opposite shore, informing them that a visitor was about to come their way. Some visitors sought charity, others intercessory prayer, many wished to be instructed by the monks, and others to become disciples of the monastery. Scots, Picts and even Irish visited Iona. Libran was one of the latter.

'What brings you here?' Columba asked when the two met in the monastery's guest dormitory.

'The hope of restoring myself after grievous sins,' said Libran, before giving a description of his misdeeds, which included murder.

'You have done well to desire a time of penance,' Columba declared, and he directed the young man to the monastery of Long on the Scottish mainland. It was one of the many new foundations under Abbot Columba's oversight.

The young man spent seven years of labour and prayer as a penitent at Long, and then he returned to Abbot Columba. But his heart was still troubled over his past misdeeds.

Serious criminals today are jailed, but this was not the case in these wild times. A serious crime could spark a family feud, and there was seldom a strong authority or government to properly punish and discipline. Often the best thing for a guilty individual to do was flee, and becoming an exile from family and friends he paid a severe penalty similar to imprisonment.

Christians guilty of grievous sin would often seek to spend their exile in a monastery. Some became monks while others only wished to spend a period of discipline and repentance, with spiritual guidance and the opportunity for good works. This period of self-denial and spiritual discipline was called penance.

'I swore a false oath to a relative of mine. He helped free me from my enemies after I committed murder, and I swore that I would serve him for life. But I soon tired of slavery to man, and wishing to serve God instead I came to you. What can I do about the man I have betrayed?'

'There is no escaping your obligation to your relative,' Columba replied. He went to a chest and took out an ornamented sword that had been donated to the monastery.

'Offer him this as the price of your release,' he said, 'but rest assured that he will by no means accept it, for he has a wife who greatly loves God.'

Libran returned to his homeland and visited his relative. He presented him with the sword as payment for his release, and the man was willing to accept it, until his wife restrained him:

'We are not worthy to take a gift from the great Columba! The holy abbot's blessing will profit us more than the cost of this sword!'

Thus released, Libran went to visit his parents. He was just in time to see his father one last time, for the old man passed away within a week of his arrival. Libran's brothers now turned on him angrily.

'Will you leave the rest of us to support our widowed mother while you run off to Iona? You must stay and do your share.'

Only Libran's youngest brother knew enough of the Spirit, which blows where it pleases, to support Libran's decision.

'Let us not detain him,' he said. 'If it comes to it I shall take on a double share of the labour, my share and his share. The work of God must come before household chores!'

So Libran bade his family farewell for the last time and headed for the harbour to inquire about a ship that could return him to Scotland.

'There she is,' someone pointed out, 'you just missed her. There'll be a long wait for another!'

Libran took to his heels and ran along the bank after the boat. 'Take me on board! I'm going to Abbot Columba at Iona!'

'Crazy monk!' one of the sailors muttered, and he turned away. That was as close as Libran got to an answer, until suddenly the wind turned and the ship was almost completely stilled. Libran could now keep up with it comfortably.

'I'm going to Iona to become a monk!' he cried. 'Please take me.'

'Do you reckon God will give us a wind if we take you on?'

Libran was soon on board, and with another change of wind the voyage was speedily underway. Libran reached Iona safe and sound, took his formal monastic vows, and spent the rest of his days as a monk at Long.

To the end of his life Columba spent a great deal of time in making copies of Scripture. Even on his dying day, in his late seventies, he spent the afternoon on a copy of the book of Psalms (the book which had played such a role in bringing him to Scotland in the first place). As he wrote the words of Psalm 34:10, 'They who trust the Lord shall not lack any good thing', he put down his quill for the last time.

'The end of a page,' he said, 'and appropriate last words.'

He went to evening prayers, and then rested, before returning to the chapel to kneel beside the altar. There his brethren found him, his soul already fled, when they came at midnight for late prayers.

THE VOYAGE OF BRENDAN; ADOMNAN, *LIFE OF COLUMBA*

The Final Defeat of Arianism

The Visigoths, after their defeat by Clovis, had resettled in Spain. Following Clovis' death, the Visigothic King Amalaric sent ambassadors to the late king's sons.

'Let there be no more bitterness between our nations,' they said. 'Let our nations be joined by a royal marriage.'

Clovis' sons thought the proposal a good one, and their sister Clotilda became King Amalaric's bride. The marriage seemed peaceful enough for some years. Amalaric was an Arian, but he allowed his wife to worship with the orthodox Christians. Proudly superior in his own beliefs, Amalaric thought it beneath him to argue with his wife.

Things changed as Amalaric came to know Clotilda better. He was confronted daily with her sincerity and faith and began to see that there was something within her which he utterly lacked. He could no longer despise her – but neither would he join her.

Amalaric turned on his wife. He said little of his change of heart, but he began to do the most insane things to annoy her.

'She can attend whatever church can bear the smell of her!'

The king encouraged a gang of Arian louts to abuse his wife, and when Clotilda went to church they would line the streets and throw dung and other filth at her. Disgraced and ashamed, the queen suffered this behaviour for several weeks, but her very patience was just the thing to push the king even further. The barbarian savagely attacked his queen, and in response Clotilda sent her brother Childebert a message as simple yet effective as could be – a towel soaked in her blood. The young Frankish king was quick to respond.

When Amalaric heard that a Frankish force was marching on Barcelona he immediately fled. He was already on a boat in the harbour, ready to sail, when he recollected that he had left a number of valuable jewels in the treasury building. The Franks were at the gates by now, but Amalaric resolved on dashing back to save his property. He collected the jewels, but Childebert had already blocked the road to the harbour before he could get out of the city. In desperation he ran for the Sanctuary of a church, but just before he crossed the threshold a Frank let fly at him with a spear, and Amalaric fell dead on the doorstep. Childebert seized the king's wealth and returned home with his sister, but Clotilda did not survive to see her native land. She died on the journey and was buried beside her father Clovis.

Half a century later there was another royal union of Frank and Goth. This marriage also seemed doomed to a gruesome end.

Ingund, a great-granddaughter of Clovis, married Hermenegild, heir to the Visigothic throne. Ingund was still in her early teens and her mother-in-law, Queen Goswinth, had arranged the marriage in the belief that she would be easily converted to the Arian faith. She had underestimated the power of the Spirit. Ingund ignored all peaceful invitations to abandon her God and receive Arian baptism, but rather than admit defeat the queen turned to more certain measures.

'Prepare the baptismal pool!'

The unwilling princess was dragged to the font, and when she still insisted on proclaiming the true faith the furious queen pulled out her hair, knocked her to the ground, and kicked her until she was covered with blood.

'Strip her,' she bellowed, 'and throw her in!' And so, in Goswinth's eyes, Ingund became an Arian!

But the pious princess was not to be deterred by such shocking treatment. Like her great-grandmother a century earlier she ceaselessly laboured for her husband's conversion, and within a couple of years of their marriage Hermenegild embraced the orthodox faith. Ingund's sufferings had made the young princess much dearer to her husband's heart.

King Leovigild was outraged at news of his son's conversion. He also was a zealous Arian and was scheming for the destruction of orthodoxy within his realm. Months of hostility between father and son ended with Hermenegild's execution and Ingund's imprisonment.

Leovigild died in 586, and another son, Recared, took his throne. Recared openly declared himself orthodox, and in 589 he summoned a council at Toledo. This council proclaimed orthodoxy as the faith of the Visigoths, and many Arian priests, including eight bishops, immediately abandoned their errors and joined the king. Arianism lingered on in Spain for several decades, but it was never again a major force in the nation.

Only one Arian tribe remained – the savage Lombards. This people had invaded Italy in the late sixth century, capturing much of the territory recently reclaimed by Justinian. They brutally afflicted the church and caused utter devastation in the north. Bishop Gregory of Rome (590–604), perhaps equally anxious to save his people from their swords as to save the Lombards' souls, worked for their conversion. Providence smiled on his missionary efforts when Theodelinda, a Catholic Bavarian princess, married the Lombard king and later became regent during her sons' infancy. By the mid-seventh century, Arianism was dead amongst the Lombards as well.

The final victory over heresy, though long delayed, had never really been in doubt. The tribes had named themselves Arian in ignorance, and as their cultures matured it was only a matter of time before the deeper truths of the orthodox faith won out.

GREGORY OF TOURS, *HISTORY* 3.10; 5.38

The Ruin of Britain

Britain's sufferings under barbarian invasion were extreme, and the conquest of the island province proved more destructive and complete than that of any other part of the empire.

As Roman power crumbled in the fifth century, the emperors were compelled to recall their troops from outlying areas such as Britain for the defence of Italy itself. They left behind them provinces quite unprepared for war, and the northern neighbours of the Britons, the Scots and Picts, seized the opportunity to invade. In their desperation the islanders sent ambassadors to the warlike Saxons, a pagan people of northern Europe.

'Come to our aid,' they pleaded, 'and you will have good pay and a fine district to settle in.'

So it was, in 449, that these European barbarians came to the British shores under the leadership of the brothers Hengist and Horsa. The Picts were crushed and sent fleeing, but the Briton's reprieve was not to be lasting. Thousands of Saxon 'reinforcements'

joined the camp over the next few months, and these formidable
allies were soon demanding extra payment and larger areas to
settle in. The Britons complied with their demands for a time,
but it required only the slightest pretence for the Saxons to take
up arms against their feeble masters. Fallen from the frying pan
into the fire, the Britons saw their cities captured with lightning
rapidity, as the Saxons seized control of much of the east coast.

Forced to defend themselves or perish, the Britons rallied
under the leadership of Ambrosius Aurelian, a descendant of
noble Roman family, and the invaders' progress was temporarily
halted. In the following years the victory went now one way,
now another, until the mighty battle of Badon Hill (c. 500), when
under the command of Arthur, perhaps the most celebrated
warrior king in history, the British achieved such a victory that
the invaders were subdued for many years to come. The Britons
did not manage to expel their unkind guests, but they did win for
themselves a long period of peace. They were once again supreme
in most of the island, and the hope of a complete reconquest
burned in their breasts.

The turning of the tide of war, however, had come too late to
save British society and culture. The island was a shadow of its
former self; the cities were ruins, the schools were gone and the
common folk were reduced to barbarous poverty. Amidst the
turmoil many unworthy men had established themselves as petty
tyrants, and in the ensuing peace they made the most of their
opportunities to exploit their own people. A British monk
named Gildas has left us a striking picture of the state of his
people some forty years after the victory of Badon Hill.

'Britain has priests, but they are fools, competing against each
other in treachery, shamelessness and greed. They teach the
people nothing but to imitate their own vices and crimes. They
bribe the princes to gain their positions, desiring to become
shepherds that they may fleece the flock. Even those who do not
dirty their own hands disgrace themselves by making no
complaint against their corrupt colleagues.'

Gildas had similar criticisms of the leading British princes of
his day, and he despaired of the future. Like a prophet of old he

warned the people to expect God's judgement unless they wholeheartedly abandoned their sins. His book *The Ruin of Britain* contains a striking pastiche of passages from Israel's prophets, unleashed against the similar evils of his own day.

Gildas' fears were realized. The last decades of the sixth century saw a Saxon resurgence, and by 600 the Britons had been vanquished and pushed back into the western provinces of Wales and Cornwall. Here, in the wild hill country, they maintained their freedom, but they had lost forever the spacious island that had once been theirs. Many fled the island to settle in the west of France, giving the name of Brittany to their new home.

But Gildas' prophetic cry had not been in vain. These decades of hardship saw a new blossoming of British Christianity, and Gildas himself led a mighty resurgence of British monasticism. As the corrupt ship of state sank the monks sought refuge in the Lord only, and like the Irish their devout energy soon became a vital agent in the mission to mainland Europe.

GILDAS, The Ruin of Britain

A Wife, a Whip and an Angel

The Saxons founded several separate kingdoms in Britain. Place names such as Wessex (West Saxons), Sussex (South) and Essex (East) mark the sites of the old Saxon kingdoms. The invaders were not only of the Saxon tribe. The Angles and Jutes were among the conquerors, and the whole body came to be known collectively as Anglo-Saxons. The 'Saxon' was later dropped, and 'Angle' became 'English'.

Regardless of tribe or kingdom, the invaders were alike in holding to the idol worship of their ancestors. The British Christians had little spiritual influence on the Saxon newcomers, and made virtually no efforts to convert them. Under the circumstances this is perhaps understandable. In the late sixth century, almost one hundred and fifty years after landing on British soil, the English were as thoroughly pagan as ever.

A Roman deacon, Gregory, was the first to concern himself with the conversion of these distant islanders. While walking through a market one day, he happened to see some slave-traders with a group of young boys. He sighed to see the misfortune which such fine looking youths had fallen into.

'Where do the young men hail from?' he asked the traders.

'From the island of Britain.'

'Are their people Christian or pagan?'

'They are most surely pagan.'

'How terrible that such bright faces should be the property of the Prince of Darkness! What is their race?'

'They are Angles.'

'An appropriate name,' said Gregory, 'for they have angelic faces, and God willing will be won to the faith of the angels in heaven! What is the name of their kingdom?'

'Deira.'

At that Gregory became quite animated, for *de ira* is Latin for 'from wrath'. 'May we live to see their people rescued from God's wrath through the knowledge of Christ! Who is their king?'

'Alle.'

'Then we must go to him immediately!' laughed the deacon. 'And teach him to sing "Alle"-lujah!'

Gregory hastened to visit the bishop of Rome and sought permission to undertake a mission to the Anglo-Saxons. It was not to be. The people of Rome refused to allow him to leave; he was already a great favourite in the city, and when the bishop died Gregory was elected his successor. We have already met Bishop Gregory, in fact, in the story of the Lombards, for it was he who aided the final overthrow of Arianism. It was also Gregory who organized the first mission to the English.

Unable to go to Britain himself, Gregory selected a group of missionaries under the leadership of a monk named Augustine. Their mission was as simple as it was daunting: go to the wild Anglo-Saxon conquerors and preach the gospel.

In 596 Augustine travelled overland to Gaul, and there he met with many British exiles and others who had seen the English firsthand. When he told them about his mission they were unanimous in their opinion.

'You won't survive a week! They are the cruellest race on earth.'

The disheartened monks delayed for some time in Gaul. 'Go back to the bishop,' they pleaded with Augustine, 'and ask him to release us from so difficult and uncertain a task.'

Augustine returned to Rome, but his complaints did not impress the bishop.

'Trust in God. In your weakness, His strength will be revealed.'

Augustine soon returned to Gaul, bearing a letter of encouragement from Gregory for the unwilling missionaries, and accompanied by interpreters the monks sailed for the island of Thanet. Thanet lay close to the coast of Kent, the most powerful of the English kingdoms, and while the monks waited there they sent their interpreters ahead with a message for Ethelbert, King of Kent:

'Visitors have come from Rome, bearing glad tidings for the English people. Their message is of the Lord Christ, and of the eternal life He offers to all who believe in Him.'

Ethelbert told the missionaries to remain on Thanet while he decided what action to take, and some days later he travelled across to meet them in person. Fearing that the missionaries might bewitch him the king requested that the monks meet with him outdoors, as it was an English superstition that magic was less powerful in the open.

'Deliver your message.'

The monks began with prayer for themselves and the English, and then, led by Augustine, unfolded to the king the basic teachings of Scripture and the life of Christ. Ethelbert was clearly moved.

'Your words and promises are very fair,' he said, 'but they are also new to me, and uncertain, and I cannot simply abandon the long-held beliefs of my people. I see, however, that you are sincere – you must be to travel so far with these tidings – and I promise that my people shall do you no harm. You may preach freely in my realm, and convert whomever you will.'

King Ethelbert granted the missionaries a dwelling place in Canterbury, his capital city, and once settled in it was not long before the mission was bearing spiritual fruit.

God had already planted a seed in the household of the king himself, for prior to Augustine's arrival Ethelbert had married a Frankish princess named Bertha. Bertha had come to Britain attended by Frankish serving girls, and a Christian minister had accompanied them as a chaplain. These Franks worshipped in an ancient church which the Saxons had left standing. The monks soon discovered this small band, and before long the rundown British church was home to a sizeable congregation.

King Ethelbert observed the pure and devout lives of the missionaries with admiration, and he was actually pleased to see many of his people accept baptism from the Italian monks. Before the year was out he also went down to the font, and from that day forth the conversion of the Kents gathered momentum.

Mellitus, one of Augustine's followers, led a missionary party to the nearby kingdom of Essex. Essex was ruled by Sabert, Ethelbert's nephew, and in 604 King Sabert became the second English ruler to receive baptism. Augustine passed away later that year, and Lawrence succeeded him as the second archbishop of the English.

The mission thrived until Ethelbert's death in 616. His son and successor Eadbald was no Christian, and even during his father's reign had been seen as the leader of the Kentish pagans. Under the flagrantly immoral Eadbald (who had married his father's second wife) the work of the church was greatly hindered, and many began to drift away from the congregation.

King Sabert's death later in the year made the situation even worse. He had left three sons behind him, all of whom were idolaters. Sabert's sons had often attended church with their father, and they continued to do so after his death, but now, when Mellitus offered Holy Communion to the worshippers, they demanded the bread and cup for themselves.

'You gave it to our father,' they said, 'now give it to us, for we have succeeded him.'

'It is impossible to offer it to you until you wash away your sins in baptism,' Mellitus answered. 'I gave communion to your father as a Christian, not a king.'

'We don't need baptism,' they insisted, 'but you must give us this bread and wine, for we know that it is a powerful thing.'

Mellitus again explained the situation, but the princes became angry.

'Hand it over or we will throw you out of our realm.'

Mellitus stood firm, and Sabert's sons meant what they said. Before evening the minister was on his way back to Kent. Mellitus visited Lawrence, and told him that he intended to return to Gaul.

'It is probably for the best,' said Lawrence. 'After twenty years' labour we thought that something great had been accomplished, but now we see the truth. What we built was so fragile that it has fallen in the first breeze. I have no hope of further success while Eadbald rules in Kent, and I shall follow you to Gaul shortly.'

Mellitus and several others sailed for Gaul the next day, and Archbishop Lawrence made what preparations he could for his Kentish flock and then arranged his own departure. On what was to be his last night in Britain he took his bedding to the church and spent the night there, heartbroken and utterly forlorn. Tears welled in his eyes as he wandered around the building he loved.

'How was I so blind?' he asked himself. 'Most of the Kents were merely following their king. These savages have done nothing but waste my time and disgrace the gospel.'

He spent several hours upon his knees, pleading with his Lord for the troubled English church, and then he fell asleep in the silent and airy building. About midnight, a troubled dream struck the old bishop's mind. A man appeared to him – a man of stern looks and powerful speech.

'A shepherd who flees at the wolf's approach is no shepherd at all.'

The stranger bared his arm and began to lash the bishop's back.

'Have you forgotten my example,' he cried. 'Have you forgotten the example of the Apostle Peter! Christ entrusted to me His sheep, and for them I endured beatings, prison and pain. I finally suffered crucifixion, all for the love of Him who sent me.'

Lawrence was catapulted out of his sleep wincing in pain, and to his amazement discovered lash marks deeply etched across his back. He abandoned his cowardly ideas of flight, and first thing in the morning he sought an audience with Eadbald. Baring his shoulders to the king's gaze, Lawrence revealed the dark welts that had appeared in his sleep.

'What has happened to you?' the king cried in shock. 'Who has dared attack a man who was my royal father's friend and guide?'

'My God has done this to me,' Lawrence answered. 'In a vision of the night I received these wounds. I was going to flee my responsibilities here, but God is so eager for your conversion that he stopped me with the lash from fulfilling my desire. I have come to tell you that nothing short of death will stop me from preaching to your people.'

Eadbald rose uncertainly, and he trembled visibly as he approached the old man.

'Is it true?' he whispered, more to himself than to anyone else. Pale and weak he fell down at Lawrence's knees. 'Baptize me.'

Messengers soon brought the glad tidings to Gaul, and at the king's urging Mellitus and his colleagues returned to their duties.

* * *

Kent was the major kingdom in the south of England, Northumbria that of the north.

Edwin was a young Northumbrian prince, son of Alle of Deira, the king whose name had once provided a pun for Gregory of Rome. Following Alle's death young Edwin was forced to flee his homeland, as a noble named Ethelfrid seized his father's throne.

Edwin wandered for many years through the English

kingdoms, until finally he found favour with King Redwald of the East Angles. When Ethelfrid heard of his location, however, he sent Redwald the promise of a large 'gift' if he should murder his guest. The offer was ignored, but Ethelfrid followed it with an even larger promise, accompanied by the threat of war if Redwald persisted in protecting Edwin. Far from the best of kings, Redwald bowed to Ethelfrid's demands.

'I shall do as your king asks,' he told Ethelfrid's messenger, who promptly returned to Northumbria.

One of Redwald's attendants, however, had formed a firm friendship with the unfortunate prince, and he went immediately to Edwin's rooms.

'You must fly this moment. The king has sealed your fate, and unless you disappear tonight you are a dead man.'

But Edwin refused to move. 'I thank you for your concern, but I cannot do as you suggest. The king and I have pledged fidelity to each other, and I will not run from the man who is my friend. I have nowhere else to go, and if I must die I would rather it be by his hand.'

The friend left, and Edwin wandered outside to sit alone and think. In fact he sat in the cool night air for some hours, his mind endlessly turning over his lamentable condition, until suddenly he was startled by the approach of a stranger.

'Why do you sit up alone, so sad and thoughtful, at an hour when others are at rest?'

'That is my concern,' the prince answered curtly, 'not yours.'

'Ah,' said the stranger, 'but it is mine! Let me ask you, what would you give to the one who could change Redwald's heart and protect you from your evil fate?'

'Anything he wanted,' said the prince, jumping up in surprise.

'What then if He also promised to restore you to your throne, and to crown your days with splendour?'

'Such a man,' said Edwin, 'would surely learn just how grateful I can be!'

'And what if you were also to receive guidance for your life on earth and for the world to come from such a man? What if He were to show your soul a path to salvation?'

'I would faithfully follow anyone who could save my life now, and restore my kingdom in the future.'

The man then laid his right hand upon the prince's head.

'When you receive this sign remember all we have said, and do not delay to fulfil your promise.' With that the man disappeared.

'A spirit!' Edwin was still sitting alone in the silence, pondering what he had seen, when his friend came out to speak with him.

'Your patience has paid off! Redwald told the queen of his plans, and she soundly scolded him for his unworthy intentions. He has abandoned the plot against you, and vowed to strike the first blow against your mutual enemy, Ethelfrid.'

Redwald was as good as his word. The two kingdoms went to war, Ethelfrid and his son perished on the field, and Edwin was restored to the throne of his father. King Edwin now sought a royal wife for himself. He sent messengers to the court of Eadbald and requested the hand of his sister Ethelberga.

'That is not so easy,' came the pious king's reply. 'My sister is a Christian, and it is not permissible to send a Christian maiden into a heathen household.'

'I shall place no obstacles in the way of her faith,' Edwin replied. 'The queen and her maids shall have complete religious freedom, and if on examination my advisers find this new faith more pleasing to God than that we now hold, I shall embrace it as my own.'

Under these conditions the marriage was arranged, and Paulinus came to Northumbria as bishop for the queen and her ladies, and missionary for their new nation. Almost a year later King Cuichelm of Wessex sent an assassin against Edwin, and the king narrowly escaped death at his hands. It was Easter Sunday, and that very evening Queen Ethelberga gave birth to the king's first child.

'Praise the gods! Today I have survived the assassin's hand, and now I am blessed with a daughter.'

Bishop Paulinus was present, and he also broke into praise as the news was announced. He then approached the king and spoke politely.

'It is not the 'gods' you should thank. Your queen has been sustained throughout her pregnancy by the Lord Jesus.'

The king was stirred by his words. 'If,' he said, 'your Christ is as great as you say, and would assist me against Cuichelm, I would abandon idols and worship Him only. As a pledge of this you may baptize my daughter according to your custom.'

So at Pentecost the royal princess received baptism, along with eleven Northumbrians converted under Paulinus' ministry. When Edwin recovered from the assassin's wound he led his troops against the West Saxons. He defeated his foe and did not neglect his promise when he returned home.

'Now you may give me a course of instruction in this faith. When I understand all that is at stake I shall discuss the matter with my advisers.'

The king immediately gave up the worship of idols, but after several months of discussion with the bishop nothing further seemed to come of it. Some began to fear that Edwin was insincere, and that he was too proud to bow his head and sincerely and humbly embrace the cross. They did not realize that there was a mighty ghost from the past tugging at Edwin's mind – for the king well remembered the night of despair outside Redwald's palace, and the promise he had made.

Edwin was torn between his conflicting desires, and daily spent long periods in thought, puzzling on the mysteries of religion. One day, sitting alone with his problem, he was startled by the quiet approach of Paulinus. The bishop laid his right hand upon the king's head.

'Remember?'

Tears stood out in Edwin's eyes, and he fell at the bishop's feet.

'Stop that,' said Paulinus, raising him up. 'He has protected you and given you victory. Now let Him save you.'

'Yes bishop,' said Edwin. 'Allow me to summon the chiefs of the nation, that we may take this momentous step together.'

The king summoned an assembly and asked the wise men to speak their thoughts on the new teaching. The chief priest, Coifi, rose first.

'I am all for it,' he said bluntly, 'and frankly confess that I hold the religion of our fathers to be worthless. I am chief priest, none has been more devoted to the gods than I, yet for all that I find myself shown less favour than many others. I would think little of a human friend who did me such poor service!'

'Your majesty,' said another adviser, 'when I compare our earthly lives to the whole span of time, I can only think of a sparrow on a winter's day. The sparrow darts in at one window of the king's banqueting hall, and then flies straight out another. For a moment he enjoys the light and warmth, then immediately returns to the merciless blizzards beyond. That is our life, a moment's sunshine in a universe that seems otherwise dark and cold. Who can tell us what went before our lives, or where we go when we die? If this new teaching offers us any surer knowledge it is only right to follow it.'

The other chiefs roared in approval, and many voiced similar opinions.

'It is done,' said Coifi. 'Let us abandon dead idols, and wash ourselves in the waters of baptism immediately. King Edwin, give me weapons and a stallion!'

Coifi, as high priest, had been banned from touching weapons of war, and from riding anything but a mare. Now he broke these taboos with delight, and accompanied by the chiefs he rode straight to the idol temple. The folk in the street looked on anxiously as he raced past.

'Has Priest Coifi gone insane?'

'You are worthless!' cried Coifi, flinging a spear through the temple doors. 'Smash the idols!' he yelled to his companions. 'Burn the worthless place to the ground!'

BEDE, *HISTORY* 1.22 – 2.16

John the Almsgiver

From the wild but glorious birth of the English church we turn again to the already ancient church of Egypt, which was graced in the early seventh century by two very striking individuals.

John, a wealthy Christian from Cyprus, was left a widower at a young age. His children also died young, and John dedicated all of his fortune and the rest of his life to supporting and providing for the poor. In time he received the nickname of the 'Almsgiver', and his fame reached the ears of the mighty. In 609 he was elected patriarch of Alexandria.

John was one of two rival patriarchs of the Egyptian church. Anastasius was the bishop of the 'rebel' Monophysite church, while the Almsgiver led the much smaller group that remained loyal to Constantinople. Immediately upon taking his position, John demanded that a list of his masters be drawn up and presented to him.

'What do you mean? Who could possibly be master of the city's patriarch?'

'I wish to learn the state of the city's poor,' said John. 'As a minister of Jesus, I am appointed to serve the poor. First I must know who they are.'

A list of 7,500 paupers was soon compiled, and the patriarch began to distribute a regular allowance to each of them. He also launched a campaign against the dishonest tradesmen and merchants of the city, whose cut-throat ways led to much of this poverty in the first place.

As the bishop was walking to church one Sunday he was met by a nobleman who told him with tears of a burglary he had suffered. His house had been completely stripped, and his extreme want had now forced him to the bitter task of seeking charity. John commiserated with him and then quietly told the keeper of his purse to give the sufferer 15 pounds of gold. It was a large amount, but nothing compared to what the man had lost. The steward thought the gift excessive and grumbled against the bishop.

'Have faith,' said John. 'What we sow today God can repay a hundredfold tomorrow.'

The steward was not impressed with such pious sentiments, and he and the church treasurer conspired to reduce the gift to five pounds.

When the service was ended and the collection taken the

bishop noted that a wealthy Christian widow had given a pledge
for five hundred pounds of gold. John, who had anticipated that
she would give considerably more than this, asked her to speak
with him later.

'I think I know why you have summoned me,' she said, 'so let
me tell you what happened. I wrote out an order for fifteen
hundred pounds, but when I happened to look at it as I was
standing in church I saw that the first digit had somehow been
wiped away. I thought to change it, but then decided that it must
be God's doing. I fear that I may have some unexpected need for
the rest of the money.'

John turned immediately to his financial stewards.

'Just how much did you give the foreign nobleman this
morning?'

They fidgeted nervously and mumbled incoherently. John
turned to another servant.

'Summon the man himself.' The nobleman came without
delay, and the deception was uncovered. 'I told you He could
repay a hundredfold,' said the Almsgiver, 'and so He has!
More's the pity for us!'

Nicetas was governor of Egypt at this time, and when he
introduced a new tax that weighed heavily on the poor John was
quick to protest. The two leaders discussed the problem, but
when they were unable to find a compromise Nicetas broke off
their conference in a black mood and stormed out. That evening
a messenger came to the governor's residence carrying a small
scrap of parchment, with only four words upon it:

'The Sun is setting.'

Nicetas pondered the strange message for a moment, until the
words of Paul, 'let not the sun set on your anger' (Eph. 4:26),
struck his memory, and with heart aflame he rushed to the
patriarch's rooms and begged his forgiveness.

On a similar occasion John himself was standing at the altar
about to celebrate communion when he remembered Jesus'
words: 'If at the altar you remember that your brother holds
something against you, leave your gift, go, and be reconciled to
him first' (Mt. 5:23–24). He recalled that he had temporarily

suspended two minor church officers for misbehaviour, and that while one of them had taken the punishment in the right spirit, the other had been furious with him as a result. With this in mind he left the altar and ran from the church.

'Just keep reciting that prayer until I return,' he called out.

He went straight to the man with whom he was at odds, and bowing before him asked forgiveness. The young man burst into tears.

'You must forgive me,' he cried, 'I have been a fool. I shall do anything to repair the damage that my pride has caused!'

'Well, not right now,' said John, hopping back onto his feet, 'we can talk again later.' With that he rushed back to the church to resume his duties!

When a prominent Alexandrian, engaged in a long-lasting feud, refused to heed the patriarch's repeated exhortations to show forgiveness, the Almsgiver invited him to a prayer meeting in his private chapel. Those present began to recite the Lord's Prayer, but on a secret signal from the bishop all ceased at the line 'Give us this day our daily bread', so that the official himself was the only one to say 'And forgive us our debts, as we also have forgiven our debtors.'

'What was that you said?' asked the bishop.

At that the man was convicted of his guilt and fell at the patriarch's feet.

'Yes good bishop,' he said, 'I shall do as I pray to be done by!'

In John's time an evil habit had spread through his congregation. The patriarch noted that immediately after the reading of the gospel many of the people would wander outside to chat, rather than remain for prayer. In response, the patriarch himself stepped down from the altar one day and wandered outside along with them.

'I think we had better finish the service out here from now on,' he said, 'for a shepherd must stay with his sheep. I come to the church for your sakes. If the service was for me I could more easily perform it at home.'

It did not take many repeats before none dared depart early again.

Patriarch John lived the simplest of lives; his food, clothing and furniture were all of the plainest kind. When a rich Alexandrian Christian learned that the Almsgiver slept with only one threadbare and torn old blanket he promptly sent him an expensive new one. John used the gift for one night, but as he went to sleep his mind was tortured by thoughts of those who had no blankets at all. The next morning he pawned the blanket and gave the money to the poor.

The rich man, hearing of this, bought the gift back and sent it to the bishop a second time. Again it was pawned, again repurchased. For weeks it bounced from the bishop's bed to the pawnshop.

'I like this game,' said John. 'Let's see who tires first, he of buying or I of selling!'

A bishop named Troilus was visiting Alexandria at this time. Wandering through the main business district one day his eye was caught by a fine silver goblet. The goblet, the trader told him, was worth 30 pounds, and notwithstanding its great expense Troilus set his heart upon it. He got together sufficient money, but as he was going to purchase it he happened to meet with the patriarch.

'You told me recently that you wanted to see the dormitories,' said the Almsgiver. 'I'm free now if it's a good time for you.'

'Oh,' said Bishop Troilus, 'well, I guess so.'

John's career spanned extremely troubled years. Throughout his patriarchate the empire was at war with Persia, and Alexandria was inundated with refugees from the affected provinces. The list of those needing the Almsgiver's aid became ever longer, and the public dormitories were just one of John's measures to help the people. Troilus and John walked over to examine the dorms, a series of large huts full of mattresses and blankets.

'They were built for the local homeless,' said John, introducing the visitor to his staff and volunteers. 'But on account of the refugee crisis they have taken on a whole new life.'

'How interesting,' said Troilus, eagerly seeking an opportunity to free himself from his host.

As the pair walked between two rows of bedding John heard the jingle of coins and looked with surprise at the hefty bag mostly concealed beneath his colleague's robes.

'God bless your charitable intention!' said the patriarch. 'I shall leave it to your discretion whether you pass this gift to the treasurer, or distribute it yourself amongst the poor folk now present.'

'Why, of course!' said the almost breathless bishop. He forced a smile at the poor folk nearby. 'Take this as a love offering from my congregation. God bless you.' Troilus was shattered by this unexpected charity. 'I, ah, must be going now,' he said faintly, and trembling with bitter emotions he rushed home and threw himself upon his bed. He lay there in anguish for several days, tossing and moaning until he developed quite a fever. When John noticed his absence he sent a servant to invite him for dinner.

'Sorry, but I can't come. I'm suffering a particularly violent fever.'

On this news the Almsgiver went to visit the sick man, but as he sat trying to cheer him he soon caught a hint of the real problem.

'You must recall,' said the patriarch, seeking a way to gently relieve Troilus' distress, 'that I borrowed 30 pounds from you recently for the support of my poor. If you wish I will return it at once.'

Troilus' heavy breathing stopped altogether. You could have heard a pin drop.

'That would be nice,' he finally muttered. Once the deal was done, and the money had changed hands, the colour returned to the bishop's cheeks.

'You look much better,' John said quietly, sadly. 'Come, we must go to dinner.'

Troilus was soon tucking into a hefty meal. He had hardly eaten for days, and at the table he drained a couple of cups more wine than was perhaps wise. After dinner he slumped into the first peaceful sleep he had enjoyed since losing his gold.

In the land of nod the bishop found himself in fields of

exquisite beauty, and he wandered until he came to a glorious mansion. Above the door was a shining inscription:

'The Eternal Mansion and Resting Place of Troilus, Bishop.'

The bishop rejoiced at the sight, but before he could enter the door a group of men dressed in shining garments came by.

'Not so,' said the leader of the new arrivals, pointing to the inscription. 'We must change it.'

Troilus watched uneasily as a new plaque was hoisted into place:

'The Eternal Mansion and Resting Place of John, Patriarch. Purchased for 30 pounds.'

Suddenly the bishop awoke, and with fear and trembling revealed what he had just seen. Almost needless to say the goblet was forgotten, the money returned, and Troilus himself from that dream forth strove to imitate the charity of his host!

As for that host, the days of his pilgrimage on earth were now drawing to a close. His last years saw greatly increased labours, as the victorious Persians began to push into Egypt itself. The aged patriarch, his health failing, gave himself body and soul to the work of relieving the refugees, but when the city itself was besieged Governor Nicetas persuaded him to accompany him on an embassy to the emperor. The patriarch consented, but before the ship had made it halfway he declared himself unable to go on.

'Let us turn aside from our course,' he said, 'that I may visit my ancestral home in Cyprus one last time. You bid me see the king of earth, but the King of Heaven has called me to Himself. I thank Him that this trip will give me the opportunity to be buried beside the wife of my youth.'

And so he was.

LEONTIUS, *The Life of St John the Almsgiver*

The Monk and the Harlots

During the patriarchate of this truly great man, another equally arresting Christian was prominent in Alexandria.

Vitalis was a monk from Gaza. He had lived in monastic calm for many years, happy to be far from the dangerous attractions of the city, until at the age of sixty he suffered an unexpected change of heart. He received a call that he could not ignore, and he could find no peace so long as he delayed obedience.

It began with his regular Bible study. Vitalis had read the Scriptures repeatedly over many years, but this time he became stuck on the eighth chapter of John's Gospel:

'Neither shall I condemn you. Go and sin no more' (Jn. 8:11).

For several days the monk could read nothing but this one passage, the story of the adulterous woman. Never could he think upon the words without tears, trembling under a powerful new impulse. Finally his mind was set, and the monk left his long familiar home. He must obey, or his swelling heart would kill him.

Vitalis went to Alexandria, where he spent some time roaming the streets by day and night. He quickly made himself familiar with the city's street life: the petty criminals, the drunkards and the prostitutes. He was soon able to draw up a fairly full list of the city's harlots.

In spite of his age Vitalis now found a job as a labourer. The work was hard, but it could not deter a man with a mission. After his first day's work he took his wages and bought some food, enough for a meal for two, and then paid an early call to the first address on his list.

'May I dine with you?'

The young woman was more than happy to receive a meal from the old monk, and afterwards Vitalis presented her with the remainder of his pay.

'This is for you, that you may spend at least one night without sin.'

Vitalis then knelt in a corner of the room, the only room in the prostitute's meagre hovel, and spent the night in prayer and psalm singing.

'Bless my toil during the day, O Lord, that by night I might save one of Your little ones from evil. Bless this girl, this poor sister for whom Christ died, that she might turn from sin and find true life in You. Help her to be what You made her for! In

Jesus' name I plead a blessing on her.'

The prostitute was astounded by the monk's behaviour, and she spent a silent and thoughtful night as she listened to the outpouring of the old man's heart before God. The following morning Vitalis returned to his labour, but before he left the poor girl he extracted a promise from her.

'Tell no one what took place last night,' he insisted. 'If word spreads that I am encouraging prostitutes to leave their sins my work will be ruined. There are many who want nothing less than for the prostitutes of this city to reform their habits. So long as I live you must keep silent as to what I have done.'

And so Vitalis lived for a long time. Each day he collected his wage, and each night he paid a visit to a harlot. This could not go on long without some word getting around the city.

'A sixty-year-old monk visiting the harlots every single night!'

It was only a few weeks before someone said something to his face. A young Christian saw him at work on a construction site and began to abuse him.

'Wretched old man! Return to your monastery and stop disgracing the name of God. If you can't control your desires then have some pride and take a wife for yourself. You are a living blasphemy!'

Vitalis was cut to the core by the rebuke; he knew how his actions looked, but the force of the Spirit, pushing him on in his work, was irresistible.

'Has the Lord appointed you as my judge?' he retorted. 'If you trust in God then leave my punishment to Him.'

Another Scripture passage came to the monk's mind now, one which spoke forcefully to his own condition: 'Take unto yourself a harlot wife, and children of adultery, for the land is doubly guilty of adultery' (Hos. 1:2).

'Lord, to teach Your people You bid Hosea marry a harlot. To myself has come a work even more evil in the world's eyes. I pray that none be wounded in spirit by my actions.'

It was not long before a report of Vitalis' conduct came to the ears of Patriarch John. A member of the Church Police, the group that investigated misconduct of priests and monks, brought the matter to his attention. The Almsgiver, however, had once before received a complaint of impropriety against a monk, and only after punishing the offender had found the charge to be groundless. He refused to rush into judgement a second time.

So Vitalis' work could continue, though the monk himself had to daily hear his name dragged through the dirt. He suffered reproach and insult without murmur, but in spite of his faith was haunted by the thought of the effect his example might be having on others.

'Lord, when I am gone I ask that you will reveal the truth of my life, so that the scandal I have created might be washed away.'

Early one morning Vitalis was leaving a brothel as a young man came in.

'How long will you disgrace Christ, you filthy old rogue?' the young hypocrite bellowed, and he struck the old man hard in the face. The monk staggered under the blow, a blinding pain racing through his skull. He swayed for a moment, and then looked straight at his assailant.

'From me, friend,' he said, 'you yourself will receive such a blow that all Alexandria will ring with it.'

The young man snorted contemptuously as Vitalis turned and left. Hearing raised voices outside her door, the prostitute came out just in time to see Vitalis depart. She saw that he was bleeding.

'What have you done, you pig?' she yelled.

'Taught a filthy old sinner a long overdue lesson.'

The girl began to cry. 'He's not like that at all! He spent the whole night in prayer, begging me to give up my ways,' the girl sobbed loudly, and then paused. 'And I shall. I'm leaving.'

She raised her head and strode out to the street, eagerly seeking the injured monk. The young man was dismayed. He stood for some moments in stunned silence, and feelings of guilt and shame welled up within him. With a sob he ran after the girl, and he began talking excitedly to everyone in the street.

'Vitalis the monk,' he cried. 'Vitalis is innocent!'

People soon gathered to hear the message of the young man and the harlot. Vitalis, after all, had been a leading topic of gossip for months.

'Innocent!'

'Where is he?' some cried.

Soon a search was underway.

'Vitalis usually prays in the church by the gate,' someone revealed.

The young man who had struck the blow was the first to reach the monk's retreat.

'Forgive me, Vitalis, man of God!'

But then he stopped and stared in silence, as the crowd continued to build up behind him. Vitalis was kneeling, his hands clasped in prayer. In this posture he was frozen, in death. On the ground before him was a small note:

'Do not judge prematurely, before the Lord comes, for He will bring to light those things hidden in darkness, and will reveal the inner workings of the heart' (1 Cor. 4:5).

The news of Vitalis' vindication, and death, soon spread through the city, and the Almsgiver and other church leaders came to take his body for burial. As they left the church they were greeted by a great assembly of women who walked before the body in solemn procession. Some were married women, some were nuns, but all had one thing in common.

'We were once prostitutes,' they testified, 'and no one in this city did a thing to help us. Now we have lost our one teacher and friend! Vitalis rescued us, each of us, from a life of misery.'

With these words ringing in his ears, Vitalis' murderer felt the promised blow. Confessing his sins, and praying forgiveness for his wicked ways, the young man gave all he had to the poor and fled to Vitalis' old monastery at Gaza. There he lived and died, in the cell that Vitalis had once occupied. And, just as Vitalis had predicted, all Alexandria resounded with the blow.

LEONTIUS, *THE LIFE OF ST JOHN THE ALMSGIVER* 36

A-lo-pen

Much has already been said of the church's missionary work in Europe. It is less well known that the same period saw equally extensive missionary work in the Far East, so that by the seventh century there were Christians from one end of the ancient world to the other.

The Persian church, sitting at the crossroads of the ancient world, was one of the most vigorous missionary churches in history. In one direction it faced Byzantium, but to the north and east it was absorbed in the view of the enormous expanses of pagan Asia.

We know only scattered details of the first Persian missionary endeavours. India was certainly an early target, and a Christian community has survived on the west coast, the Malabar Coast, from the fourth century (or earlier) to the present. Cosmas Indicopleustes, a Christian merchant and author of the early sixth century, records the existence of large Christian congregations in both India and Sri Lanka in his time.

A long overland route stretched through central Asia, connecting Persia and China, and many Christians were settled in the major stations along this ancient highway. From the fifth or sixth century onwards these Christians had a considerable influence on the wild central Asian tribes, and though records are scanty, we know that numerous tribes embraced the faith over the centuries. A-lo-pen is one of the few Persian missionaries of the period known to us by name. Well might he be remembered, for he was probably the first missionary to take the gospel to China.

A-lo-pen arrived in Changan (modern Xi'an), the Chinese capital, in 635. He was well received by the Chinese emperor and provided the court with copies of the Gospels and other Christian writings. These books were translated, and the emperor was most impressed with the teachings of the faith. He declared that the gospel proclaimed a path of truth, and ordered the construction of a church in his capital.

The Chinese mission blossomed for several generations, and

there were soon churches and monasteries established throughout the empire. But the church was not to experience a lasting missionary success. In fact the very words of the emperor's first declaration about the gospel, positive as they might sound, contained within themselves the bitter seed of the mission's ultimate failure.

The emperor, Tai-tsung, had called the gospel a way of truth, and in the centuries that followed no Chinese emperor went further. The missionaries received many privileges, but no ruler embraced the faith in a wholehearted manner, and the church never succeeded in becoming a major movement amongst either the lower classes or the ruling elite. When persecutions eventually came the church was barely able to withstand them, and though for centuries the Chinese church remained a factor in society, it was never to rise to the heights that the western church experienced, and which led to the creation of a new civilization in Europe.

CHING-CHING, 'THE HSIANFU MONUMENT'

The Rise of Islam

We have already heard, in the story of the Almsgiver, of the bitter warfare between the Byzantine Empire and Persia in the early seventh century. The seventh century, after the glory days of Justinian, was a new period of decline for Byzantium. The barbarians won back many of the newly captured territories, and Persia, the ancient enemy, seized the opportunity for plunder and conquest.

Between 611 and 616 King Chosroes of Persia conquered the provinces of Syria, Palestine and Egypt, stripping the empire of her very heartland, and it was not until 622 that Emperor Heraclius was able to strike a telling blow in return. Under this great emperor the Byzantines recaptured the provinces and then avenged their sufferings by carrying the war deep within Persian territory. By 627 the tables were turned, and Persia herself had been brought to her knees. As it happened, she was never to rise again. Both nations were exhausted by the long war, and when a new power came onto the scene neither was in a fit state to resist.

The power in question was the newly united Arab nation. The world map was about to be changed for centuries to come by the appearance of a new empire and a new religion, and Christianity was to receive one of its greatest challenges ever. To understand this revolution we must take a closer look at the history of Arabia.

The Arabs, or Saracens, inhabited the vast expanses of desert to the south of the boundary between Rome and Persia. Their land was poor, and the Arabs tended to live in small and scattered tribes. They were best known to their more civilized northern neighbours as bandits, and the name Arab was synonymous with theft, murder and kidnapping.

Over the centuries many of the northern Arabs had converted to Christianity, and some of their tribes had settled in small towns on the borders of Rome and Persia. Christianity was less widespread in the south of Arabia. The southern population was mainly pagan, though with a sizeable Jewish population and scattered members of several heretical Christian sects. It was a fact of enormous importance for later history that there was no major missionary activity in southern Arabia in this vitally important era. The pagan Saracens were more familiar with the beliefs of Jews and heretics than with true Christianity.

In the late sixth century a strange religious movement began in Arabia. The 'Hanifs', as they were called, were inspired by the confusion and variety of ideas about the 'One God' which they heard around them. They abandoned the old Arab idolatry and sought inner peace through prayer and meditation. They professed belief in One God but confessed that they knew little about Him.

The Hanifs, self-confessedly seekers rather than teachers, had little effect on the lives of their pagan countrymen (several, incidentally, eventually became Christians). This would change, however, when a Hanif named Mohammed came on the scene.

Mohammed claimed that the God of the Bible, the God of the Jews and Christians, had sent the angel Gabriel to speak with him. He proclaimed himself God's prophet to the Arabs, sent to save them from ignorance, and claimed that his teaching, preserved in the Koran, was the same as the teaching of Moses, the prophets and Jesus. Mohammed repeatedly asserted that his own book agreed with and confirmed the Bible, and that both books were true and divine. Amongst a nation ignorant of the true Scriptures such a claim was hard to disprove; we, however, can compare the two books for ourselves.

Mohammed had never read the Bible, in fact he was probably illiterate, but he did know many Jewish and heretical stories by word of mouth. The Koran contains a number of stories from the Old Testament, and some are quite accurate retellings. There are, however, very striking errors. The twelfth chapter, in which Mohammed responded to a challenge from some Jews by attempting to tell the story of the patriarch Joseph, is one of the more notorious. Mohammed skips constantly between scriptural truth and wild legend (for example, King Solomon could control the winds, owned a fountain which ran with liquid brass instead of water and had supernatural spirits at his beck and call!), and it has exhausted all the ingenuity of Muslim commentators on the Koran simply to putty up the cracks in the supposed revelation.

When it came to the New Testament, Mohammed was quite out of his depth. Jesus is repeatedly mentioned, and is even proclaimed the greatest teacher prior to Mohammed, but there are virtually no stories about him. Mohammed knew only a few stories about his birth and childhood, as well as some heretical legends (he even claims, like the ancient Docetists, that Christ was not truly crucified). Not one of the apostles is so much as mentioned by name, and besides a brief mention of three disciples of Jesus preaching in Antioch (completely dissimilar to the account in the book of Acts), and a legend about certain Christians who escaped their persecutors and slept in a cave for three centuries (one of the wilder folk tales of the early Christians, and one which Mohammed evidently believed), the story of the church after Jesus' ascension is not even touched upon. The claims of the Koran are easily dismissed. Mohammed asserted in plain language that his new 'scripture' agreed with the Bible – and that simply isn't the case.

On a moral level the Koran is open to equally grave criticisms, and nothing so reveals the Arabian prophet's imposture than the goings on in his own household. A genuine prophet, of course, can have failings, but when he justifies them by 'divine revelation' one sees the wolf within the wool!

The Koran permits a Muslim (a word derived from Arabic 'surrender', meaning those who have surrendered in obedience to 'god' and Mohammed's 'revelation') to take up to four wives, and to treat as concubines any female slaves in his possession. Mohammed, much addicted to women, tired of this restriction in his later years, and he received new revelations to the effect that God had made him the one exception to this rule, and had permitted him to take as many wives as he pleased. And take he did! While visiting the home of his adopted son one day he caught a fateful glimpse of the younger man's wife in a scanty gown, and he made no secret of his appreciation of her beauty. His son caught the hint, and he offered to divorce his wife so that the prophet might have her. Mohammed at first refused. Marrying a divorced woman was not a problem (Mohammed permitted his followers to divorce their wives on a whim), but marrying so near a relation was unheard of. In this anxiety he was seized by the spirit of prophecy in a public place.

'Go quickly and congratulate Zeinab,' he announced, 'for the Lord has now joined her unto me in marriage!'

A new chapter of the Koran quickly followed, in which all Muslims were given the right to marry the divorced wives of their adoptive sons.

On another occasion Mohammed's wife Hafsa returned home unexpectedly to find the prophet misbehaving with a slave in her own bed, and fearing for his reputation Mohammed vowed that he would never again lay hands on the girl. Hafsa made the scandal public nonetheless, and Mohammed found himself receiving the cold shoulder from all ten ladies of his house. The fact that he had made a rash vow to abstain from the beautiful slave girl, an Egyptian named Mary, made the situation even more bitter. In his plight, a new revelation absolved Mohammed from his vow to abandon Mary, and even reproached him for fearing the ill opinion of his wives! To punish his wives Mohammed threatened them with divorce (which he said would last to all eternity – his tastes are revealed in the fact that he taught that every Muslim man would receive 70 beautiful virgins in heaven), and to really rub their noses in it he locked himself away with the slave girl for a month! Nothing could better illustrate the darkness of men's hearts than that such a religion is today second only to Christianity in numbers.

The first years of the prophet's ministry saw little success. The pagan elders of his people were unimpressed with the new message, and when they once accosted him the fearful prophet assured them that he honoured their pagan goddesses in addition to the one true 'Allah'. Soon repenting of this backwardness, however, Mohammed became much bolder in his preaching.

Slowly the prophet gained a following and over the course of 20 years, and through various battles and plots, he became the greatest leader amongst the southern Arabs. When the great capital of Mecca finally fell to him in 630, virtually the whole of the south was united in obedience to Mohammed. With such an army behind him the ambitious prophet saw that the present distresses of the nations to the north opened even greater

---

Mohammed had such an inflated idea of his writings that he made claims for the Koran greater than any that Christians have made for the Bible. To Christians, only Jesus Christ is the *eternal* Word of God. The Bible, wonderful as it is, is only a revelation of God – not part of God Himself. The Muslim, however, sees the Koran as being equally fundamental to the universe with God. It is as ancient as God, and the prophet Mohammed had no part in writing it. The Koran, complete and perfect, was chapter by chapter shown to the prophet that he might report it to others.

In view of this it is surprising to find that the strange principle of 'correction' should apply to the Koran. Mohammed knew that he was in danger of contradicting himself as he wrote, and of accidentally making statements in one part of the Koran that disagreed with statements in other parts. So he declared from the outset that if such should occur, the latter revelation should be taken as authoritative! How could an eternal and infallible book need correcting?!

Nothing is more striking than the fact that the Bible, written by dozens of authors over hundreds of years, is more consistent within itself than the work of one man written over a couple of decades.

prospects of conquest. Not since the Huns had such a formidable force threatened the great kingdoms of the day.

Mohammed died in 632 (his death was hastened by poisoning – a prisoner, a Jewess, had tested his supposed prophetic insight by feeding him a poisoned leg of lamb), and shortly thereafter his followers marched upon Persia, still in ruins after its defeat at the hands of Heraclius. The Persians crumbled quickly, and most of their territory was gone before the survivors put up even a semblance of resistance. Within two decades the ancient enemy of Rome was almost completely destroyed, and with Persia's fall the religion of Zoroaster virtually disappeared.

In these same years the Arabs launched separate assaults on the nearest Byzantine provinces – those very areas which had recently suffered under Persian invasion. Even as poorly organized nomadic raiders the Arabs had been an ongoing danger to the empire, which for centuries had been unable to find an effective remedy for their destructive frontier incursions. But now, with the whole Arab people following one banner, with zealous armies propelled forward by the earnestness of their faith in Allah, and the belief that he had called them to jihad ('holy war') against unbelievers, the Saracens looked to be all but unstoppable. In 636 the flower of Byzantium's troops perished in the battle of Yarmuk (in Syria), two years later Jerusalem fell to the Arabian scimitar, and within another decade virtually all resistance in Syria and Egypt had been snuffed out, and the Muslims, almost surprised with themselves, were contemplating the destruction of Constantinople itself. A people who had so recently been dismissed as no more than bandits now seemed capable of sweeping all before them.

MOHAMMED, *THE KORAN*; IBN ISHAQ, *LIFE OF MOHAMMED*

Aidan of Lindisfarne

Before further exploring the Byzantine plight, however, we must wing our way back to the west and the infant church of the English.

Oswald succeeded Edwin as King of Northumbria. He was the son of Ethelfrid, Edwin's predecessor and rival, and fleeing to Scotland after his father's death had been converted to the gospel there. Now, following Edwin's death, he returned to take the throne that had once been his father's.

Oswald asked the Scottish church for a missionary bishop to aid him in spreading the knowledge of God amongst his people, and an Ionan monk soon arrived in his capital of York. This monk laboured several months amongst the English, before returning home utterly disheartened. At an assembly of Scottish Christian leaders he explained the reason for his return.

'It is an impossible task,' he complained, 'the English have hearts of stone. They are too wild ever to submit to the gospel.'

At these words a great debate began amongst the leaders. How could they help these wild English? After a time a monk named Aidan called for silence and addressed the unsuccessful missionary.

'Brother,' he said, 'I can only imagine that you were too hard on the people. Heed the advice of Scripture, and give milk to babes and solid food to more mature believers. If they are wild, meet them where they are. Don't try to change them in a day!'

All eyes fell upon the speaker, and the decision of the assembly was unanimous:

'Aidan for the English!'

Aidan, in the Spirit's power, proved as good as his word, and he spent the rest of his life as missionary bishop. The king granted him a small island, Lindisfarne, which became the monastic centre of Northumbria – a new Iona. It was the Celtic monks of Lindisfarne, not the Italians who had laboured so worthily in the south, who would be chiefly responsible for the development of a strong church in the north of England. Within a few years after Aidan's death the last strongholds of Anglo-Saxon paganism would be gone.

A touching anecdote illustrates the relationship of Aidan and King Oswin, Oswald's successor. Oswin gave the bishop a fine horse, that the monk might no longer need to undertake his missionary journeys on foot. The gift was appreciated, but it was not long before Bishop Aidan encountered a beggar on the road.

'Have you something for a poor man?'

Aidan dismounted. He looked at the beggar, and then at his horse. His very saddlecloths were a thousand times finer than the beggar's thin clothes had ever been!

'Take it and sell it,' said Aidan, handing the reins to the pauper.

Oswin heard of this surprising generosity and brought the matter up the next time he dined with the bishop.

'That was a fine horse – I chose it with great care for your personal use. I have many less valuable horses and other belongings. In future ask for these if you wish to make a gift to the needy.'

'Is that true, your majesty?' asked the bishop. 'Do you really have more care for the child of a mare than you do for a child of God?'

Aidan sat down to eat, and Oswin went over to the hearth to warm himself. He stood there silently for a moment, turning over in his mind the bishop's words. Suddenly he felt very deeply the presence of God, and casting off his sword he ran to the bishop and knelt at his feet.

'Forgive me, bishop,' he said, 'I shall never again question the ways of charity.'

Aidan raised the king, and the two men embraced.

'Sit and eat with thanksgiving,' Aidan said, 'for the Lord delights in you.'

As the meal progressed the king became very merry. The bishop himself, however, became sombre, and a fellow minister questioned him about his long face.

'Brother,' he said privately, 'I know that King Oswin will not be with us much longer. I have never before seen a humble king, and perceive that this people is unworthy of him.' His words were soon proved true.

BEDE, *History* 3.1–17

Caedmon's Call

One of the most intriguing characters of the seventh-century church was a Northumbrian by the name of Caedmon.

The English loved singing and poetry, and during their feasts a harp would be passed around the table for each of the guests to entertain the party in turn. Caedmon loathed the very sight of the harp. To be sure he loved music and poetry, and would sit for a moment and listen to the others, but he would always depart before the harp reached his own chair.

'Where are you going Caedmon?'

'I am suddenly exhausted,' was his perennial reply.

Caedmon had never sung in public, and he flushed with embarrassment at the mere thought of doing so. Sometimes in private he would try to prepare a song or poem, but somehow the words would just not come.

On one such night he abandoned the party and went out to the nearby stable. It was his duty that night to mind the livestock, and Caedmon was glad of the excuse to leave early. After a few moments of sitting with his thoughts he curled up to sleep on the hay.

'Caedmon, sing for me.'

Caedmon looked up in surprise and saw a stranger standing nearby.

'I can't sing,' Caedmon confessed, for the first time in his life. 'That is why I always leave when the harp comes my way.'

'Caedmon,' said the stranger, 'you shall sing for me.'

'What about?'

'About the creation!'

Suddenly Caedmon's tongue was loosed, and a song in praise of God the Creator poured from his lips:

Now we must praise the Maker of Heaven,
His glorious power and His mind's wisdom.
    We praise the great Father's deeds,
The eternal God, Worker of wonders.
    He made Heaven our glorious canopy
And Earth a home for the race of men.

With a start Caedmon woke, the new verses deeply embedded in his mind. Gingerly he recited them, and to his surprise he found himself adding more and more verses in a torrent of unexpected eloquence.

Caedmon visited a priest the next day and unfolded his remarkable story. An assembly was called, and in the presence of the wisest men of the realm Caedmon repeated his verses, and many others like them. All agreed that this was a gift from God, and Caedmon abandoned his humble calling and entered a monastery, where he spent the rest of his life in the composition of spiritual songs. The man who had blushed for shame at the sight of a harp now became known as the father of English sacred verse, and Caedmon's songs thrilled the heart of his nation for centuries.

BEDE, *HISTORY* 4.24

The Mission to the Netherlands

Columba had been the first of many brothers. Throughout the seventh and eighth centuries a great wave of missionaries poured from Ireland into mainland Europe.

Columbanus was one of the greatest among them. He settled amongst the Franks about 590, and it was to the labours of his monks that France owed its greatest debt as it emerged from the barbarism of the sixth century. Columbanus' leading disciple was Gall, a missionary whose labours focused on what is now Switzerland, and who founded a monastery there that became one of the greatest centres of learning in Europe.

A barbarian town, a remote rural area, a lonely island – any of these places might become a mission base for the Irish wanderers. Many have been almost completely forgotten with the passage of centuries, but the effects of their labours are with us to this day. They were seldom the first missionaries to visit a country, but their energy and zeal was vital in revealing the true life of the Spirit to the barbarian churches.

From the middle of the seventh century onwards many Englishmen joined the Irish in the great missionary adventure. A Northumbrian named Willibrord spent many years in Ireland under the direction of that nation's leading monks, and late in the seventh century he was selected to lead a mission to the Frisians, inhabitants of what is now Belgium and the Netherlands.

The mighty Frankish kingdom, immediately south of Frisia, proved a mixed blessing to Willibrord's mission. The Franks often controlled parts of Frisia, and Willibrord could rely on their support and protection, but this relationship with their warlike neighbours tended to make the Frisians suspicious of him. The progress of Willibrord's mission often fluctuated in line with the political relations of the Franks and Frisians.

The pagan Frisians followed the abominable practice of child sacrifice, and it once happened that Willibrord's colleague Wulfram was at the court of King Radbod when the day arrived for the performance of this bloody rite. Horrified at the news, the missionary rushed to the king and began to plead with him.

'Sire, I know that you are not yet prepared to accept the teachings of the gospel, but I beg you, while you are contemplating the message we have brought you, to put a ban on these detestable rites. The Bible, the book of the true God, speaks many times of the wickedness of child sacrifice. Sire, it is evil demons who have commanded this rite, not "gods".'

'Believe what you will,' King Radbod replied, 'we must do as we have always done. If we fail to make sacrifices to Odin, our gods will destroy us.'

And so the ceremony went ahead just as planned. The children of the nobles were gathered, lots were drawn, and the unfortunate child chosen by the gods was hung from a tree.

'Oh Lord!'

Wulfram went down on his knees, and while the Frisians performed the other abysmal rites of their religion he poured out his soul in fervent prayer.

'Lord, show your power!' he cried. 'May this evil never take place again!'

Two hours passed like this, when suddenly all were silenced

by the unexpected breaking of the noose. The lifeless child fell to earth, and Wulfram rushed forward and took the victim in his arms. Cradling the child he groaned forth prayers beyond words, until suddenly a ripple of surprise and wonder passed through the watching pagans and the child trembled and opened his eyes.

'The Lord returns your son to you,' said Wulfram, taking the boy to his parents.

Many of the astonished Frisians were led to embrace Jesus in spite of themselves. The Christian God could rescue a victim even from Odin's bloody grasp! King Radbod himself asked for baptism, but before entering the water he turned to Wulfram with a question.

'Where are my ancestors now? Have they a share in the heaven that you promise me?'

Wulfram answered without hesitation. 'Not likely,' he said. 'Your ancestors, in fact, are in the place of eternal torment.'

With that Radbod turned his back on the stream and remained a pagan until his death.

Perhaps Wulfram could have shown more discretion. Radbod was still a spiritual infant, and he was clearly unprepared for such 'solid food' as Wulfram's teaching on damnation. It might have been more appropriate for the missionary to simply answer: 'God knows.'

However that may be, we can at least admire Wulfram's honesty and conviction. Perhaps after such long experience of the hate-filled barbarism of the Frisian religion he could not bring himself to say anything else. Whichever way we look at it, Wulfram's answer and Radbod's response provide food for thought – the question is perhaps the hardest that a missionary can be asked.

The Oak of Thor

The English church was thrilled by stories of the Netherlands mission, and there was no shortage of fresh recruits for the work. Amongst those who embarked for the continent, none would be so well remembered as Boniface, a monk and lecturer in Bible studies from Wessex, destined to be the greatest missionary of the age.

Boniface left England in 716, in his early forties. His arrival in Frisia was ill-timed, for Willibrord's team had just been scattered and virtually silenced by an outbreak of persecution, and after delaying some months in the hope of a change for the better the somewhat disheartened novice returned to England.

Back in familiar surroundings, however, Boniface could not return to life as usual. The Lord's call to the mission field became even more insistent, and with a new determination he returned to the continent. This time he made the city of Rome his first destination, and in 719 he shared his dream with the Roman bishop.

'The Lord has charged my soul with a mission to the Germans.'

Bishop Gregory II wrote letters in the Englishman's favour to the relevant authorities.

'Do as the Lord directs you,' said the bishop, 'and in so far as we can help you we shall.'

Boniface travelled into Germany, but his preaching there met very limited success. He was encouraged, however, by news that Willibrord's mission was now enjoying more peaceful times, and after several fairly disappointing months he resolved on revisiting Frisia. The next three years proved to be pivotal in his life and ministry. The Frisian church enjoyed a period of rapid growth, and Boniface himself so impressed the ageing Willibrord that he was urged to remain and succeed him in the Frisian bishopric. Here was a temptation – a dignified role in a now established church – but the monk refused it.

'I have been given the mission to the Germans, and to that I shall return.'

It was a very different Boniface who returned to the wild German forests. His experience under Willibrord had sharpened his vision, and his energy and devotion were now fortified with experience.

Boniface was not the first missionary to brave the German forests, and there were already numerous small Christian communities scattered through the vast land. Most of these converts, however, tended to be dangerously ignorant of deeper Christian truths and continued to follow ancient pagan practices. A visit to the local wizard right after church was nothing unusual.

'Where else could we get our magic potions?'

Even the few converts from Boniface's own earlier mission were living like their neighbours by the time the monk returned.

'Yes, we believe in Jesus,' they said. 'And we believe in Odin, and Thor, and the spirits of the streams and trees . . .'

Boniface saw that he must do more than simply preach and teach. Something had gone wrong with the former missionary efforts; somehow the Germans had not been able to see that the gospel message demanded a radical change of the whole of life. How could he clearly show the division between Christian and pagan, God and the 'gods'?

The Germans were a warrior race. They worshipped gods of war and dreamed of a heaven where each day was filled with bloody battles and each night with drunken feasting. No greater obstacle than this love of war stood in the missionary's way. How could such a savage people be brought to full acceptance of the life and teachings of a man who said 'turn the other cheek'? How could the gospel of peace and love replace the worship of Odin and Thor, gods of battle and thunder?

Germany needed a hero. Boniface came up with a plan.

The holiest site of the German religion was the Oak of Thor. The warriors would congregate at the foot of this mighty and ancient tree and join with deafening cries in the worship of the god of thunderbolt and storm – a terrifying spectacle indeed! It was during one such assembly that the Lord called Boniface to one of the boldest steps in the history of Christian mission. Taking a hefty axe, the monk joined the German warriors at their holy place.

'Who is Lord?' he asked. 'Who is the God of thunder?'

With fearless step he approached the trunk of the mighty oak, and swinging with all his might he made a dent in the hard wood. Blow followed blow, and the sound of the axe was all that could be heard for miles around. The warriors stood in complete silence, dumbfounded by the foolhardy antics of the slight bodied monk. Who, indeed, was Lord? They waited in shock, but sure nonetheless that some terrible fate must soon befall the Christian. The monk had as yet made little impression on the mighty tree's girth when a distant rumbling fell upon the assembly's ears. Sweating and exhausted Boniface stepped back from the tree, and his axe fell to the ground. The silence of the pagans was broken, as a cry of triumph shook the forest.

'THOR!'

The pagan chants were struck up with a tremendous ferocity. All stood back and waited for the punishment that must soon befall the monk. The treetops began to shake and sway, and a mighty wind came crashing through the forest.

'WHO,' Boniface cried, 'IS THE GOD OF THE STORM?'

With a numbing roar the wind struck the tree, and the pagans were sent scattering as Thor's Oak came crashing to the ground. The storm immediately died, and left the idol shattered in four pieces on the forest floor.

This display preached louder than any sermon to the German heart. All the warriors went down upon their faces, and with fear and trembling they begged to be told how they could appease this mighty and angry God. Within a few days the whole region was baptized, and the mission to the Germans had begun! Boniface set to work on the construction of the first Christian church for the area, and with a poetic master stroke built it from the massive timbers of Thor's Oak.

Now Boniface was confronted with a new problem. The nation was prepared to listen to the gospel, but who was to teach them? An urgent call went back to his fellow English Christians, and soon the German forests were flooded with willing hands. Scores of monks travelled over land and sea to aid the German mission, and a surprising number of nuns came with them.

Unlike other missionaries of his time, Boniface ensured that

Christian women took an important place on the mission field. At the frontiers of the mission, where life was hardest and the threat from the pagans greatest, only men laboured by his side, but once a degree of safety and stability was assured Boniface encouraged his devout sisters to come and settle in the newly Christianized towns. Soon the whole land was dotted with monasteries and convents, each one of them a centre of Christian education and outreach.

Boniface was a gifted communicator, and both in person and by letter he was able to create enormous interest in his work. A less engaging and affable man would have found it practically impossible to create such zeal for the venture into the wild forests of Germany. We still have many of the letters that Boniface sent back to England, and we can read in his own words the requests for helpers, Bibles, Christian books, etc. A number of Boniface's sermons have also been preserved. They show the clear and simple style that the great missionary used to teach his infant churches:

'Far away in the land of Italy, there is an ancient city named Rome. In this city there was once a mighty chief named Augustus Caesar, who made peace in all the world. While he ruled, a child was born in Bethlehem . . .'

In this straightforward manner Boniface communicated the teachings of Scripture. His sermons also reveal his unrelenting war with the lapses of his converts into pagan practice. Witchcraft, the use of magic amulets and fear of werewolves in particular proved very hard to eradicate.

Boniface never stayed long in any one location. Once the foundations of a church were laid he would immediately move on, deeper into the German forests, seeking new areas to sow. Even in his sixties and seventies he showed energy such as few other missionaries before or since, and he seems to have thrived on the danger of his explorations – not in some sort of thrill-seeking way, but because the very fact of persecution convinced him of the need for more preaching. His career was dogged by the fact that there were always more pagans just beyond his present location. Pagan neighbours frequently launched attacks upon new converts, and during Boniface's own lifetime he saw dozens of churches burned to the ground by extremists. Few missionaries have been so visibly engaged in spiritual warfare. Town by town his troops conquered, pushing the remains of paganism ever further back into the north and east of Europe.

More dangerous than pagan persecution in Boniface's opinion, however, was the growth of wealth and ease within the church. After more than twenty years of labour a great deal of Germany had come under the Christian sway, and many of the churches in the west of the land were becoming affluent. Perhaps, thought Boniface, too affluent.

'In the early days of the mission our communion cups were made of wood, and our priests were made of gold. Now we have golden communion cups, and rather too many wooden priests.'

But Boniface was not the type to content himself with complaints about declining standards. He accompanied words with action, and by his frequent travels, and his display of septuagenarian sprightliness, he sought to inspire his co-workers to greater exertion. He appears to have taken a great interest in each of them personally, and in spite of his high demands there has seldom been a great Christian leader so well loved by his assistants. Through friendship and deep fellowship, imparting to others his own fire, he endeavoured to improve the service which each was able to give to the mission and to God.

Soon after the fall of Thor's Oak, Boniface was made bishop of Germany. Later in his career, when the German church had swelled to more than one hundred thousand people, he received the title of archbishop. By 753, his eightieth year, Archbishop Boniface appeared to have achieved everything a heart could desire. Surely he could now sit back and take life a little easier, resting secure in the glory of his achievements.

'I wish to resign the archbishopric.'

What? All Germany held its breath at the stunning announcement.

'The Lord has put a new call on my heart. I must return to Frisia.'

And so it was that this incredible man departed on his last missionary journey.

The Frisian mission had fallen on hard times since the death of Willibrord. There had been a pagan revival, and life was now very dangerous for the Christian communities. Boniface was unable to sit at ease in Germany while such was the case in a land so dear to his heart, a land whose bishopric his beloved mentor had so earnestly desired him to shoulder three decades earlier.

Boniface knew that this journey would be his last, and that the site where he had first learned the ropes would be the site where he bid the earth farewell. In his case of books the old man packed a burial cloth.

'Lord, wherever You lead.'

The venerable old preacher enjoyed tremendous success amongst the Frisians. Some remembered him from his younger days, and Boniface planted many churches in the most hostile locations. At Easter 754 a great number of Frisians were baptized, and Boniface requested that the new converts return to him at Pentecost for confirmation. He and his party were established in a temporary mission base on the banks of the river Burde. (Confirmation involved anointing with oil and laying on of hands. To those who had been baptized as infants it was performed as a sign of their coming to maturity as believers. Those baptized as adults usually received the anointing in the weeks following baptism.)

A group of pagan extremists saw this as their perfect opportunity to strike. They were enraged at Boniface's success, and they determined to attack early on the morning of Pentecost. The missionaries heard the clang of weapons and the war cry, and then they saw the plain before them filled with pagan warriors.

'Prepare to resist. We are lost if we flee, so we must fight!'

Boniface emerged from his tent and calmed his co-workers.

'Return good for evil,' he cried. 'Strengthen yourselves in the Lord, and He will redeem your souls. Fear not those who kill only the body.'

The Frisians were soon upon them, and within moments the entire company was dead. The pagans ransacked the missionaries' tents, but finding only books and other religious materials they left in disgust.

The new Frisian converts arrived at the riverside later that day, and discovering the bloodbath they swore revenge. Within a few days most of the assassins were dead, and the pagan resistance in Frisia was forever crushed – and with that, ironically, the purpose of Boniface's mission was achieved, however little the means would have pleased the martyr.

BONIFACE, LETTERS & SERMONS; WILLIBALD, *THE LIFE OF ST BONIFACE*

The Muslim Menace

While missionaries were winning new lands to the Christian faith in the north, Arab armies were making life very difficult for the Christians of the south.

Syria, Palestine and Egypt were in Muslim hands and the Arabs, not satisfied with these provinces, had made Constantinople itself the focus of repeated attacks. By the late seventh century things looked very grim in the Christian east, and many thought that the days of the final antichrist must be at hand. The Byzantine Empire was tottering on the edge of extinction, and without a timely invention would probably have disappeared altogether.

That invention was one of the most revolutionary weapons in history. Discovered by the Greeks in these years of their greatest distress, it decisively turned the tide of the Arab war. It is usually known as 'Greek fire'.

Greek fire was a devastating weapon, both in land and sea battles. It was a secret mix of highly inflammable ingredients which, once alight, was almost impossible to extinguish. It was used in several different forms.

One form was the grenade, a small cylinder which, thrown onto enemy ships, would begin a fierce blaze wherever it landed. On a larger scale pots of Greek fire could be propelled from a catapult, and the burning liquid would run everywhere and cause enormous damage on the enemy's deck. The most effective kind of Greek fire, however, was a flammable liquid fired at the enemy by gunpowder – indeed the first recorded use of gunpowder in warfare. These ancient flame-throwers must have been as terrifying as they were deadly.

These new weapons kept the Arabs at bay and Byzantium became the chief defence of eastern Europe – an immovable obstacle in the Muslim path. If Greek fire had not been invented at this critical moment, if Constantinople had fallen, it is hard to imagine just how great the Saracen victories in Europe may have been.

Thwarted by the resistance of Constantinople, but their appetite for plunder by no means sated, it was not long before the Arabs were launching an attack on Europe from the opposite end!

North Africa fell to the Muslim armies in the course of the late seventh century. The Muslims first entered North Africa on thieving raids, but finding the land poorly defended they began to dream of a complete conquest. The Byzantines were too busy saving Constantinople itself to give effective aid to these distant territories, and though the invasion of North Africa proved costly to the Arabs, who suffered several major defeats from local forces, by 703 the land was entirely theirs.

The conquest of North Africa proved far more destructive to the church than that of any other area of the empire. Many of the leading Christians fled to other lands, and those who remained were slowly crushed out of existence. It took centuries, but the ruin of the North African church was eventually complete. Whereas the churches of Syria and Egypt live to this day, the North African church was entirely extinct by the fifteenth century. The destruction in North Africa was the most comprehensive defeat that the church has ever endured. The land which gave us Perpetua and Felicitas, Cyprian and Augustine, to this day has fewer Christians than almost any other place on earth.

The Arab conquest of Egypt and Syria did not prove a complete disaster to the local church, and the conquered Christians even perceived certain benefits in a change of masters (they did not, however, actively welcome the change). The Copts and Syrians had long been alienated in spirit from Constantinople, and religious interference was a great source of resentment; the Saracens, at least, did not care at all what form of Christianity their subjects believed. Coptic religion and culture went on to flourish under the Muslims in a way it could never have done under the sway of Christian Constantinople, and to this day the Coptic church remains strong, accounting for a tenth of the population of predominantly Muslim Egypt.

With North Africa in their grasp the Muslims began to cast their eyes across the Mediterranean. Western Europe beckoned, and the troubled nation of the Visigoths offered easy pickings.

The North African cities were founded by settlers from other lands, conquerors, who never became integrated with the native inhabitants, the Berbers. For centuries the North African cities lived at war with the surrounding tribesmen, and this situation continued when the city dwellers embraced the gospel. Many of the settlers fled when the Muslims came, and they left the Berbers behind. As with Arabia, there had been no major mission work amongst the Berbers, and the pagan Berbers now became Muslim. In a very real sense the church of North Africa disappeared because it failed to evangelize its neighbours.

The kingdom of the Visigoths, the rulers of Spain, was in disarray. There were battles within the nobility for the kingship, but the exact nature of the civil troubles are not clearly known to us, as the Muslim conquest caused such a catastrophic upheaval that little precise knowledge of the era was preserved. At any rate, we know that the divisions amongst the Goths were so bitter that some even took sides with the Muslims against their fellow countrymen.

The Muslims invaded Spain in 711, and within six months almost half of the country was theirs. By 714 only tiny pockets of resistance remained. The Muslims now had a foothold in Europe, and there were no signs that their conquests were at an end. How many more Christian lands would be swept away in their onwards march? Constantinople was maintaining some resistance, but who could actually defeat the Arabian foe?

In 718 the Muslims crossed the Pyrenees, the border between Spain and France. Puffed up with their amazing successes, the followers of the warrior prophet were captured by a new dream. France was badly governed, Italy was crippled by the cruel Lombards, and Germany was wild and undisciplined. If these three nations fell, Christendom would be theirs. Muslim armies would unite at the gates of Constantinople, having conquered everyone else both east and west! The destruction of the whole Christian world was almost within their grasp.

Charles Martel

The kings of the Franks were beneath the contempt of their Muslim foes.

The history of the successors of Clovis is one of the blackest pictures ever painted in Christian Europe. The church was struggling to lift the nation from the depths of barbarism, but the kings themselves were descending into a decadence that it would be hard to equal. By the late seventh century the French monarchs were so weak and detestable that they had become known as the *Rois Faineants*, or 'Royal Sluggards'.

With one brush we can paint almost all of the French kings of the period. They were simple-minded, drunken and immoral. Some fathered children while still children themselves, and it is little surprise that each generation was worse than the preceding one. All that can be said in their favour is that they at least did not interfere with the management of the nation! It was their people's greatest good fortune that the kings lived in luxurious and secluded idleness, drinking away their days, while others held the reins.

The real control of the kingdom was usually in the hands of the 'Mayor of the Palace', a type of prime minister. These were often men of piety and wisdom, and it was only through their efforts that France retained any power at all.

When the Muslims crossed the Pyrenees and began to harass southern France, there was no question of the king leading his nation out to confront them. That task would fall to Charles, Mayor of the Palace. After more than a decade of minor raids upon Frankish territory the Muslims gathered a formidable force for an assault on Tours. They hoped to conquer the whole nation, but they were drawn first to this city by greed for gold. Tours was France's spiritual capital, and the church of St Martin was full of wonderful riches – three centuries worth of pious donations from kings, dukes and commoners. All this, the Muslims hoped, would soon be theirs.

Charles responded to the crisis immediately, and with a large army he was soon encamped beside the road leading to Tours. Here the two forces met in October 732, one hundred years after the death of the Arab prophet.

The armies stood their ground for seven days, each warily observing the other, and it was finally the Muslims who launched the attack, their light cavalry pouring upon the French ranks like some mighty torrent. The Franks stood firm. Clad in heavy armour they were slower than the foe, but like a wall of iron they resisted and beat back the repeated surges of the Arab horse. The battle was evenly poised until fresh war cries sounded in the rear of the Arab army.

'The Aquitans!'

The Aquitans dwelt in the south. Prior to the Arab invasion they had been in rebellion against Charles and the Frankish kings, and they were one of the few tribes which had not joined Charles in the field. Their timely arrival now apologized for all past sins, and thrown into confusion by the attack from the rear the Muslims were cut down in their thousands. Their leader Abd-ar-Rahman was struck dead, and only the approach of night saved them from complete annihilation. Both armies returned to their camps, but when the Franks awoke the following morning to finish their work they found that an eerie silence had descended on the scene of slaughter.

'The Muslims have fled!'

Indeed they had. Only the countless bodies of the fallen

showed that the mighty Arab force had ever existed. Europe was safe. Charles was celebrated as the saviour of his nation, and a grateful Christendom gave him the nickname of 'Martel', or 'hammer'.

'Charles Martel. Hammer of the Saracens.'

Timothy's Stones

With Greek fire and French brawn Europe was safe. But what was life like for the Christian communities already subject to Muslim rule?

There were several obvious negatives. Christians were treated as second-class citizens, and all men had to pay a 'non-believers' tax, an oppressive penalty which could only be escaped by conversion to Islam. The law courts were biased, the scales of justice tipped decisively in favour of Muslim citizens, and Christians were banned from preaching to Muslims, and even in private they were forbidden to speak against Mohammed.

> Mohammed and his followers gave the victims of their aggression a famous threefold choice: 'The Koran, the non-believers tax, or the sword'.
>
> Those who accepted the Koran, that is who became Muslims, were granted equal citizenship, while Christians, Jews and Zoroastrians could maintain their faith only as members of a heavily taxed underclass. The situation, however, was still worse for members of other religions, who must embrace the Koran, or perish by the sword.

But, especially for the more talented Christians, there could also be certain advantages under Muslim rule.

The Arabs, generally speaking, were unschooled barbarians, and the Christians formed the best-educated and most talented section of the community. Christian architects were employed to design the great Muslim mosques and palaces, Christian doctors led in health care, and Christian scholars translated the great works of philosophy into the Arabic tongue of their masters. Christian scribes, tradesmen and civil servants thronged the courts of the Muslim rulers, and some rose to the highest positions in the state. A caliph (Arabic 'emperor') once pronounced the following striking judgement:

'In affairs of state I would rather employ a Christian than anyone else. The Muslims, puffed up with their military might, are oppressive rulers. The Zoroastrians, regretting the power from which they have fallen, are bitter and resentful. The Jews, awaiting a Messiah who they believe will crush our government, are hardly to be trusted!'

With the help of its Christian subjects the Muslim empire rose to great heights of learning. We shall hear more of this later, but we must point out now that these Muslim glory days lasted only so long as the subject church remained strong and vibrant. When the Muslims eventually crushed the church, their own era of excellence in science and art came to an end.

There were severe laws against Muslims converting to Christianity, but the Muslims seldom forced the Christians themselves to accept Islam. To do so would be to lose the lucrative non-believers tax. Nevertheless, in spite of the positives we have noted, Muslim rule was ultimately extremely detrimental to the life of the church.

The caliphs treated the Christian patriarchs as important government officials. They were, after all, the chief representatives of their 'nations', and the emphasis of their position slowly changed, until they were as much politicians as they were spiritual leaders. Such a position became the envy of all ambitious men, and scandalous scenes of bribery and fraud accompanied many patriarchal elections. Betrayed by worldly and wicked rulers, the church slowly lost its stature and authority.

Even in the late eighth century, little more than one hundred years into Muslim rule, there were terrible signs of the church's moral decay. When the patriarch of the Persian church died in 779 the bishops gathered in the Arab capital of Baghdad to elect his successor. Some candidates were not ashamed to offer bribes and make large promises to ensure the vote for themselves, and though there were many who rejected such offers with scorn there were enough worldly bishops to ensure that graft would probably win the day.

A minister named Timothy came to the election hall with a great many servants. The servants wandered through the crowd, and each singled out one man and placed a linen sack at his feet. With a subtle cough they drew the voters' attention to the sacks.

'It's yours,' they whispered, 'if you vote for Timothy.'

Eyes bulging at the sight of such a hefty 'gift', most of the ministers nodded their consent – all other offers seemed paltry in comparison. Timothy easily won the vote, and the victorious priest rushed immediately to the caliph's court to have his election ratified. His electors now went to accept their earnings.

'You must wait,' Timothy's servants replied. 'The master commanded us not to hand over the presents until after the election is approved.'

Timothy soon returned, his election sealed, and his servants gladly stepped back as each of the corrupt ministers dived for the loot.

'Stones!'

Timothy laughed out loud at the consternation on the bishops' faces.

'What did you expect? The priesthood is not to be purchased for money – so what did you think was in there?'

The furious voters fumed and swore, and cast their votes again! They elected a replacement for the deceiver, but when this new 'patriarch' presented himself before the caliph he found an unsympathetic audience.

'Do you mock me?' asked the caliph. 'I have just given my seal to one man. Who dares appoint another?'

Thus it was that the greatest of the Persian patriarchs came to power! Timothy survived the anger of the electors, and he went on to lead his church for more than forty years. Throughout that time he laboured tirelessly, and successfully, to eradicate the evil which had brought him to power in the first place. His story is a clear illustration of how God uses even the corruption of men's hearts to further His church.

The Iconoclasts

The eighth century brought the first relief in the war against
Islam, but it also witnessed one of the most furious internal
battles the church has endured.

Holy pictures, usually known as icons or images, had become
an everyday part of the spiritual life for many Christians. These
pictures might be of Christ, the Holy Spirit (in the form of a
dove), angels or saints. Most churches contained them, as did
many private houses.

As we have already noted, most Christians did not pray
exclusively to God. Many prayers were directed to martyrs and
other saints, and also to angels, in the belief that these beings
had been given authority from God to aid and answer prayer.
The most popular recipient of prayers was the Virgin Mary,
who was thought to have a supremely close relationship with
Jesus.

It should be plain that such prayers in themselves were
treading on dangerous ground. With dozens of saints to choose
from, God Himself could be restricted to a very small part of
one's spiritual life. Why, in fact, need we pray to saints at all, if
God is capable of meeting all our needs? We dealt with the
question earlier, and we shall return to it again. For the moment
we are chiefly concerned with the icons of these saints.

It was common for Christians to pray before an icon of Christ
or the saint to whom they spoke. The believer felt closer to the
heavenly listener while gazing upon the icon, and the supporters
of this form of prayer said that pictures were of great benefit to
the uneducated, to whom it gave a precise focus as they opened
their hearts. It filled them with devout feelings, and for the
illiterate could almost function as a Bible in pictures.

Others thought differently. They believed that such pictures
were extremely dangerous, and for no one more so than the
'simple folk'.

'It is a return to idolatry. The pagans worshipped wood and
stone, and these supposed Christians worship their icons. The
pictures are not some innocent reminder of Christ or the saints –

the common folk believe that the icons themselves have miraculous power.'

This dispute came to a head in the early eighth century when Leo III rose to the throne of Constantinople. Leo was a bitter opponent of icons, and he and his followers became known as the Iconoclasts ('picture smashers'). Though a gifted ruler, Leo was a savage foe to all who differed from his opinions, and Jews, heretics and the patrons of icons all suffered from the blasts of his rage.

Leo's first move was to crack down upon the 'reverence' of icons, the custom of kissing or bowing to icons as a mark of respect to the person represented. Leo ordered that all church icons be raised to such a height that none could reach them, insisting that it was 'to stop them getting dirty'(!), but after thus testing the waters the emperor soon made his intention plainer by banning them altogether. The only image retained was the unadorned figure of the cross.

Iconoclasm reigned in Byzantium for 60 years, and the removal of icons was attended with scenes of wild disorder. Some imperial employees were attacked by angry mobs as they destroyed the images, and many supporters of the icons were tortured, imprisoned or executed by the emperors. When a church council was called in 754 the emperor's stooges ensured that both icons and their supporters were formally condemned, and it appeared that Iconoclasm had won. The reality, however, was far from being so simple.

Most of the people detested the iconoclastic emperors and longed for the return of the old forms of their faith. Governments simply cannot tell people what to believe, and how to worship – reform must start with the people, it cannot succeed if bloodily thrust upon them. When Leo IV, grandson of Leo III, died, the movement collapsed with him. His own widow, Irene, called a new council, the seventh and last ecumenical council, and the decrees of 754 were reversed.

The icons were restored to their places, but the peace was not to last. A revolution brought the Iconoclast Leo V to the throne in 813, and he pursued the same policy as his earlier namesakes.

We have briefly discussed each of the ecumenical councils, save only the sixth, 'Monothelite', council.

Monotheletism was the last chapter in the Monophysite debate. In an attempt to woo those who believed that Christ has only one nature, some emperors proposed a new belief – that Christ has two natures, but only one will. This teaching, Monotheletism ('one will-ism'), failed to win over the Monophysites, and was itself ultimately condemned as heresy – for if Christ had only one will, the divine will, how could He have been tempted, how indeed could He have been human at all? Monotheletism nullifies the incarnation by robbing Christ of genuine and complete humanity. The two wills of Christ were not conflicting and contrary, but His obedience was shown by the exercise of human will in submission to divine will. The complete list of Ecumenical Councils is as follows.

- I. Nicaea I (325) – Arianism condemned.
- II. Constantinople I (381) – decisions of the first council reaffirmed.
- III. Ephesus (431) – Nestorianism condemned.
- IV. Chalcedon (451) – Monophysitism condemned. Clear statement on the incarnation.
- V. Constantinople II (553) – further debate on Monophysitism.
- VI. Constantinople III (680) – Monotheletism condemned.
- VII. Nicaea II (787) – icons approved.

The life of a monk named Methodius illustrates the troubles of the period well.

Methodius, as a member of the pro-icon party, fled to Rome when Leo V rose to power. Upon Leo's murder in 820, however, the Roman bishop sent Methodius back to Constantinople as an ambassador.

Unfortunately for Methodius the new emperor, Michael the Stammerer, was cut from the same cloth as his predecessor, and the would-be ambassador was arrested and imprisoned in a tiny dungeon, as narrow as a tomb in the rock. For nine years he lived in this squalid hole, his only company being two violent criminals whom the considerate emperor interred with him. When one of the criminals died his corpse was left to rot beside his fellow prisoners: an odd punishment from an emperor who claimed to be the restorer of a purer form of Christianity!

The Spirit within Methodius triumphed over this dismal scene, and the monk won the heart of the surviving criminal and the two became close as brothers. When the criminal was offered his freedom he refused to leave.

'Methodius is my spiritual mentor, and I cannot desert him!'

With the death of Michael in 829 Methodius was released from prison. He was withered to the bone, his skin almost colourless, his hair gone, and his clothes reduced to a few straps of filthy rotten rag. The wretched man was given an audience with the new emperor, Theophilus.

'Why have you so long persevered in your faith?' asked the emperor. 'They are only pictures after all.'

'Your majesty,' the worn old man replied, 'destroy them if you must, but at least be consistent. If the pictures of Christ must go, then so should the statues of yourself.'

Methodius had made a good point, and one that can help those who live in a different age understand the controversy a little more deeply.

The Iconoclasts criticized their enemies for kissing or bowing before icons, and insisted that these practices were superstitious and idolatrous. No doubt there was merit in their complaints, and many simple people did have superstitious ideas about the power of icons. But, the supporters of icons insisted, that wasn't the point.

In Byzantine culture people were expected to show respect to statues of the emperors and governors as though they were before the ruler in person. It was a way of ensuring complete respect for government, and not bowing to the civil statues was taken not only as a sign of disrespect, but even of treason. Most Christians argued that icons should be treated the same way.

'If we bow to the emperor's statue, how much more should we bow to Christ's picture!'

Methodius made this very point to the emperor. If bowing to icons was to be banned, then the whole culture of bowing to superiors and their images must be reviewed. Who, after all, was the more worthy of respect? Theophilus did not think much of the monk's argument.

'Whip him!'

The frail monk's frailer rags were torn from his back, and

A major cause of the failure of Iconoclasm was its own inconsistency. It was promoted by emperors who expected people to bow before the royal statues, yet denied similar treatment to pictures of Christ. But Iconoclasm was even less consistent when it came to relics.

The bodies of departed saints were treated with a far more superstitious reverence than their icons, and most people believed that a saint was more likely to hear prayers if one visited his tomb. It was even better to possess some object that had belonged to the saint, or, grotesquely enough, a fragment of one of his bones, and the saint's power could then be carried wherever one went. Not only were relics like a telephone to the saints in heaven, but they were thought to have a great power in themselves. A saint's remains could cast out demons, cure sickness and save travellers from trouble.

The most famous of all relics, incidentally, was not a bone. It was a wooden cross, claimed to be the very cross on which Christ suffered. This cross was supposedly discovered in Jerusalem in the fourth century, and a beautiful church was built to house it. Its splinters were thought to have wonderful healing powers, and the person or church that received one considered itself supremely blessed. Surely this reverence for splinters and bones is no less dubious than the use of icons? The Iconoclasts showed their own folly by fully accepting the use of relics, while slaughtering the supporters of simple pictures.

Methodius was whipped until he fainted and collapsed into a pool of his own blood. He was returned to prison, and he might have died soon after had not some supporters secretly come to his rescue. In the dead of night the monk was carried into hiding, and there he remained until Theophilus' death in 842.

Theophilus was the last of the Iconoclasts, and history repeated itself when his widow, Theodora, restored the icons. The empress then sent messengers to Methodius and urged the old monk to accept the patriarchate. Methodius had never fully recovered from his flogging at the hands of Theophilus. His jaw, broken that day, had never quite healed, and for the rest of his life he wore a cloth strap under his chin to hold the damaged bones and muscles in place. During his short four-year reign, the sight of this conflict-stricken old man was a perpetual reminder to the people of all they had suffered. Iconoclasm had fallen, never to rise again in the eastern church.

Pepin and the Popes

Iconoclasm had repercussions of enormous magnitude in the west.

The Iconoclastic emperors ordered the Roman bishops to outlaw the use of icons, but as they were safe from the emperors' military might the Romans could treat such commands with scorn. It was the beginning of a serious breach, one which events in the west would soon exacerbate.

At Charles Martel's passing in 741 his sons Carloman and Pepin (Pepin the Short) succeeded him in the mayoralty. Six years later the pious Carloman relinquished his position to become a monk, and Pepin assumed sole rule. In 751, desirous of establishing his family's position on a more formal basis, Pepin sent ambassadors to seek the advice of Bishop Zachary of Rome, bearing a thinly veiled plea for support.

'Is it good,' they asked, 'that a man should bear the royal title, while another exercises the royal power?'

'It is preferable,' Zachary responded, 'for the power and the title to meet in one man.'

This sanction was just what the mayor needed, and early in the following year a bloodless revolution saw Childeric III leave the palace for a monastery, as Pepin himself took the throne. The Merovingian puppet-dynasty of Clovis' unworthy successors was at an end.

It soon became apparent that the Roman bishop had even more need of the new Frankish king than the king had of him. The Lombards were by now masters of most of Italy, and at this time they were threatening to attack Rome itself. The eastern empire, which had held parts of Italy since the conquests of Justinian, could no longer be relied on for help. The Byzantine emperor and Roman bishop were at war over icons, and there was little that Constantinople could have done anyway – at this very time the Lombards were actually seizing the empire's last Italian strongholds. Bishop Stephen, Zachary's successor, soon saw that there was only one hope of deliverance.

In late 753 Stephen travelled to France to lend the new ruler the added authority of his spiritual approval, and to plead for his aid against the Lombards. Pepin was consecrated by the bishop's own hand, and when summer returned he marched into Italy to chastise the bishop's foes. The swords that stemmed the Muslim tide had little difficulty punishing the Lombards, and a large tract of land was wrested from the Lombard king and put directly under the control of the Roman bishop. None could have guessed the implications of this new alliance, of the bishop of Rome and the king of France. It was an alliance destined to bring to birth a new empire.

The France of the eighth century was entering upon a new maturity. In the midst of barbarism a higher culture was coming into being, and when Pepin's son Charlemagne, who became sole king in 771, invited the leading scholars of the time to his court, the royal city of Aachen became a centre of learning such as Europe had not seen in centuries.

The successive waves of barbarian invasion had destroyed the schools, the books, and even the teachers of what had once been the western empire. The barbarians had little learning of their own, and the riotous disorder of their kingdoms usually prevented the reestablishment of a high level of culture. In spite of the church's best efforts, ignorance and illiteracy, brutality and superstition, reigned supreme.

For some generations Ireland was one of the few places in the west to preserve the flame of Christian scholarship; oddly enough the best Greek scholars of western Europe lived in this distant island, as far as possible from Greece itself. In the late seventh century a period of peace in northern England saw that area gradually overtake Ireland as Europe's capital of learning, and Northumbrian scholars were prominent among those called to the court of Charlemagne, to inspire there a great blossoming of the arts.

Charlemagne founded impressive libraries and initiated sweeping reforms of public behaviour (no longer were drunken revels welcome in the royal palace). He urged all monasteries and cathedrals to operate schools, and he even (unsuccessfully) promoted the idea of universal literacy. His scholars reformed

the written language and promoted a new style of lower-case
writing, which with little change is with us to this day. EARLY
LATIN AND GREEK HAD ONLY UPPER CASE with little punctuation
and nospacebetweenwords Most manuscripts from the centuries
immediately prior to Charlemagne show a terribly dense and
messy style. The new Frankish script facilitated both ease of
reading and speed of writing. Perhaps chief among the king's
achievements was a codification of the law of his people.
Charlemagne, feeling himself divinely called to the role of a new
Moses, revised the barbarian laws in the light of Scripture, and
for the first time much unwritten custom was committed to
paper, thus ensuring the consistency of the courts.

> Charlemagne and the leading figures of his court each took a nickname.
> Charlemagne, for obvious reasons, was David; a certain Einhard skilled in
> metalworking was Bezalel (Ex. 31:2); and others took the names of famous
> poets and thinkers of days long past.

Rome also was entering a new age.

Following the grant of land from Pepin, the Roman bishop
was now a political chief, with a region of Italy obeying him as
prince. This was not a radically new development, as the gradual
destruction of Byzantine power in Italy had already forced the
bishops to take on many governmental duties. Gregory I (590-
604) had led the way, and while his treaties with the Lombards
had saved the region around Rome from devastation, his charity
had made much of the Roman population reliant on him for their
very survival. Gregory had made the church's huge Italian
landholdings (centuries of pious donations) the breadbasket of
the poor, ensuring their careful administration and the
application of their produce to those impoverished by invasion.

The Roman bishop had traditionally been one of five
patriarchs. Because of Rome's history as the imperial city he was
usually considered the highest of the five, but only in a very
limited sense. Christians of early times called the Roman bishop
'first among equals'.

The Muslims and Iconoclasts were changing that. Antioch, Alexandria and Jerusalem were in Arab hands, Constantinople was ruled by the Iconoclasts, and Rome alone was free of unbelievers or heretics. The 'equals' were gone, so Rome now boldly stood forth as the 'first' bishopric in Christendom.

Rome, further, had been the chief authority behind much of the missionary work in the north and west of Europe. Gregory had sent Augustine to England, and missionaries like Willibrord and Boniface had sought approval and encouragement from Rome before undertaking their own labours. The belief in the power of relics added a unique extra dimension to Rome's claims to authority. The tombs of Peter and Paul and the dozens of Roman bishops were not just a tourist attraction, they were centres of real supernatural power. One gave allegiance to the Roman bishop not as to a man, but as to the earthly representative of so many generations of now glorified Christian leaders.

Rome's influence had proved beneficial in many ways. There was a danger of poor management in the barbarian churches and of heresy and division amongst the wild warriors, so the growth of a powerful central authority was quite advantageous. Boniface, for one, frequently sought Roman advice on difficult issues, and with their long Christian history and wealth of literature and learning the Romans usually gave wise judgements. Many far-flung missionaries were saved from serious error.

But the Roman supremacy did not go unchallenged. Churches that had been planted before the fall of Rome were more likely to consider themselves free and independent. They had never relied on Rome for advice, they had traditions and learning of their own, and thus their attitude was quite different to that of the younger churches. The Celtic churches of Ireland, Scotland and Wales were the most striking examples of this. While the rest of Europe was centring on Rome, these areas were ruling themselves in complete isolation. Trouble arose when the countless Celtic missionaries came into conflict with the established Roman churches, especially in France and England.

There were numerous differences between the Celtic and Roman churches – everything from the calendar they used to the tonsure of their monks (monks of this time shaved a part of their heads as a sign of their vocation). Celtic monks also tended to be more severe and ascetic than Benedictine monks. These differences had existed, almost unknown, for centuries. With the Irish monks settled amongst the Romans, however, they became a serious source of division.

'Are you Celtic, or Roman?'

In those times there was no concept of different denominations. All Christians believed that the church must have the unity for which Jesus prayed:

'Father, I ask that they may be one, just as You are in Me, and I in You' (Jn. 17:21).

The Celts were left with a choice. They could split the church, or they could abandon much of their independence. It took many generations, and many bitter arguments, but to maintain peace between believers the Celtic church finally came into line with the rest of western Europe. The decision, in the end, had to be made between the way of freedom and the way of peace.

With Celtic resistance quieted, and the other patriarchs gone from the scene, a new era was dawning for the Roman bishop. He was slowly embracing a new role – that of pope of the western church.

The names patriarch, papa and pope had been used of bishops for many centuries; all emphasize the fatherly role of the ministry. In western Europe, however, only the bishop of Rome has retained the name of pope, and it is now associated with a role and power which was completely unknown in the early church. The modern pope has an authority formerly undreamed of, and hence this book has not used the word pope until the Roman bishop was beginning to claim these powers for himself.

Charlemagne

Pepin followed established Frankish practice by dividing his realm between his two sons, but Carloman, his youngest, died only three years after him, and the whole Frankish realm thus came into Charlemagne's hands. It was not long before the great prince began adding to the inheritance.

Fresh troubles broke out in Italy, and the pope again called for French assistance. Charlemagne joined the pope against the Lombards, and in 774 he completed the conquest of their nation. At the age of thirty-two he was now king of both France and Italy.

Charlemagne, like his father and grandfather before him, fought short campaigns against the Muslims of Spain, but to his mind the barbarian territory stretching away to the north and east of his kingdom posed a far greater danger to his people than did the followers of Mohammed. His efforts to establish a progressive intellectual culture, he perceived, were of little avail while the forces of barbarism still hung like a deadly axe over his realm. Christian Europe could never think itself safe while hordes of wild pagan barbarians lived just outside her door. Scandinavia, north and east Germany, central Europe – all of these lands were peopled by formidable pagan warriors, with the Vikings, Saxons and Avars chief among them.

In an attempt to forestall a new wave of barbarian invasion Charlemagne set about the conquest of the foes of civilization. For 30 years he led campaigns against the Saxons of north and east Germany, and by 804 the whole of Germany acknowledged his sway. Southern and western Germany, Boniface's territory, were already Christian, but the tribes of the north and east, the Saxons, were almost entirely pagan. Victory did not ease Charlemagne's dread of this powerful nation, and in his desire to permanently pacify the Saxons he perceived that the only way forward was their conversion. Here, however, he made a drastic departure from the Christian past, and to expedite the process he resolved upon the use of force.

Many Saxons were compelled to undergo baptism. Missionaries were supported by armed soldiers, and the payment of a tithe to the church was rigidly enforced. The effect is not hard to imagine. Whenever opportunity offered, the Saxons rose in rebellion against the hated opponents of their nation and religion, the missionaries would be murdered, and again the Saxons must be punished with the sword – certainly a wrong-headed manner of making Europe safer and more civilized!

Charlemagne also led successful campaigns further east, against the savage Avars of central Europe. Few reigns have seen such consistent and widespread military success, but for all that Charlemagne never dispelled his own fears for the survival of his land. The enemies the king most feared were beyond the reach of his arms.

Charlemagne once spent the night at a seaside resort in southern France belonging to one of his nobles. While at dinner he spotted several ships coming to shore.

'I imagine they're Jewish merchants,' his host declared.

'More likely English traders,' another decided.

Charlemagne shook his head. 'They are loaded not with goods, but with our foes.'

At this news the king's retainers leapt to their feet and made haste to meet the ships as they landed. The ships, for their part, saw the formidable reception party awaiting them and disappeared into the night. When the soldiers returned to the hall they found the king staring out of the window with fresh tears on his cheeks. No one dared ask why. When the king finally spoke there was an indescribable sadness in his voice.

'I fear no danger from these bold pirates in my lifetime, but I weep for the misery they will bring on my kingdom when I am gone.'

The age of the Vikings is almost upon us.

It is interesting to note the differences between the Greek and French culture and religion of this period. Charlemagne and his court were intrigued by reports of the iconoclastic debate, and they requested that the minutes of the eastern councils be translated into Latin for them.

Charlemagne disagreed with the iconoclastic council of 754, and thought the destruction of the icons a sign of ignoble fanaticism. His disagreement with the council of 787, however, was even sharper. He thought the practice of bowing before or kissing icons absurd, and virtual idolatry. Such things were unknown in France, where no one would dream of bowing to a king's statue. The more democratic Frankish mind could simply not understand the Greek culture of reverence.

This disagreement was not at all helped by the poor standard of the translation made for the Franks. The Greek word for the supreme act of worship is *latria*; hence words such as ido*latry*, that is, idol worship. The council of 787 said that true worship should be for God alone. However, another Greek word indicates a display of profound respect. This includes bowing and can be done to a person or a picture as a sign of reverence and humility. As there was no clear Latin word with the same meaning (we might call it reverence or obeisance), the translator made the fatal choice of rendering this word as *adoro* – the same Latin word he had used to translate *latria*! This unhappy choice of words has caused problems to this day, with the Greeks being accused, by those who do not understand their language, of icon worship – a charge they vehemently deny.

So it turned out that Rome and Constantinople were in agreement on the council of 787, while Charlemagne and the Franks had gone over towards the side of the Iconoclasts. The Franks did not push their disagreement with Rome, but Charlemagne did point out a fact that was about to become brutally apparent to the Roman bishop.

'Forget about looking to the east. The Greeks are your past. The west is your future.'

EINHARD, *LIFE OF CHARLEMAGNE*

The Holy Roman Empire

Pepin and Charlemagne had freed Rome from the Lombards, but the great city's turbulence ensured that life was still dangerous for a Roman bishop. In 799, two high church officials, Paschal and Campulus, launched a dramatic attack on Pope Leo III. They were relatives of the previous pope, and while their motives are not quite clear, it is probable that they hoped to take the bishopric for another member of their family.

It was the day of a major festival, and Leo, riding a white horse and flanked by Paschal and Campulus, was leading a procession through the city. The pope was slightly ill at ease. He had a sneaking suspicion that something was amiss, but Paschal and Campulus kept him engrossed in conversation and left him little time to review his doubts. Suddenly, as the procession passed a monastery, a crowd of armed men burst out of ambush. The crowd and priests were scattered, and Leo was knocked heavily to the ground. Campulus grasped Leo's feet, and Paschal grabbed his head.

'Fix him, quick!'

One of the ruffians drew a knife and slashed at the struggling minister's face.

'Blind him!' Campulus cried. 'Cut out his tongue.'

The ruffian completed the task and turned to run. 'Let's be gone before the whole city is after us!'

Paschal and Campulus were not slow to heed the advice, and dragging the mutilated pope into the privacy of the monastery's chapel they beat him unconscious. After nightfall they dragged him to a nearby convent and locked him in a small cell. They were observed, from a distance, by Albinus, a personal assistant to the pope. In the dead of night Albinus entered the convent, and with difficulty aided Leo's escape.

'Your life is not safe anywhere in Rome. Until we can arrange for your deliverance you must take Sanctuary in St Peter's church.'

Paschal and Campulus dared not snatch the pope from Sanctuary, and instead they contented themselves with looting Leo and Albinus' homes. Word of the outrage drew Duke Vinegis of Spoleto to Leo's aid, and he arrived in Rome with a large force and released the pope from his Sanctuary. Only now could Leo receive medical assistance.

As it happened, the attempted 'surgery' of the pope's enemies had been a failure. In their hurry they had severed only a small part of the bishop's tongue, and only one of his eyes was badly damaged. His speech and sight were restored within a few weeks, and once recovered he departed for France. Never had a pope been so desperately in need of Frankish backing.

Leo received a warm welcome from the royal court.

Charlemagne embraced the fallen bishop, and he shed tears at the sight of the jagged scars that marked his face.

'Glory to God in the highest!' cried the pope.

'And peace on earth to men in His favour,' Charlemagne's ministers responded spontaneously.

But the season of joyful greeting was short-lived. Messengers from Campulus and Paschal were close on the bishop's trail, and these men laid serious allegations against Leo before the king. Charlemagne continued to treat his guest with respect, but he insisted that the charges should be thoroughly investigated. Leo was escorted back to his city, with the promise that the king himself would soon follow.

Leo's progress to Rome was a very different affair to his flight. Every city he passed sent a delegation to greet him, and when he finally arrived at the ancient capital he was welcomed wholeheartedly by an enormous crowd. The pope resumed his ministry, and the nobles and bishops who had accompanied his homewards march established a commission to examine the charges against Leo. A verdict of not guilty was returned a week later, and the conspirators were sent into exile.

Charlemagne reached Rome in November 800 to find the city already at peace with its bishop. The king remained for the celebration of Christmas, and it was then that the most significant moment in the relationship of his dynasty and the popes took place. As he knelt before the altar on Christmas Day Leo approached him unseen and placed a crown upon the Frank's head.

'I crown you,' he said, bowing in reverence, 'emperor of the Romans!'

With that the cry sounded throughout the church.

'Long live Charles, great, pacific! Emperor of the Romans!'

Charlemagne was displeased. 'Had I known you intended this, Christmas or not, I'd have stayed away from church today.'

Why? And what did Charlemagne's coronation as emperor of the Romans really mean?

Europe had never accepted the fall of the Roman Empire.

For centuries Rome had united North Africa, south-west Asia, and the civilized part of Europe in one empire. The enormous

Mediterranean Sea was flippantly called 'the Roman lake'. It was natural to feel that Rome would last forever.

When Rome became Christian, new ideas made these feelings even stronger. The church was one. Jesus had prayed that His followers might be one just as He and the Father were One. If there was one church for all believers, why should there not be one nation as well? The Roman Empire seemed to provide the very structure the church wanted – a Christian Roman Empire seemed to be God's own design. Had not Jesus come to unite mankind?

The fall of Rome did not destroy this idea. The eastern empire, of course, kept some hope alive, but there was more to it than that. The tribes who conquered the west could scarcely believe that Rome was gone. The empire, in fact, seemed such an important part of the world that the barbarians gladly kept the fiction of Rome alive. Theodoric the Ostrogoth, conqueror of Italy, and to a lesser degree Clovis of France, accepted titles from the hand of the eastern emperor, and allowed the Byzantine emperor to use the language of a superior. Though they wouldn't dream of obeying him, they bowed to the fiction that they were ruling the provinces in his name. They were kings, but he was *emperor*.

The citizens of their realms felt the same way. Rome, with all its faults, had provided stability, peace and intellectual culture. The barbarians, as we have seen, destroyed all three. The rule of barbarism seemed so terrible, so wrong, that it was usually viewed as a punishment. Surely God would eventually restore true and just government? The survival of Byzantium, especially the conquests of Justinian, provided some fuel to this hope.

By the eighth century, however, the west could no longer look to Greece for help. Too many obstacles divided west and east. But the need for the empire seemed more real than ever. Western Christendom must unite, or it would be in a poor position to resist the Muslim and Viking hordes.

Charlemagne himself had given thought to this problem. His conquests already gave him the substance of an empire, but until he bore the imperial name he would be viewed as nothing more than a foreign conqueror by most of his subjects. In view of this he had proposed marriage to Irene, widow empress of Constantinople; her hand could bring him both the imperial title and the Byzantine territories. This was why he was displeased to receive the crown from Leo. He knew that the east would be furious at his coronation, and his own plan had been to acquire the title more diplomatically. But the die was now cast. The empire born on Christmas Day 800 was dubbed the Holy Roman Empire. All hoped and prayed that a new age was beginning.

That Charlemagne deserved the title of emperor can hardly be doubted. In terms of the modern map his kingdom stretched over France, Belgium, the Netherlands, Switzerland, Germany, Austria and Italy. It is some measure of the French emperor's importance that his name has been forever mutated as a tribute to his achievements. Alexander will always be surnamed 'the Great', but Charlemagne alone has received an altogether new name – Charlemagne means literally Charles the Great.

We have now witnessed the birth of the two most powerful influences in the next period of European history: the papacy and the empire.

The Dreamer of the North

Anskar was born in northern France, near the town of Amiens, just a few months after the founding of the new empire.

Anskar's parents were devout Christians, and the boy's first years were happy and carefree. He would never forget those early days – of sitting on his mother's lap and hearing stories about Jesus, about the life to come, about the work of the great missionaries. The greatest lesson that Anskar learned in these first years, however, was of the fragility of all things in this world. He was only five years old when his beloved mother died.

Anskar's father, unable to raise his son alone, soon sent the child to live in a nearby monastery. There, he hoped, his spiritual life would be nourished and encouraged; he already felt that the boy had a calling from the Lord.

For Anskar, this move was the most traumatic event of a very traumatic life. He already loved Jesus, but the Jesus he loved was one who spoke in soft storybook tones and a mother's warm embrace. The Jesus he was now confronted with spoke in hour-long prayer sessions, formal choir chants, and long and difficult readings and lessons. The boy could neither understand nor embrace this Jesus.

The monastery was a harsh home for one so young, and Anskar rebelled against his surroundings. He began to live in a world of dreams, a world where mothers didn't die and young boys never had to grieve. His lessons were ignored or fled, and Anskar spent his time in riotous play with the other boys from the monastery school. How he envied those who came to the monastery to learn, not to live! His behaviour continued to slide until one night, tossing fitfully in his corner of the dormitory, Anskar experienced an incredibly vivid dream.

He was stumbling barefoot through a wide muddy field. Every step he took was an immense labour, as the mud was so thick and sticky that it seemed to be clutching at his feet. He looked up and noticed a fence some distance away. The ground beyond looked firm and grassy, and Anskar struggled towards it with a new urgency. He was sick to the stomach with exertion, but the fence never seemed to come any closer.

'I'll never reach it!'

A broad and dry path ran along beside the fence, and Anskar saw a fine looking lady walking past. Behind her were many ladies dressed in white, and amongst them all the struggling lad saw his own mother.

'Mo . . .' he began to cry, but the word would not emerge as he thrashed along pathetically in the mire. His sobbing caught the attention of the leading lady.

'Do you want your mother?' she asked kindly.

Anskar's furious but fruitless strides said more than words.

'Fear not, for she shall again be yours. You will arrive where she now is, but you must know that none of us arrived on this side of the fence by being lazy. You, too, must work.' The scene clouded over, and Anskar awoke.

'I shall,' he promised. 'I shall work!'

The monastery may not have been the best home, but it was his home. He had to make the most of it. Years passed, and the lad grew and strengthened in the knowledge of God. In those years of monastic routine little out of the ordinary happened, except just once, when Anskar's home received a visit from Emperor Charlemagne.

'Incredible!'

All the boys were gathered at an upper window, staring in awe as the procession of this mighty monarch came along the road towards them. First were the emperor's baggage bearers. Some of these men were extremely finely dressed, and the boys clambered over each other to gain a better position, as they tried to work out which one was the emperor himself.

'The man on the horse, the one who's telling everyone what to do, that must be him.'

One of the monks came past at this moment, and he stopped behind the boys with a look of amusement.

'Actually these men carry the food and clothes. The man on the horse you pointed out is just a servant.'

The boys treated the monk's words with scepticism, until another group of men came into sight behind the baggage bearers. The pick of the Frankish knights rode along proudly in this next division. The chiefs rode upon fine dark horses, their heads held high and rigid as they trotted along.

'Which one is Emperor Charles?' the boys asked in amazement.

'Not yet,' said the monk, 'just wait.'

Next came the officers of the royal escort, and each high official was scrutinized by the boys and dismissed by the monk in turn.

'Well, where is he then?'

The monk did not need to answer, as it was just at this moment that the emperor came into view. The boys were speechless.

Charlemagne was surrounded on all sides by his highest officials. All kept a respectful distance, and the emperor rode alone in the centre of a small oval of men and horses.

The boys had never seen such a horse as the one the emperor rode upon. Its hair was like shining iron, and its head and body were elegantly draped in fine purple. The emperor himself wore a purple robe across his shoulders, and it fairly seemed to blaze in the late morning sun. As Charlemagne came nearer, however, all attention was engrossed in his face and bearing. His head was crowned in blazing gold, and his face was so firm and unchanging that it seemed to be set in stone. His beard was extremely long, and the colour of whitest wool. So awesome was his majesty's appearance that the boys remained silent long after he had slipped from view beneath them.

The memory of this day profoundly moved young Anskar. His whole existence, the daily life of the monastery, seemed very small and inconsequential.

'Imagine the life of an emperor!'

The dream of power, dignity and riches began to exercise a great fascination over him. Before Charlemagne's visit all he had known of riches was what he had learned in the monastery: 'You cannot serve both God and Mammon' (Mt. 6:24). This lesson seemed a little harder now than it had been in the past, back before he had known what riches were!

In 814, however, when Anskar was thirteen, Emperor Charles died, and news of his passing affected the young monk most powerfully.

'Dead!'

The man who once had everything now had nothing but eternal things.

'The only wealth he now possesses, is the wealth he stored in heaven.' Anskar was thunderstruck by the unreal nature of worldly wealth. 'Lord, be my Master! I see now that Mammon can give us nothing just when we most need help!'

Anskar now applied himself to his Christian training with a new fire. His desire was to serve; to hear God's call, and then enter the field of labour. It was during this time that the teenager had another striking dream.

He again dreamed of being trapped in a dark and awful place. This time, however, it was unlike anywhere on earth – a searing land of misery and pain. Panic and all the sensations of nightmare tormented mind and body, until suddenly the darkness parted, and Anskar found himself in a world of brilliant colour. His spirit burst out into exclamations of joy, and he looked about him at a crowd of radiant and exuberant beings. He felt a fellowship with those around him such as he had never even imagined before. His world was flooded, utterly filled with light, and the longer he looked the brighter it became.

'Go forth to your labour,' came a voice that filled his whole being. 'Then return to this place with a martyr's crown.'

'Yes, Lord! Yes!' cried the young man as he awoke. 'I shall go wherever you send me!'

Christians had been attempting for more than a century to get the gospel into Denmark. Willibrord, missionary to the Frisians, was probably the first to try, but his venture was a failure and those who came later fared even worse. The result, after several attempts to set up missions, was less than a handful of conversions. But God's time had now come.

During the reign of Louis the Pious, son of Charlemagne, the Danish throne became the focus of a bitter civil war. In 826 King Harald II of Denmark was forced to flee his land and make his way to the emperor's court.

'Aid me in regaining my throne,' he pleaded, 'and the Danes will ever be your allies.'

This offer appealed greatly to Louis' political wishes, and when Harald requested baptism for himself, his family and his followers, the pious emperor could scarcely refuse. Louis was a great patron of missions, and it was this interest that had won his unusual surname. He provided Harald with military aid and then sought a minister to accompany the Danes as priest and missionary. Volunteers were hardly fast in coming.

These early years of the ninth century were the dawning of the Viking age. Danish, Norwegian and Swedish pirates had become the great scourge of Europe, and nowhere accessible to their ships was safe. Coastal towns were worst hit, but anywhere along the great rivers of Europe might be a target. The Franks were terrified at the growing might of their pagan northern neighbours, and the prospect of going to live amongst them was likely to be welcomed by but very few. Louis called a council of abbots and bishops.

'Who will go?' he demanded. 'Is there not a single man fit for the task in the whole empire?'

There was a long silence. It was finally broken by Abbot Walla.

'There is a young man in my monastery,' he offered quietly. 'He has a definite missionary calling, but whether he will go to Denmark I dare not guess.'

'I wouldn't ask you to,' said Louis. 'Summon him immediately.'

More than ten years had passed since Anskar had received his call to missions. He had completed his studies, become a teacher, and at the age of only twenty-five was now the principal of his monastery's school. It was no small surprise to be called from his classroom by a summons from the emperor's own hand. Within hours, in the echoing halls of the royal court, he was to make a promise that would engross the rest of his life.

'Yes, your majesty. I shall go.'

Anskar's calling was from God, so the choice was clear. It was, however, far from easy.

In the weeks before his departure many of Anskar's friends tried to dissuade him from leaving. Some thought him foolhardy; a few insisted that he was only taking on such a difficult, indeed preposterous, task out of pride.

'Convert the Vikings will you!'

The young man was tossed by doubt. God seemed to be saying one thing, while everyone else he respected was saying the opposite, and encumbered with this unexpected trouble Anskar spent his days in prayer and mental struggle. Actual preparations for departure were neglected. He was sitting in a favourite spot one day, a small orchard, painfully grinding away at his problem, when a friend named Autbert approached.

'Are you really going to the Danes?'

'I think I've already said so often enough!' Anskar spat through his teeth. 'And if everyone would just mind their own business I might actually be able to start packing.'

'I didn't mean to be a nuisance,' said Autbert, taking a step back. 'I just wanted to say that if you really are going, that I'd like to go with you.'

Anskar almost exploded. 'YES!' he cried. 'PRAISE THE LORD!' And within a week the friends were on their way.

On their way to Denmark, it did not take the monks long to discover the way the ground lay with King Harald. The Dane was not very interested in speaking with them, and Anskar soon realized that Harald had been baptized simply to please Louis.

'But don't be discouraged,' he said to Autbert. 'If that be the case, then King Harald himself is our first mission field.'

In this narrow field the pair went to work, and by the time they reached Denmark the king was as enthusiastic for the mission as the monks themselves!

Harald succeeded in gaining control of a large part of Denmark, and the monks established a small school in the town of Schleswig. They dreamed of training up a number of Danish youths in the ways of God, so that they might have native help in the work of evangelism. Harald, however, moved too fast for his pagan kingdom.

The king had only a precarious grip on the throne. His enemies were many, and when he began closing down the pagan temples a reaction was sure to follow. After only two years he was again forced to flee his country, and the monks and their school were thrown into great peril. Both men would probably have soon been martyred, had not Autbert become extremely sick and wished to return to France. Anskar had to accompany him, and the disillusioned missionaries returned to their monastery. Here Autbert's condition became worse, and he died soon after. Anskar's own future seemed more confused than ever. He was still pondering the meaning of it all when he received a second imperial summons.

'Come immediately. Don't even stop to shave.'

He arrived at court to find the emperor engaged in discussions with ambassadors from the king of Sweden.

'King Bjorn has asked for missionaries,' said Louis. 'Will you go?'

The Swedes had learned much about Christianity over the course of the last few decades. Their traders paid frequent visits to Christian lands, and they had brought back many reports of the southern faith. More importantly, the Viking pirates brought back Christian captives, and these believers provided a more exact knowledge of the faith to their unwillingly 'adopted' home. The Swedes now wanted to know more.

'We would like experienced teachers of these beliefs to come to us.'

Anskar immediately went into action, and he soon found two other monks who shared his passion for the north. To one, Gislema, he handed responsibility for whatever may happen in Denmark, while the other, Witmar, he made his colleague in the Swedish mission. Anskar and Witmar were soon on their way, but again things did not go as planned.

The monks made part of their journey on a trading ship, and it was here that disaster struck. Viking pirates attacked their ship, and after a fierce resistance most of the sailors and passengers were forced to leap overboard to save themselves from slavery. The two monks were among the weary band that was forced to swim for shore, with everything lost but their lives. They were now faced with a dilemma. Was it worthwhile continuing their journey when they did not have so much as a single Bible left to take to the Swedish king? Their small Christian library, 40 books in all, was gone.

'But we've come too far to go back now.'

The monks found passage aboard another ship, and after a harrowing journey, and near starvation, the bedraggled pair found themselves in the Swedish court.

King Bjorn greeted them warmly and granted them permission to preach and baptize freely throughout his realm. The monks established their mission in the town of Birka, and after some inquiry they discovered a small number of Christian slaves in the neighbourhood. These victims of the Vikings were soon formed into the first regular fellowship in the Scandinavian peninsula.

Anskar and Witmar remained in Birka for 18 months. The crowning triumph of their mission was the baptism of the

Governor of Birka, Herigar, who built a church upon his estate. But without books and other supplies the church was rather lame, so once the work was well established the monks returned to Emperor Louis.

The emperor and his ministers discussed the Scandinavian situation with the missionaries, and it was decided that another monk, Gauzbert, should be sent back to Birka. Anskar himself was made archbishop of the whole north and was given a base in Hamburg, a town near the frontier between the empire and Denmark.

'You will be more useful closer to home.'

And so it was for a little more than a decade. Archbishop Anskar began the arduous task of organizing the Danish church: visiting the heathen towns, appointing missionaries for the various regions and training Danish children in the faith. Progress, on the whole, was fairly slow. Anskar was never to see the dramatic successes of such earlier missionaries as Boniface; and few missionaries can have met with more causes for discouragement. The reasons for this are not far to seek.

Boniface's triumphs had been achieved during the years of France's rise to power, and the support of Charles Martel and Pepin had given the German mission great advantages. By Anskar's day, however, the Franks were falling into a period of weakness. The raids of the Vikings left their fairest cities in ruins, and their wealth was stolen or expended in war. Louis the Pious was a good man, but he had little of his father's political and military skill. His sons and grandsons were even worse, and the Frankish realm slowly sank beneath the Scandinavian assault.

Few towns escaped the ravages of pirates, and in 845 it was Hamburg's turn. The archbishop and his congregation were put to flight by a furious Viking assault, and from a safe distance they could only watch as their monastery and church went up in flames.

'The Lord gave, and the Lord has taken away,' said the archbishop, in the spirit of Job. 'Blessed be the name of the Lord!'

Equally grave troubles struck the church in Sweden almost simultaneously. Gauzbert had successfully taken over the Swedish mission, and over the years a number of French monks had joined him in the work. His successes had infuriated many Swedish pagans, and at this time a bloody attack was made upon the Birka mission base. Nithard, Gauzbert's nephew and fellow missionary, was killed in the assault, and the rest of the monks were forced to flee the country. They were never to return.

In the course of the attack, however, one of the pagan soldiers had stolen some of Gauzbert's belongings. Amongst the spoils was a Christian book, and the soldier decided to keep this as a trophy of his gang's victory over the church. He could not read a word of it, but it was colourful and handsome and looked extremely fine upon his wall.

Only a few days after the attack the soldier sickened and died. His sister and mother soon followed him to the grave, and his father was left as almost the sole relic of the family. Even the family's livestock were struck by illness, and the father, astounded by these misfortunes, decided that they must be the result of divine vengeance. He called upon a pagan soothsayer, hoping to learn which deity was angry with his household. The soothsayer cast lots to test the ill will of each of the pagan deities against the man and his family, but found that he had angered none of them.

'It must be some foreign god,' he declared.

'What foreign god has visited Sweden?' the father asked in surprise.

'The God of the Christians!'

Perplexed by this response the father returned to his home. There, as though for the first time, he noticed the Christian book upon the wall.

'There is death in the book!'

With pounding heart he took the book down and went straight to the town market. There he addressed his fellow townsmen.

'I wish the citizens and elders to hear my words. You all know that my family has been destroyed by some ill fate. Today I have discovered the cause. My son took part in the raid that expelled the Christians, and from the church ruins he brought home some booty, which included one of their holy books. This book has been in my house ever since, and I have had nothing but misfortune so long as it has been there. Now I seek a word from the wise, as to how I can erase my guilt. I cannot just throw the book away, for that would be even worse than keeping it. What can I do?'

No one had any suggestion to make. None dared take the deadly treasure, so the man was forced to come up with a plan of his own. He wrapped the book carefully and tied it to a post near his house. Beside it he placed a sign:

'For the theft of this book my family has been destroyed. I wish to repent of this sin. Any who dare may take this book and relieve me of the guilt of keeping it.'

A convert of Gauzbert's mission heard of this state of affairs and gladly took charge of the dreaded volume. No sooner had he done so than the disease destroying the pagan's flocks disappeared, and his run of misfortune came to an end. Thankful and relieved, he soon sought out the local Christians.

'I too want to know this Mighty God!'

In Hamburg, meanwhile, Anskar was rebuilding on the ruins of the Viking attack. His work in Denmark was gaining momentum, but the archbishop could not rest easy as long as the infant church of Sweden was without a regular ministry. Gauzbert refused to return there, and for six years no one was found to replace him. Herigar, the Christian governor of Birka, sent repeated requests for new missionaries, and when all other preparations failed Anskar determined to return in person.

Things had greatly changed in the 20 years since his last visit to Sweden. The pagan priests now knew much more about the church, and the name of Anskar was dreaded amongst them. News of the archbishop's coming long preceded him, and he found a country already up in arms against him.

'The gods have spoken,' the pagan priests assured the people. 'Everything you have is a gift from them. Embrace a new god, and all will be lost.'

The Swedish king, Olaf, was no slave of the priests. He welcomed the archbishop, but in order to maintain the peace he forbade the preaching of the gospel.

'I understand your position,' said Anskar. 'But I have been commanded by my God to preach here. Can we not come to some arrangement pleasing to my God and your priests?'

'That would be difficult,' Olaf said thoughtfully. 'All I could suggest is that we put the question to the sacred lots. Thus the gods themselves will decide.'

Olaf took this suggestion to the chiefs and priests, and all agreed that this was the only way forward. The priests busied themselves with preparations, and a holy day was appointed as the one on which they would receive the word of their 'gods' . . .

Anskar was at first troubled by this development, but as the days passed he felt a great assurance grow within him. When the chiefs congregated at the Field of Decision the archbishop was sure of the outcome.

'Favourable!' the pagan priests declared in horror. 'The gods have smiled upon the mission of the Frank!'

The news created quite a riot. The people were in a state of great excitement, and the decision was taken as a sign that the gods themselves were betraying them.

'The gods have lied!' said some. 'They are so furious at us for receiving this Anskar that they have abandoned us to the will of his God!'

Things looked black indeed, until a Swedish elder finally brought the mob to order.

'Many of us have found that the God of Anskar answers prayers,' he said. 'It is true. Why would so many nations worship Him if this were not so? And why should we alone hate and dread Him? If we allow His ministers into this country it can only be for our good. When our gods turn their backs on us, we can pray to the new God instead.'

The Swedes were silenced.

'We never saw it quite that way before!'

And thus Anskar's mission went ahead in safety.

Anskar laboured beside the Swedish Christians for two years, and many new believers were brought into the fold before he returned south. In Hamburg and the surrounding region he spent his last 11 years, strengthening the Danish mission and guiding the efforts in Sweden. He did not live to see either land wholly embrace the gospel, but he did do much to create the solid core of Scandinavian believers who were later to be part of that revolution.

Anskar died in 865, in the peace of his own home, but to those who knew the story of a certain dream in his early teens, Anskar would always be remembered as a martyr.

'He went forth to his labour, and all his life died daily for the souls of the North men.'

RIMBERT, *LIFE OF ANSKAR*

Cyril and Methodius

Towards the end of Anskar's life God was raising up two missionaries at the opposite end of Europe. They were to be the evangelists for an important area of central and eastern Europe.

Cyril was born to a wealthy Byzantine family about the year 827. He was educated by the leading teachers of his nation, and in his early twenties he retreated to a secluded monastery. His elder brother, Methodius, had already risen to a high position in the government, but he was inspired by Cyril's example to adopt monasticism. For seven years the brothers lived together, a life of religious study and prayer.

In 858 an ambassador of the Chazars, a barbarian people from the region between the Black and Caspian Seas (now the far south of European Russia), asked the eastern emperor for missionaries to instruct his people in the Christian religion. The Chazars had long been in contact with Christians, Jews and Muslims, and they now desired more precise knowledge of the 'One God'. The imperial officials committed the task to Cyril and his brother, and the monks embraced the charge with enthusiasm. In a little more than two years they had gathered the scattered local Christians into a church, instructed several ministers, and won many pagans to the gospel. When the church of the Chazars was able to stand on its own feet the brothers returned to Constantinople.

A new assignment soon followed. Ambassadors came to Constantinople from the Slavic barbarians of Moravia (present-day Slovakia and the eastern part of the Czech Republic) in 862. The Moravians wished to forge an alliance with the Byzantines, and to make their nation more attractive to the empire they expressed a willingness to receive Christian missionaries. The brothers were delighted at the opportunity, and they were already preparing to depart when a fresh request arrived at the royal court – this one from King Boris of the Bulgarians:

'Knowing the excellence of the Greeks in painting, I have hope that a skilled artist might be found to take in hand the adorning of my new palace. His payment will be more than adequate.'

The Byzantines here saw an opportunity to sneak a missionary into Bulgaria. Methodius was a gifted painter, and here he was already preparing for just such an expedition. It was decided that the brothers should travel to Moravia by way of Bulgaria, that neither opportunity need be put in less experienced hands. On arrival in Bulgaria Methodius was immediately given an audience with the barbarian king.

'I love nothing more than hunting,' Boris revealed, 'and I want a picture of the chase that will cover a whole wall in the main hall. It must be a good picture, large, and awe-inspiring.'

'So it shall be,' said the missionary painter, 'but there is a condition which I always place on my work.'

'Name it.'

'I must not be disturbed while I work on the picture. None can see it until it is finished.'

Boris agreed, reluctantly, and the painter was locked in the hall. There he remained, unseen by the outside world, for several weeks.

The king became increasingly impatient as the days passed, and his fiery barbaric blood was almost boiling when Methodius finally threw open the doors and invited the king to view his masterpiece.

'What is it?'

Boris stood still as a stone, his eyes engrossed in the wonderful scene before him.

'Explain it.'

Methodius had depicted in striking colours an interpretation of the Last Judgement. Above was the figure of Christ upon the throne; below were the just and the unjust, the two classes being divided by the angels.

'The figure above is Jesus Christ, the Son of God,' Methodius began, and the king stood entrapped while the artist unfolded the story of judgement and sin, repentance and redemption.

'Such is the final fate of all people,' Methodius ended. 'There are only two eternal homes for mankind.'

The king bowed low before the artist.

'Take me, teach me,' he said, 'that I too may cross over to the beautiful side of the picture.'

King Boris and several of his court were soon baptized. The royal court formed the nucleus of the first Bulgarian church, and though Boris would endure many problems with his pagan nobility, the church ultimately triumphed and spread throughout the nation. Cyril and Methodius did not remain to see this take place, for once a regular ministry was established in Bulgaria they moved on to the beckoning wilds of Moravia.

Moravia proved an even more fertile field for their labours. In the course of five years most of the nation accepted baptism, and Cyril took on the enormous task of making a Moravian translation of the Scriptures. In this the first obstacle was the greatest – for the Moravians had no written language at all!

The peoples of that region used the Slavonic language, and Cyril now made an alphabet to fit their speech. Over the course of some years he made translations of the Bible and other Christian works, and of the traditional Greek prayers and hymns, until finally the church services could be conducted entirely in Slavonic. Trouble struck the mission from an unexpected corner in 868.

The Roman pope and the patriarch of Constantinople were engaged in a fierce quarrel at this time (of which more in the next story), and Moravia, midway between Rome and Greece, was greatly stirred by the disagreement. Only a short distance west of Moravia were areas under Roman influence, and the bishops of these districts laboured to make life difficult for the two eastern monks. They had no real grounds for complaint, but they were jealous that Moravia had been converted by the Greeks and not by themselves.

The brothers received a summons from Pope Nicholas, who demanded they visit Rome to defend their ministry against certain accusations that the western bishops had made against them. The brothers, knowing that a refusal would worsen the division between Greece and Rome, obeyed immediately, but they arrived in Rome to find Nicholas already dead. His successor, Hadrian II, quizzed the visitors.

'We hear,' said Hadrian, 'that you have abandoned the use of Greek in the church services. Why so?'

Cyril began to answer, but the pope's attendants, itching for a fight with the Greeks, interrupted and objected to everything he said. Tiring of their pettiness, Cyril snatched up a copy of the Psalms:

'"Let everything that has breath praise the Lord" (Ps. 150:6)' he read aloud. 'If God wishes this to be so, why do you quibble about performing divine service, or translating Christian books, into Slavonic? Should the Greek and Latin tongues praise the Lord, but not Slavonic? I went forth to a people ignorant of our Lord's salvation, and by the inspiration of God I found this way of reaching many. You should follow the example of Paul, and "forbid not to speak with tongues" (1 Cor. 14:39), whichever tongue it might be that the people understand.'

The Romans were momentarily silenced, and Hadrian was the first to respond.

'You have said well. You may continue in this work just as you have begun.'

Unfortunately for Moravia, however, it was only to be one of the brothers who would continue in the field. Cyril fell ill in Rome, and feeling his end near he retired to a quiet monastery. His dying words were an exhortation to his elder brother:

'Do not put down what we have once taken up!'

Methodius was not to disappoint the great translator. Once Cyril was laid to rest Methodius returned to central Europe, and

there he laboured another 16 years. The strife of Greece and
Rome was to cause him much more anguish of heart, as he
endured repeated attacks from the western clergy, but in
adversity his greatness shone all the brighter. Raised to the
dignity of archbishop in 874, Methodius rode through the storms
of his time, and rose above the attacks of his foes, to emerge in
the light of history as a man worthy of the respect of all
Christians. To this day he and his brother are remembered by
east and west alike as the greatest missionaries of central Europe.

The East/West Divide

The battle between Rome and Constantinople had been brewing
for quite some time. Iconoclasm had soured relations, the
declaration of the Holy Roman Empire had made the breach
worse, but it was the rising power of the pope that made a
permanent division almost unavoidable.

In 858, Emperor Michael III of Constantinople unjustly
deposed Patriarch Ignatius of Constantinople, and Photius, one
of the most brilliant scholars to grace the eastern church, was
elected in his place. Such an election almost inevitably led to
division in the Greek church, with many ministers, quite rightly,
refusing to acknowledge the new patriarch. Photius responded
by despatching ambassadors to Rome, hoping that the followers
of Ignatius might agree to make peace if Rome were to back his
claims.

Pope Nicholas, however, was not one to be easily swayed. He
knew that Michael's proceedings had been improper, and he
saw the present strife as an opportunity to test his own strength.
He pronounced Ignatius the rightful patriarch and wrote sternly
to both Photius and Michael. Asserting himself the supreme
head of the church, east and west, he condemned Photius and
declared the acts of his administration null and void:

'The Greek church is led by an impostor.'

Few Greeks were prepared to swallow this. Even Photius'
enemies were wary of Nicholas' claims to authority over the

east, and Photius soon countered with a council of his own.

'The Roman church,' this council declared, 'is the real impostor. Rome has fallen from the true faith, and the pope's decisions are to be considered worthless.'

Here, in a nutshell, is what has become known as the Photian Schism. In claiming to be master of the Greek patriarch, the pope had overstepped the mark. The breach was not yet complete and final, but so long as Rome maintained its pretensions a lasting peace between the two churches would be impossible.

Closer to home, Nicholas' policy of papal supremacy was much more effective. As the ninth century progressed the new western empire slowly crumbled, and most Europeans stopped looking to the emperor as the man who could hold Christendom together. The Frankish emperors still divided their realms amongst their sons, and thus it was only rarely that one man held sway over the entire area that had been ruled by Charlemagne. In this chaotic state of affairs the popes declared themselves the

---

In declaring that Rome had fallen from the true faith the Greek council named several points on which they held that the west was in error. Most were trivial, and would not have been an issue if anti-Roman feelings had not been running hot, but there were two significant points.

- I. That Rome had introduced a new word into the Nicene Creed.
- II. That Rome had taken moves to ban the marriage of ministers.

The original creed said that the Spirit 'proceeded from the Father'. During the debate against Arianism in Visigothic Spain, however, it became popular to add the Latin word *Filioque* ('and the Son'), that is, 'from the Father *and the Son*'. The whole Latin church eventually adopted the new word as a way of emphasizing the equality of Father and Son. They said that the original creed was not wrong, but that it did not contain the full doctrine – a point that the Greeks did not dispute, though they insisted that it was nevertheless wrong to make a change to the creed. The controversy brings out a distinctive difference between the two churches. The west, rightly or wrongly, has always felt free to improve and innovate, while the east has declared itself eternally bound to follow the practices of the past.

The other point, clerical marriage, will be explored in the next volume.

superiors of the Frankish monarchs and claimed the right to settle disputes between them. In time they went a step further and claimed the right of actually giving away the crowns.

'Your crowns belong to God; we are God's chief servants; we can give the crowns to whomever is most worthy.'

Put another way: Europe needed unity, the Franks had failed to provide it, so the popes were taking over.

While asserting their authority over the Frankish rulers the popes were attempting to bring the whole western church under their personal control. In pursuit of this goal the western archbishops, their nearest rivals in authority, were naturally the first targets. The archbishops had certain powers over their bishops; if a bishop was accused of misconduct his archbishop would sit as judge, and according to a law of Charlemagne only the emperor himself stood above the archbishop.

Pope Nicholas insisted that the pope, not the emperor, was the only power above the archbishops. He urged bishops who had a disagreement with their archbishop to bring their cases to his court for a retrial, knowing that if this right of appeal could be established the power of the archbishops would be largely broken, and he would reign supreme. It was a bold attempt, but it received great help from the strangest source.

An unknown writer, or writers, of the mid-ninth century composed one of the most stupendous frauds in history. They were known at the time as the Decretals of Isidore; they are known today, more appropriately, as the False Decretals.

The False Decretals are a series of letters and laws which claim to have been composed by the first bishops of Rome, leaders during the first four centuries of the church. The False Decretals claim that the Roman bishop has power over all other ministers, and that the church has complete authority over the state. There is scarcely an atom of truth in the whole collection, and some of the letters contain the most ridiculously obvious mistakes, but circumstances of the late ninth century prepared the way for the west to swallow the amazing fraud whole.

The lower ranks of bishops were the first to use the False Decretals. To escape the power of their archbishop, certain bishops used the False Decretals to prove that Rome was the chief judge. They saw that with the archbishop weakened they themselves would become stronger.

Strangely, the False Decretals were next put to use by an archbishop, Hincmar of Rheims, the highest figure in the French church, who used them against the emperor to prove the church's superiority over the civil power. It was an unwise move.

The pope was the next to discover this magical source of power. To bishops and archbishops the False Decretals were useful – in the hands of a pope they were a devastating weapon. Nicholas, ironically, first used them against Hincmar of Rheims himself, and when a French bishop appealed to Rome against an unjust decision made by Hincmar the pope reversed the decision and pointed to the False Decretals as the basis of his authority. Hincmar now rued the day he had allowed the forgery to go unchallenged.

'I thought those documents useful to myself,' he declared. 'Now I see that they are a mousetrap to catch unwary archbishops.'

Rome was removing the last obstacles to complete control of the western church. It now had a claim to great authority, but would it be able to use it?

The Western Scholars

Fortunately the west produced much more than forgeries in the ninth century, and while the pope and archbishops were arguing the schools of the early empire produced work of a standard such as had not been equalled for centuries. We note two controversies illustrative of the times.

We have already seen that the Franks tended to view the Greek use of icons as superstitious, if not idolatrous. Two western bishops, Agobard of Lyons and Claudius of Turin, went even further. Agobard, like the Iconoclasts, wished the simple figure of the cross to replace all other pictures and believed that the reverence of saints and the use of icons were snares of the devil, designed to pollute Christian worship. Claudius was more extreme. He opposed all religious artwork, even the simple cross, taught that intercessory prayer ended with physical death (and that calling upon the saints was therefore pointless), and even dared attack the supremacy of the Roman bishop. Agobard enjoyed considerable support; few joined Claudius. Both, however, kept their bishoprics in spite of their outspokenness. The points in dispute were not yet such an everyday part of life in the west that opposing them could endanger one's position.

Not all radical thinkers were so fortunate. The mid-ninth century witnessed the tragedy of Gottschalk.

Gottschalk had been sent to live in a monastery as a child, but coming of age, and knowing that he had no calling from God to be a monk, he had applied for permission to leave. Permission was granted, but the new abbot of his monastery, Rabanus Maurus (who also happened to be one of the greatest teachers of the age), opposed the decision and appealed to the emperor. He argued that the decision of one's parents should be as binding as one's own decision as an adult.

'We do not allow adults to come and go as they please. We can't set an example by allowing just this one class, involuntary monks, to leave. Entering a monastery should be final, at whatever age it is done.'

The emperor agreed, and Gottschalk was forced to remain a monk against his will. He was, however, allowed to move to a different monastery.

The unhappy monk devoted his life to theological study, and in time he won wide respect for his learning. This very learning, however, would prove his eventual downfall. An admirer of Augustine, Gottschalk claimed that the great North African had taught the doctrine of double predestination, and so he began earnestly to preach the same.

Predestination has to do with the way in which God orders the salvation and damnation of men. Single predestination teaches that God's elect are chosen from before the world, called by God's grace, and saved by His power (Rom. 8:30). Double predestination goes further, and insists that those who are not saved were created by God specifically for damnation, thus to reveal His justice through the punishment they suffer for sin. Gottschalk's teaching sparked debate on a double-headed question: who did Jesus die for, and why are some people saved and others not?

Gottschalk argued that Jesus did not die for the sins of all mankind. His proof was simple: not everyone is saved; God can't fail; therefore God did not intend to save everyone through Jesus' blood. If Jesus had died to save everyone, He had failed in His task. Gottschalk also stressed that people are saved or condemned solely by the inscrutable choice of God. God rules the world in such a way that, with Him, foreknowing something and willing it are the same; whatever happens, happens because God wills it. There is no human freedom of will to repent and turn to God. Those who die as sinners do so in consequence of God's unchangeable decree against them.

Such teachings met much opposition and led to vigorous debate in theological circles. Some leading scholars agreed with most of Gottschalk's system but were more careful in describing the nature of predestination. They said that God has predestined the elect to receive saving grace in this life, and a heavenly reward hereafter, and that He is responsible for all that is good in them. The damned, on the other hand, are predestined to hell on account of the sins which God has foreseen in them. God, however, has no part in leading them into those sins. The guilt is wholly their own.

Other scholars, among them Rabanus, objected to Gottschalk's teachings more broadly, and particularly to his teaching that Jesus' blood was shed for the elect only. They maintained that God 'wishes all men to be saved' (1 Tim. 2:4), and that the reason that many are lost is because they reject the offer of grace. They urged that Christ's sacrifice is of infinite worth in God's sight, and sufficient to redeem all the sins of mankind. They also insisted that God foreknew sin, but did not will it to happen. Sin is, in fact, disobedience to God's will.

All sides acknowledged Augustine's teaching, but each interpreted his words and the biblical testimony in different ways. The differences between the combatants were in many cases slight, and were more about forms of expression than real substantial issues. Gottschalk himself, however, was clearly pushing an extreme. In Augustine's many hundreds of pages on the question of election there are but a few isolated passages in which he intimates that the damned are predestined to their fate by God. It was something to which he gave little attention – his real concern was to prove quite different points. Gottschalk, however, took hold of this obscure doctrine as though it was of fundamental importance to all theology.

The debate over the exact nature of God's foreknowledge and predestination has been carried on in the church throughout the centuries, and we shall examine it in more detail later. It was a valid enough topic for the new Frankish schools to concern themselves with no doubt, but the temper of the times is revealed in the controversy's gruesome end. Hincmar of Rheims objected to Gottschalk's teachings and summoned the monk to a council. The council condemned Gottschalk's views and the monk was scourged to within an inch of his life and compelled to burn his writings with his own hand. The teacher remained firm, however, and refused to deny his beliefs. Hincmar threw him into prison and there he remained until his death, prisoner of an archbishop as once of an abbot.

Alfred the Great

Leaving the cloister for the high seas, we find the Vikings spreading terror throughout northern Europe.

Ireland suffered repeated attacks in the ninth and tenth centuries and most of the North Atlantic island monasteries were destroyed, never to be rebuilt. Irish monasteries had probably spread as far as Greenland prior to the pagan devastation.

England suffered a similar fate. The eighth century had seen England become the intellectual centre of the west, but by the late ninth century this glory was completely gone, vanished in the smoke of burning monasteries. Some of the English kingdoms were completely overthrown, all were harassed, and thousands of Danes (like the Anglo-Saxons themselves four centuries earlier) made their home on the conquered land. Never had the land so needed a hero.

Alfred, brother of King Ethelred of Wessex, was the first English general to defeat a major Viking force in battle. The year was 871, Alfred was twenty-two, and when Ethelred died later that year Alfred himself took the throne.

The early years of Alfred's reign enjoyed an extended truce with the Danes, but this ended disastrously in the first week of 878. The king and his soldiers were celebrating Twelfth Night, the final day of the Christmas festival, when a Danish force launched a surprise attack. Wessex fell entirely into Danish hands, and Alfred himself was forced into hiding.

Alfred is the only English king to bear the surname of 'the Great', and this quality was never more apparent than in defeat. The king, always disguised, travelled throughout his vanquished realm, organizing the remains of his forces and spying out the weaknesses of the enemy. Within months he was confident of his opportunity, and the English rallied to his banner when he put forth the call. He met the Danes in battle, one of the most furious to stain English soil, and comprehensively defeated them. The survivors begged for peace and offered to leave Wessex.

Alfred had a better plan. He knew that if the Danes left now they would be back later, so he encouraged them to stay and to learn to live peacefully beside his own subjects. The Danish leaders were invited to meet him, and Alfred encouraged them to embrace the gospel and learn the way of peace. The conquered Danes were baptized and then feasted by the West Saxon king.

In the years of peace that followed Alfred threw himself into the activities which have made his name immortal. He reformed the law of his nation, founded a formidable defensive navy to deal with the Viking scourge, and took the lead in a progressive spiritual and intellectual movement.

Collecting and committing to writing the laws of his nation, laws that had previously been a confusion of local customs and rules, Alfred endeavoured to conform the old system to the Law of Moses and the precepts of the gospel. He was thus the father of the English Common Law that stands to this day.

Alfred was passionately concerned for the revitalization of the church. Knowing that good education, especially in the truths of the gospel, was the best way to achieve this, the king established schools throughout his realm. As the scholarly language of Latin was little known in England, Alfred determined to translate a range of useful books into the native Anglo-Saxon tongue.

Alfred himself spent much time in the work of translation, and he gathered a group of scholars to aid him. Amongst his translations were parts of Scripture, Bede's *History of the Church of the English People* (the finest work of the eighth-century flowering of English scholarship), Aesop's Fables, and books on theology, philosophy and world history. Thus he became the father of English literature as well – and all from a man who was plagued by ill health throughout his life and died (in 899) at the age of fifty!

Alfred's contribution spread far beyond his own borders. Wessex was but one of the English kingdoms, but the strength it gained under Alfred made it far outshine its rivals. In the four decades following Alfred's death the kingdom of Wessex subdued each of the other kingdoms, and soon all England bowed before Alfred's dynasty. Alfred's grandson Athelstan was the first King of England. A united nation had emerged from the chaos of the centuries.

Rome's Darkest Night

While a new age was dawning in England, a dream seemed to be dying in Italy.

The empire had promised a new age of peace and unity in Europe. When it fell apart the pope had attempted to hold the broken pieces of Christendom together. Now he too fell a victim to the troubles of the times. The popes were respected, even obeyed, throughout western Europe. Everywhere, it seems, but in their own home town.

A handful of petty rulers battled for the supremacy in Italy. The late ninth and early tenth centuries were a miserable scene of turmoil and civil war, terribly aggravated by repeated Muslim incursions into southern Italy. The Muslims already held much of the nearby island of Sicily, and from here their pirates made devastating raids on the Italian cities. Large areas of the south bowed to the Saracen yoke for many decades, and the infidels once plundered the outer suburbs of Rome itself. One can imagine the church's trembling at the prospect of the pope becoming a slave to the Muslims!

As it happened the popes did become slaves, but of Christian rather than Muslim masters. The civil wars and Muslim assaults plunged Italy into barbarism, and it was not long before the popes became pawns in bloody political battles. The popes had brought this situation on themselves. They had wanted the right to appoint kings and emperors, and this right now backfired. In the Italian anarchy, rival factions would capture the pope in the hope of forcing him to give them his support, and leaders from every corner of the empire joined them in besieging the pontiffs in search of a crown.

In 878 Pope John VIII was imprisoned by an Italian noble named Lambert, who attempted to starve the bishop into joining his political faction. For a month the city of Rome was without religious services, as the unfortunate minister languished in a small cell. Upon release John covered the altar of St Peter's (the main Roman church) with sackcloth, shut the doors and fled to France. There he saw for himself the truth of Jesus' saying about a prophet in his home town – for in France the king himself bowed before him.

From the time of John onwards the Italian nobles were not to be satisfied with manipulating the popes. They began to battle for the right to put their own stooges on the papal throne.

When Pope Formosus died in 896, one of the noble houses raised Boniface VII to the throne. Boniface was one of the most scandalous priests in the empire, and his chequered career had seen him twice deposed for immorality – first as subdeacon, later as priest. This mattered little to his supporters; he was an ally, and that was what counted. Europe breathed a sigh of relief when he died of the gout within a fortnight of his election.

The relief was premature, for another faction now proceeded to the election of Stephen VII. Stephen was a bitter enemy to the recently deceased Formosus, who had opposed his political faction. Not content with reversing the policies of his predecessor, Stephen ordered that Formosus be exhumed.

'Dress the body in papal robes and present Formosus for trial.'

Stephen summoned a council, and one of his deacons was appointed as the deceased pope's lawyer.

'Explain your conduct, Formosus,' challenged Stephen. 'What excuse can you offer for your wicked ambition, which saw you unjustly become Roman bishop?'

The deceased, and his deacon, remained silent.

'Have you no answer?'

The silence deepened.

'You are in contempt of court! All the decisions of your pontificate are null and void. We sentence you to be stripped of your papal robes, to have three of your fingers severed, and to be cast into the river Tiber!'

Such was the fate of Formosus; Stephen's was no better. A few months later he was imprisoned by his opponents and secretly strangled afterwards. Formosus' body was fished from the river and reinterred in a solemn service.

From this time onwards a confusion of short-lived popes followed each other in rapid succession, seven in seven years, until Sergius III came to the throne in 904. With Sergius begins the blackest period of Roman history – the era known as the 'Papal Pornocracy' (*porne* is the Greek word for 'prostitute').

Control of the papacy now slipped into the hands of Theodora, wife of a Roman senator – a woman equally famed for her power, beauty and crimes. As the lover of Sergius (she was known as the papal prostitute), Theodora manipulated the fate of both the church and city.

While living in sin with the ageing Sergius, Theodora was also having an affair with John, a much younger Italian bishop.

John, however, was bishop of a city many days' journey from Rome, and Theodora longed for a way of bringing her man to town. When Sergius died in 911 she went to work on her lover's behalf, and after two short-lived pontiffs had come and gone, John was ordained pope in 914. As John X he ruled for 14 years, a longer reign than Rome had seen for some eighty years. His criminal rise, however, was to be matched with an equally criminal fall.

In 925 Theodora's daughter Marozia attempted to conquer the papacy for herself. With her lover Alberic (she equalled the beauty and outstripped the vices of her mother) she led an army against Rome.

John himself rallied his flock for battle. Decked out in the papal robes, slightly modified so as not to encumber his iron armour or his sword arm, John rode at the front of a motley mob that cut down and scattered the invading force. Alberic did not long survive the defeat, and Marozia soon began the search for a more powerful support. Spreading her favours far and wide she won herself a loyal band of followers, and after marrying the best of these, Duke Guido, she returned to Rome in 928. This time she met with better success, and John X was captured, imprisoned, and later smothered with a pillow.

Marozia had a bastard son, another John. Some said he was the child of Alberic, while others believed him the son of Sergius, the pope who had also been her mother's lover. He was still in his teens, but his mother was determined to install him as the next pontiff. Guido disapproved, so Marozia bided her time. Two popes came and went in three years; Guido died; the boy became pope.

John XI began his reign as a puppet, and ended it as a prisoner. At first it was Marozia who reigned supreme. Soon after her husband's death Marozia wrote to Hugh, Guido's half-brother, and offered her hand in marriage. Hugh had recently become king of Italy, and Marozia offered him undisputed rule over the city of Rome if he would allow her to share his throne. The king agreed, the pair met in the Roman suburbs, and the harlot's triumph seemed complete.

It was not to last. Alberic, Marozia's son by Alberic, resented his mother's favouritism to John and gathered an army and led a rebellion against his family. Within a few months he was undisputed ruler of Rome, Marozia and John were imprisoned, and King Hugh was forced to retreat. For 22 years the son of Marozia ruled Rome with an iron fist. The papacy was his personal puppet, and during his reign he appointed a succession of four popes.

It was Alberic's death in 954, however, which sank the papacy to its very nadir. His son Octavian succeeded him as Roman tyrant, and at the age of only eighteen this grandson of Marozia assumed the papacy as well. He was the first pope to take a new name at his ordination – he is known to history as John XII, the tyrant pope.

The tyrant pope scarcely even pretended to be a minister of religion. He always appeared in public wearing full armour and carrying sword and spear. An eager gambler, he would invoke the aid of pagan gods at the gaming table. He never made it to church for either the early or the late services. He ran a brothel in the papal mansion, loved hunting above all else, and drank extremely heavily.

'Good health to the devil!' was his way of saying grace.

He made a ten-year-old a bishop, forced certain ministers to receive their ordination in a stable, mutilated his enemies, and made concubines of nuns, widows, and whoever else fell in his way – including the mistresses of his deceased father. For eight years he remained the supreme minister of the western church!

Good King Wenceslas

We shall return to John later. With a sigh of relief we turn from the vileness of Rome to mountainous Bohemia, now part of the Czech Republic, and the most famous Christian of the age.

The gospel first entered Bohemia in the late ninth century through its ruler Duke Borivoj. The duke and his wife Ludmila were baptized by Methodius while visiting nearby Moravia.

Most of their realm remained pagan, however, and it was not until the reign of Borivoj's son Wratislaus that many of the citizens accepted Christian teachings.

Wratislaus, a devoted Christian, was married to the violently pagan Drahomir. The couple had two sons, Wenceslas and Boleslas, and the duke wisely had the elder boy educated at a Christian school far from his mother's influence. Throughout his youth Wenceslas spent more time with his godly grandmother Ludmila than with his idolatrous mother.

Wenceslas was still in his mid-teens when his father died, and Drahomir took the government into her own hands. Within weeks Bohemia's churches were closed, and the preaching of the gospel was entirely banned. The Christian schools were boarded up, and Drahomir's cronies killed several believers.

Drahomir dreaded the influence of Ludmila, both over her eldest son and over the nation, and feared that the older woman might rally the Bohemian Christians against the pagan 'reforms'. Assassins were dispatched, and Ludmila was seized and strangled at prayer. It was an unwise move. Ludmila was well loved, and her murder caused outrage. Wenceslas, now eighteen, rose in rebellion against his mother, and with the support of the people he asserted his right to rule his father's realm.

The reign of the new duke was nothing short of a revolution. Wenceslas had drunk deeply at the gospel fount, and his heart was so completely set on Jesus that nothing he touched as ruler could remain the same. The pagan shades must go, and all things must conform to the golden precepts of the word of God.

Within weeks of his accession the young duke had banned the use of torture to extract confessions in criminal cases. The public gallows of the major towns, upon which the corpses of executed criminals were displayed as a terror to the public, likewise disappeared.

'Such barbarity only hardens hearts. There are better ways to deter the people from crime.'

Wenceslas himself found several such ways. He reopened and improved the church schools, provided for the poor and encouraged Christian missions in his realm. In all his good works, however, he was zealous to maintain as low a profile as possible, often keeping his own involvement a complete secret, that he might receive his reward from God alone (Mt. 6:6). By night, with one servant accompanying him, he would visit the fields to gather with his own hand the wheat and grapes used in the bread and wine of Holy Communion. Also by night he would pay secret visits to the poor and sick. One such night-time charity call is remembered throughout the world.

It was Boxing Day (then known as the Feast of Stephen the Martyr), and the good duke, looking out at the wintry night, saw a poor man gathering firewood. The thought of this man returning to his draughty hut was too much for Wenceslas, himself about to sit down to a hearty meal in his warm palace, and he decided to follow the pauper home.

'Let's share some of our cheer this evening!' he told his page.

Flesh and wine were brought, and the rest is history.

The duke, incidentally, was known throughout Europe as King of Bohemia. From his own people, however, he refused to hear any other title than that which his father had borne. Bohemia might have basked for decades in the calm of this golden age had not the hatred of an unnatural mother, and the greed of a brother, brought it to an untimely end.

Wenceslas had vowed not to marry. His intention was to pass the inheritance to his brother Boleslas and his nephews, and from the very beginning of his reign he divided his authority with his younger brother. Boleslas, however, was not satisfied with such brilliant prospects. Urged on by the bitterness of his mother he conspired against the life of the duke and found that a sizeable faction would support any move he might make against this destroyer of the old ways. Still he dared not rise in open rebellion, and months passed by as he planned the coup.

Finally, in mid-autumn 929, Wenceslas paid a visit to his brother's territory. It was the time of a major Christian festival, and the duke and his companions were amply feasted by the treacherous Boleslas. Wenceslas wished to begin his return to Prague, his capital, before evening, but Boleslas fervently entreated him to spend the night, and he arranged a series of entertainments to keep him occupied. Fatefully, Wenceslas consented to stay.

As always, the duke rose early the next morning and made his way to church before dawn. Boleslas was waiting for him on the church steps.

'Dear brother,' said the unsuspecting duke, 'your hospitality has been a great joy to me. You have left nothing to be desired!'

'Ah, but brother,' said Boleslas, 'there is one more gift you must accept!'

With that he drew his sword and struck a blow at the unarmed man's head. Wenceslas received a severe wound, but he grappled with his brother, and disarming him knocked him to the ground.

'God forgive you, brother,' he cried, looking with sorrow and amazement at the prostrate villain.

'Now!' screamed Boleslas. At the call three armed men appeared from a hiding place beside the church, and the duke, with his servants, were overpowered and killed on the spot. Boleslas was now ruler of the land.

Drahomir repented somewhat too late of her part in the crime. Catching wind of the deed she made haste to the church, and in tears she fell upon the body of her son. The cost, her son a sacrifice to her idols, was too great even for this mother's heart. It was a price but ill rewarded anyway. Boleslas himself eventually abandoned idolatry and he and his son, Boleslas II, almost entirely extinguished the paganism of Bohemia. To this day the church of the Czechs remembers two names above all others: that of the good duke, and of the grandmother who nurtured his faith.

The Saxon Empire

Charlemagne had dreaded the power of his Saxon neighbours. With force he had made them part of his empire, and with force he had brought them to baptism. Now, one and a half centuries later, these very Saxons were not only the main strength of the empire, but they were soon to become the reformers of the church which their fathers had so unwillingly entered.

Charlemagne's Holy Roman Empire had slowly died in the late ninth century under the misrule of a confusion of warring factions and tyrants. From this confusion one man eventually arose greater than the rest – the Saxon Duke Henry the Fowler, and in 919 he was elected King of the Germans. Henry restored order to the eastern parts of Charlemagne's realm and conducted significant campaigns against the more dangerous barbarians of the surrounding lands.

The Magyars, or Hungarians, were one of the most dreadful enemies to afflict Europe during the centuries of barbarian invasion. In the first decades of the tenth century they destroyed or subdued several of the smaller states of central Europe and made bloody assaults on both Italy and Germany. For some time the mighty Saxons themselves paid regular tribute to preserve their lands from fire and sword.

In 933 Henry determined to throw off this shameful yoke. He defied the Hungarian tribute collectors, and within days the barbarian war cry (a guttural 'Hui! Hui!') was heard on the borders of the land. The Hungarians were divided into two armies; the smaller tackled a frontier force, while the larger marched against the king himself, spreading out to plunder the nearby towns as they went.

The Hungarians had poorly judged their adversaries. Their smaller force was vanquished on the frontier, and when news of this defeat reached the main force the Hungarian leadership decided that they must come to blows with Henry immediately. They lit huge fires to attract the stragglers who were plundering the surrounding towns and farms.

'We must gather quickly, and join battle tomorrow.'

Henry the Fowler and his men prepared for battle with a night of prayer and waiting on the Lord. At daybreak they went to battle bearing before them an enormous banner of the Archangel Michael, Prince of Armies. To the 'Hui! Hui!' of the Hungarians they responded with the cry of 'Kyrie eleison!' ('Lord, show mercy!').

The battle raged through many a dreadful hour, but Saxon valour finally prevailed. Broken and put to flight, the barbarians left behind them hundreds of Christian slaves. Troops and rescued slaves alike knelt in the field of victory, and the king himself led in thanksgiving and praise. A season of joy had opened to Saxony.

The Hungarians were now as much terrified of the Saxons as the Saxons had so recently been of them. The image of the Archangel Michael was burnt into the nation's memory, and the Hungarians were sure that this supernatural agent had aided the Saxons. How could they get this heavenly power for themselves?

'The wings!' they decided. 'The Saxon victory god has wings. Our gods can only walk!'

From then on the Hungarian idols were decorated with golden wings, in imitation of pictures of angels.

Henry lived three years after this great victory, and on his death his son Otto rose to the German throne. In Henry's time there had been no emperor – none worthy or able to bear the title had arisen in the confusion of the last decades. The concept of the Holy Roman Empire itself might have perished altogether but for the appearance of this powerful new Saxon dynasty.

Otto took the Saxon power to new heights. He led campaigns against the Hungarians and the Danes, and it was an attack from his Saxons that first forced Boleslas of Bohemia to favour the church. The German king had a reasonable claim to the imperial crown, and he contemplated the journey to Rome to receive it. Events, however, conspired against him. These were the last years of Alberic's reign in Rome, and the tyrant was unwilling to receive the mighty Saxon in his city. Wars also cropped up in the north, and Otto was kept more than ordinarily busy.

Strangely enough it was only a few years later that the Saxon received urgent pleas from the pope himself to come to Italy. The tyrant Pope John XII was now on the throne, and his violent rule was being challenged by certain Italian nobles. John promised Otto a crown as the price of conquering the upstart Italians, and in 961 the Saxon led a formidable army into Italy. At Pavia, in the far north, he received a crown as King of Italy, and from thence he proceeded to Rome, where on 31 January 962 he received the imperial crown from the hands of the tyrant pope himself.

The reign of Otto is the true birth of the Holy Roman Empire. France, the nation from which the new empire had originally sprung, has dropped out of the equation; in Otto's time France was already a separate nation under rulers of her own. The empire in the new age opening before us is based on the unity of Italy and Germany. We shall soon see just how fascinating a cocktail this would prove.

Once freed from danger, John XII began to regret his choice. He had rid himself of the petty Italian nobles at the expense of bowing to the mighty Saxon as master, and he now invited even his recent enemies to join him in rebellion. News of the Italian conspiracy reached Otto, but he refused to believe such ill reports of the head of the church.

'News must travel slowly in Saxony!' his Italian informants decided. They then ventured to advise the emperor of some of John's more public crimes and immoralities, but Otto rejected their stories with scorn.

'The pope is young, perhaps he has made some errors of judgement,' he said, 'but I cannot believe one man guilty of all the crimes you speak of!'

Hard facts soon convinced Otto of the treason against him, however, and he returned to Rome to put the pontiff on trial. John fled at his approach, and a council of leading Italian ministers was summoned to investigate the accusations.

'Why is John himself not present?' asked Otto.

'He knows his own guilt!' the people and clergy of Rome cried with one voice. 'From Spain to distant India his monstrous crimes are known. He is the only wolf of the church who has scorned to wear sheep's clothing! Were he here he would scarcely be able to deny his sins to you – daily they were on proud display before the whole city!'

'How do I know that this is not the voice of envy?' asked Otto. 'List his crimes. Be precise – don't simply throw curses at his name.'

The tale was not soon told! Incest, adultery, assaults – including castration and blinding . . . the list went on and on, and the people also complained that under John the churches had been left in such a state of disrepair that some roofs were threatening to fall in. With this list of charges before him Otto summoned John to come and clear his name. John sent a letter in reply:

'John, servant of God, to all the bishops of Italy.

'I see that you mean to elect a new pope. I forbid it. As supreme head of the church I hereby excommunicate you all. I am the only minister left. No one else may conduct religious services.'

Otto again summoned the tyrant. This time there was no answer from John himself.

'John is presently unavailable,' his servants affirmed. 'He is out hunting.'

The emperor was left with no choice. John was deposed, and Leo VIII appointed in his place.

The papacy had been rescued from its lowest depth, but the relief was only temporary. When Otto departed the exiled tyrant returned, and his powerful allies and cronies welcomed him with open arms. Leo was forced to flee, and John took gruesome vengeance on the friends of the emperor. A presbyter lost two fingers, another minister lost his tongue and nose, a third lost his right hand. In this horrid state they were thrown from the city, and thus they soon after appeared before Otto. The emperor marched on Rome for a third time.

John did not live to see this final showdown. The husband of a woman he had ravished fell upon the tyrant in an unguarded moment, and with a single blow delivered Rome of her shame. The Romans, however, were not inclined to attribute their deliverance to the vengeful husband:

'The hand of God has finally struck him down!'

Otto returned to find the tyrant already in the grave, and Leo was smoothly reinstated in his position. Rome had been rescued from the dynasty of Theodora and Marozia, but the troubles of the papacy were far from over.

Monastic Revival

It is not surprising that these evil years saw a new and powerful revival in monastic life. Thousands, disgusted with the sin and danger of the world around them, retired to what they hoped would be the sanctity and safety of monasteries.

The western monasteries, however, were in many cases little different to the outside world. Ironically, one of the greatest evils afflicting the monasteries was the high esteem in which they were held. A popular monastery would receive countless gifts over the years, from kings, nobles and commoners alike. Thousands left their whole estates to the monks, and thus the monasteries grew to enormous sizes.

The problems that this caused were manifold. The larger a monastery, generally speaking, the poorer the standard of discipline which could be enforced amongst its members. The richer a monastery, the more likely it was to attract people with no real calling; luxury and ease prevailed in many of the monasteries and convents. The countless involuntary monks did not make things any easier – the unfortunate individuals who had been sent to the monasteries as children and now longed to be free of them. All added up to ensure that the monasteries did nothing like live up to their claims.

Monasteries, like many other areas of Christian life, are in constant need of revival and reform. It was in the first years of the tenth century that just such a movement began – a powerful monastic revival such as Europe had not seen for many generations.

In 910 a monastery was founded at Cluny in France. From its inception its founders preached a thoroughgoing return to the Rule of Benedict. The other western monasteries had slipped away from many of the old regulations, and their monks had become at best worldly, at worst positively wicked. The ideals of Cluny inspired men throughout the west, many new establishments were created on a similar pattern, and a succession of brilliant and holy abbots saw Cluny maintain its high standards for centuries to come, 'a leaven in the lump' to the whole western church.

A significant revival in monastic life began in Italy a few decades later.

Nilus was born in the year of Cluny's foundation. A married man, a sincere and earnest Christian, Nilus was sickened in spirit by the state of the church of his day. Rarely blessed in owning a few Christian books (few could afford books of their own, and one of the benefits of joining a monastery was access to a library), he spent much time in reading and prayer.

With the passage of years, however, Nilus' zeal waned. Bad company rubbed off on him, and earning a living replaced the things of the Spirit in his most solemn thoughts. At the age of thirty, however, he was thrown from the slippery path of the backslider by a severe shock. The death of his dear wife reawakened him to an appreciation of the nature of worldly happiness, and he abandoned his empty home and entered a monastery.

The monastery was no great spiritual haven. The monks, unlike many, were not particularly wicked, but their love and devotion were cold. Wicked monks might have hated Nilus for his sincerity; these monks were simply amazed by him. Nilus spent hours in prayer every day, and he was always willing and able to instruct those around him. His fellow monks had not seen anyone like him before, and they began to call Nilus a second Apostle Paul!

Disenchanted with the life of the monastery, and inspired by the example of the earliest Egyptian monks, Nilus sought permission to retire into the forest to live as a hermit. His abbot agreed, and Nilus and two companions departed.

In time Nilus' name became renowned throughout the land, and his return to the old hermit ideal proved a great inspiration to his people. Many followed in his footsteps, and everyone from commoners to the emperor sought his advice. Hermits had long ago given way to monasteries, which provided better spiritual support and fellowship. With the decline of these institutions, however, the trend was now reversed.

Shortly afterwards another arose in Italy to reform the monasteries themselves. Romuald, like Nilus, was disgusted by the state of the monasteries, and like the founders of Cluny he became the father of a whole chain of vibrant and disciplined monasteries. The movement he sparked is known as the Camaldoli Order, and it had a major impact on the next few centuries. It catered for both types of monks, those seeking a 'cenobitic' life (i.e., living in a monastic society) as well as those wishing to be hermits.

England also experienced monastic revival in the tenth century.

Monasticism had become virtually extinct in the Viking years. Alfred had made moves to restore it, but the traditional discipline of the monks was almost completely forgotten. Some monastery buildings had been taken over by the kings and nobles, while married ministers and their families now inhabited others.

Dunstan, Archbishop of Canterbury, was the man who brought monasticism back to life in England. Dunstan himself, as a young man, had no intention of embracing the life of a monk. In his late teens he fell madly in love with a beautiful young woman, and had it not been for his elderly relative, Alphege the Bald, Bishop of Winchester, he would probably have been happily married, and lived and died quite unknown to history. It was not to be.

'The church needs young men like you,' old Alphege insisted. 'There are few true monks left in England. It is a disgrace.'

'Thank you uncle,' Dunstan answered curtly, 'but I know what I need. I'd prefer the company of a pretty lass to a monk's coarse woollen smock!'

And that was where matters stood, until Dunstan came down with a terrible skin disease. His whole body raw, and fearing for his life, he decided that the illness was a divine punishment, and upon recovery determined to follow Alphege's (painful) advice. It is hard to view Dunstan's decision without some sadness for him. However that may be, though he may have become a monk for dubious reasons, it is certain that he did not look back.

In a time when true monks were few and far between Dunstan quickly made a name for himself. He was still in his twenties when he was appointed abbot, and his climb through the ranks saw him become in time both archbishop of Canterbury, the highest rank of the English church, and chief adviser to the English king. Dunstan was a man of the widest interests and talents. He is mainly remembered as a politician, minister and monastic reformer, but that is only half the story. In his own time his skill as a worker in metals, and his abilities in other arts and crafts, were quite legendary. He immersed himself in books from a young age, and he ensured that the men whom he inspired to adopt the woollen smock were the best educated in the kingdom.

Dunstan's name is especially associated with the reintroduction of the Benedictine Rule. He waged a virtual war against the lax English monks, and he led hundreds of them to adopt the principles of Cluny. Many monasteries were reclaimed from the nobles and the married clergy who had taken them over, and they were filled with Dunstan's energetic and zealous followers.

Had the monastic revival ended there Dunstan's movement would have created few complaints. He took, however, a fateful further step. Dunstan, like most monks, believed celibacy a far superior and more spiritual state than marriage, and with the hope of improving the standard of Christian ministry strove to oust the married clergy from the churches and to replace them with his monkish followers. Such a move could be nothing but turbulent, and it created terrible problems in the ministry and the wider church. It was, however, only the smallest foretaste of violent changes that would assault the church in the following century. For his part in preparing the ground for these changes Dunstan's name has ever lived under a cloud. But, cloud or not, it is on all hands acknowledged that Dunstan left the English church stronger, more spiritual, and better educated than he found it.

The Apostle of the Alps

The internal health of the churches and monasteries, however, was only one part of the west's problem. The church still had battles ahead with paganism yet alive and well throughout supposedly Christian land.

In times of peace the church could almost forget that the idolaters existed. When the church and Christian rulers were strong the pagans slipped into the shadows, hidden behind the day-to-day life of Christian Europe. When chaos prevailed, however, idolatry returned to the open, and many, especially in the wilds, relapsed into the old ways. Missionaries had again to sally forth to the lands already once won.

Bernard de Menthon was the only son of a noble French family. From his earliest youth he was sickened with the constant round of war and strife which was the lot of a nobleman, and he longed to escape and adopt a celibate life. His father, however, anxious to perpetuate the family name, refused to hear his pleas and arranged his marriage to a rich young heiress named Marguerite.

Bernard was carried to the estate of his bride to be, and was kept there as a virtual prisoner. He tried to resign himself to his fate, but his whole will screamed against it. On the evening before the wedding he left a short note upon his dresser and ventured onto the ledge outside his window. He crouched, grasped the ledge with both hands, and dropped over the edge. He was suspended for a moment, before he braced himself and let go. Unperceived, and with heart pounding, he escaped into the night.

The fugitive dared not stay in his homeland, and he directed his steps to the Alps. He crossed the mountains on foot and finally came to rest at Aosta, a northern Italian town. Here he was befriended by the local archdeacon, Peter, under whose guidance he entered the ministry.

Aosta lay at the foot of two major Alpine passes which were used by the thousands of travellers coming to Italy from the west. Many of these travellers were pilgrims, drawn to Rome by the fame of the ancient church of that city. Even in this time of degeneracy and vice many sought the advice and approval of the Roman bishops.

Crossing the Alps was dangerous. In winter the passes were

choked with snow, and even at the best of seasons the journey was no affair for the faint-hearted. The crossing of the Alps has claimed countless thousands of lives over the centuries, but in the tenth century the dangers of the landscape were eclipsed by those of the Alpine dwellers themselves. The Alps were always regarded as a wild and violent region, and paganism still abounded there. The crags and valleys swarmed with dreadful bandit gangs, and pilgrims were fortunate if they lost only their money.

It was to the bandits and their victims alike that Bernard de Menthon devoted his days. He wandered the frozen mountain tracks, and falling in with the robber gangs he boldly shared the gospel story. In time the pagan temple which stood by the major Alpine pass was replaced by a Christian church. Bernard also built rest huts for weary travellers on both passes, and the Alpine churches and huts eventually became bases from which mountain rescue operations could be launched. Many were inspired to join this Alpine ministry, and Bernard's twin dreams of a secure route to Rome and the conversion of the neglected mountain folk were finally realized.

> Bernard is known as the 'Apostle of the Alps'. The name of 'Apostle' has commonly been given to the greatest early missionary to work amongst a particular people. Thus Boniface is the 'Apostle of the Germans', Anskar of the Danes, Patrick of the Irish, and so on.

With the passing of his mentor Peter, Bernard became archdeacon. His fame spread throughout western Europe, and many came to Aosta simply to meet him. Among these visitors were two elderly nobles, a man and wife.

'Archdeacon,' said the man, 'we know you for a man of honesty and wisdom, and we know also that pilgrims from all over Europe are familiar to you. Perhaps you have some time heard of, or met, our son.'

The old man went on to tell the story of his only child, a bright lad who had promised to one day be someone great.

'He was all we could have asked for,' put in the woman. 'His marriage was planned, all was well, but on the wedding day itself his beautiful young bride was left standing at the altar.'

'And this note,' said the father, presenting the worn old parchment, 'is all that remains of him.'

The old couple described their fruitless searches, and they pleaded with the archdeacon to offer them some hope before they went sorrowing to the grave.

'Just one sight of him!' the father moaned.

The archdeacon allowed none of his emotions to show as he gave the couple his consolations, and with a pounding heart he begged a moment's leave and promised to do whatever he could for them. Withdrawing, he almost collapsed and spent several minutes in a confusion of passionate prayer. Left to themselves the old couple whispered seriously for a moment. There was something uncanny about the famous archdeacon's appearance – and his name!

'Remember, it was partly that which brought us here in the first place,' said the man. It was only the hope of a moment, however, and soon both had agreed that the thought was an impossibility – a futile hope. A moment later Bernard returned, and their doubts were erased.

'Father!'

The bliss of reunion could scarcely be described. 'We sought to load you down with children of the flesh,' his father said in apology, 'we wanted our name to live in you. Praised be God for the countless spiritual children He has given you instead!'

But there was to be more to it even than that. Bernard, who cared not for the preservation of his name, has an undying fame even on earth. The two Alpine passes above Aosta were later renamed the Greater and the Lesser Saint Bernard, and the whole world remembers him for the hardy mountain dog bred by his followers to aid them in search and rescue work. To this day the St Bernard brings relief to injured and lost travellers in the Alps.

The Conversion of Russia

The late ninth and early tenth centuries saw little missionary work undertaken beyond the boundaries of the established western church. Anskar's work in Denmark slowly unravelled in these years, and the church planted in Sweden almost completely vanished.

As the tenth century drew to a close, however, exciting new developments took place in Scandinavia. Kings of both Denmark and Norway accepted Christ, and they eagerly promoted the faith amongst their peoples. King Olaf of Norway, who came to the throne in 995, not only laboured for the spread of Christianity amongst his own people, but he also promoted a mission to the distant Viking settlement of Iceland. It was the east, however, which enjoyed the most significant missionary success of these twilight years of the first Christian millennium.

The Viking expansion did not trouble western Europe alone. In the mid-ninth century a Swedish tribe known as the Varangians crossed the Baltic Sea and conquered the northern Slavs. They made a new home in the vanquished land and established their capital in the city of Kiev. From this Kievan state, a union of Viking conqueror and native Slav, a nation was eventually born – the nation of Russia.

The River Dnieper provided a natural highway from Kiev to the Black Sea, and hence to Constantinople, and the new nation soon made its presence known to the Christians of the south. From the 860s onwards the Greeks were startled into awareness of this new barbarian threat, as the aggressive Varangian rulers attempted to plunder the rich cities of Byzantium.

No sooner did the Russians and Greeks first meet in battle than Patriarch Photius of Constantinople began organizing a mission to the new northern power. It is curious to consider just how mysterious the conduct of the Christian nations must have seemed to their pagan enemies.

'We send raiders to rob, murder and enslave, and they respond by sending unarmed priests to save our souls!'

In this way missions have often been a beautiful fulfilment of the command to turn the other cheek, and to return good for evil.

The church grew quietly and slowly for several generations. In 954, Princess Olga became the first Varangian ruler to receive baptism, but she did not spark a major move to the gospel. The church continued to grow in the shadows until the reign of her grandson Vladimir.

Vladimir's reign began with the darkest days the Russian church had yet seen. Vladimir was a pagan, and when a sacrifice was required for Perun, the Russian thunder-god, he demanded one of his nobles to provide it.

'Give up your son,' Grand Prince Vladimir insisted. 'The sacred lot has decreed that your family must provide the blood of sacrifice.'

The noble refused, emphasizing both his faith and his humanity. 'As a Christian, and a man, I cannot allow the fiend you call a god to feast his eyes with human gore!'

'You shall replace your son then!' and with that the noble and a friend who defended him were put to death. It was Russia's first martyrdom, but it sparked no wider persecution.

Religious affairs remained much as they had been until ambassadors from the region north of the Caspian arrived in Kiev some five years later. They were the first to stimulate the Kievan prince's interest in religious questions.

'Prince Vladimir,' they said, 'you are wise and prudent, but your people are ignorant of true law and religion. Follow us, and honour Mohammed!'

'What is your religion?' Vladimir asked the strangers.

'We believe in one God,' they answered, 'and we believe in all that was said by the prophet Mohammed. You must be circumcised, and you must abandon wine and pork. After death our God will give all of his followers 70 beautiful concubines in heaven.'

'The concubines sound like a good deal,' said the prince, 'but I'm rather fond of wine. I don't think my people would be very happy without it.'

So the Muslim mission failed, but that same year representatives of another faith arrived at court.

'Where do you come from?'

'We are sent by the pope.'

'What does this pope want?'

'He wishes to have you know that the religion of your people is not right. You should worship the One true God, and not idols made of wood and stone.'

'You can tell this pope,' said the Prince, 'that neither I nor my fathers have ever taken such orders from a foreigner.'

Some Jews from the land of the Chazars heard of the two failed missions and came to Kiev.

'We hear that the Muslims and Christians have attempted to ensnare you,' they said. 'Do not believe their tales. The Jesus whom the Muslims admire, and the Christians worship, is a rebel whom our fathers put to death.'

'What is your religion then?' asked the bewildered Prince.

'We circumcise, we ban pork and rabbit, and we do no work, not even good deeds, on Saturday.'

'Where is your nation?'

'Jerusalem,' said the ambassadors with a sigh.

'Where is that?'

'It is far, far away,' they said, 'but our people live there no longer. God was angry with us, and he scattered us over the face of the earth.'

Vladimir's face reddened, and he sat forward with an angry countenance.

'What? You seek to lead me into a religion that God punishes! If your ways were pleasing to Him would your nation be a nation of exiles?'

Thus the Jews also failed. It was not long after that Vladimir's court was host to a Christian philosopher from Greece, and the prince summoned him for a similar discussion.

'I have heard about the various religions of the One God,' said Vladimir. 'But one thing especially perplexes me. You worship Jesus, while the Jews boast of having killed him. What I want to know is why was He crucified?'

'The opportunity to share that with you,' said the Greek, 'will be my greatest pleasure.'

The Greek scholar proceeded to not only answer the question, but to bring out the whole story of sin and redemption that stands behind it. The prince was impressed, but he was far from being able to accept the story as the absolute truth. In his indecision he summoned the elders of his people.

'The Muslims, Romans, Jews and Greeks have all presented me with their ideas of the One God,' he said. 'Each denies the beliefs of the other, and all extol their own excellencies. How can we choose between them?'

'All men think their own ways best,' his council declared. 'The only way to judge between them is to send ambassadors to observe the ways of the various nations.'

The prince was pleased with the advice, and ten trusted men were given the important work. They first visited the Caspian Muslims, a tribe related to the Bulgarians of Europe. They soon returned to Kiev.

'We saw the worship of the Bulgarians,' they declared. 'At prayer they fall on their faces, and then look about them as though possessed. There is no happiness there, only sorrow and an awful stench.'

'Go next to the western Christians,' said Vladimir, 'and before you return visit the Greeks also. You can forget the Jews. Not even their own God agrees with them.'

When the envoys returned the prince was eager to hear what he felt would be a decisive verdict.

'We saw the churches of the Germans,' they said, 'but we saw nothing in them to compare with what we later saw in Greece. In the churches of the Byzantines we knew not whether we were on earth or in heaven! Wherever else God may be among men, He is certainly there amongst the Greeks!'

The Russian elders were greatly moved by this report.

'Prince Vladimir,' one said, 'if this faith were evil your grandmother Olga, wisest of women, would not have embraced it.'

'What say we then of Christianity? Are we prepared to accept baptism?'

'The decision,' said the elders, 'will rest with you.'

And rest it did, indeed it verily slept, for almost a year. Russia and Byzantium were frequently at war at this time, and Vladimir was not eager to take a step that would submit his nation in some sense to the Greeks. How could he ask the enemy for baptism? In the end he chose a truly Russian way!

In 988 the Russians captured the Greek city of Kherson, and Vladimir sent a peremptory message to the Byzantine emperors.

'Kherson is mine. Give me your sister in marriage or Constantinople will be next.'

'We cannot give our sister to a pagan,' said the joint emperors, the brothers Basil and Constantine. 'However, if you are baptized, you will have the princess, eternal life and our friendship to boot.'

'I accept the conditions,' ran Vladimir's reply. 'In fact I have already given your faith much thought and study. Send the princess and some priests immediately.'

Thus it was, in the Greek city of Kherson, that the prince and his nobles received baptism into the Christian church. When he arrived back in Kiev the Russian prince ordered the destruction of the city's idols. With hammer and fire all were reduced to fragments or ashes – all but Perun, for whom the prince planned a special fate.

'Tie the thunderer to a horse's tail,' he commanded, 'drag the bloodthirsty wretch down to the river, whipping him all the way, and then cast him in. Watch him float downstream. If he strikes the bank push him back into the stream with a pole. Ensure that he goes over the waterfall, then you may return.'

As the order was obeyed the Russian prince exulted over the fallen foe.

'I offer this insult not to the wood of the idol,' he proclaimed to the Kievans, some of whom were weeping for the loss of their god, 'the wood is utterly dumb and senseless. I offer the insult to an evil demon who has kept us bound for centuries! Never will he feast on a child's blood again.'

Soon afterwards a proclamation was addressed to the whole nation.

'Join your prince at the river tomorrow. Any who refuse shall lose his friendship.'

Most of the common folk were perplexed. The smattering of Christians, however, were overjoyed, and they spread their enthusiasm to the crowds.

'Would the prince and the boyars have accepted this religion for themselves if it were not good?' they asked.

Few refused Vladimir's invitation. The scene on the following day is hard to imagine.

All went together into the River Dnieper. Some were immersed almost to the neck, others to the middle, children crowded the shallows by the bank while the sturdy tall warriors waded far out. From the shore the priests recited the baptismal prayers, and the prince raised his hands to heaven as he cried out his joy.

'O Mighty God, Maker of heaven and earth, look down upon this, Your new people! Grant them to know You as You have been made known in the Christian lands. Give them a true and unfailing faith.'

At first, obviously, this new faith was little more than a matter of follow-the-leader. But churches and monasteries were soon springing up throughout Vladimir's realm, and a multitude of Christian teachers travelled the land to explain the gospel to the people. Beyond this, however, there was nothing that preached louder to the common people than the change in the prince himself.

Before his conversion Vladimir was a harsh and often cruel ruler. His command for the people to receive baptism was perhaps the last instance of this overbearing temper, but as he grew in the faith the gospel so softened Vladimir that he became a danger to his friends rather than his enemies. Vicious robber bands troubled Russia in the latter part of his reign, and the Christian priests themselves were compelled to accost the prince.

'Why have you allowed these bandits to rove about unpunished?'

'I dread the judgement of God,' said the prince. 'I dare not do other than turn the cheek to them.'

The Russian bishops were rather startled by this attitude, and though they were delighted by the prince's sincerity, they feared the ill effect of his error.

'God has appointed you as ruler,' they assured him. 'Into

your hands has been given power to punish and to show mercy. Treat as you will those who sin against you personally, but as a prince it is your obligation to defend the safety of your people.'

Vladimir took this necessary advice to heart, and the bandit gangs were soon brought to justice. The Russians were relieved at their deliverance from the thieves, but it is the story of Vladimir's hesitation that has ever made the prince most dear to the hearts of his people.

THE PRIMARY CHRONICLE

The Death of a Pope

The last years of the tenth century were a jubilee period for Russia, rejoicing in the glorious youth of its national church. The years were bright in Greece as well, as the emperors Basil and Constantine led victorious armies against the Saracens. The state of affairs in the west was not so clear.

The new Saxon Empire, and neighbouring France, were slowly restoring stability. Peace had been made with many of the Vikings, and many thousands had become Christian. The monastic revivals were also an inspiring and uplifting element in western life. But in a church that had come to look to Rome for leadership, the state of that one city alone was of enormous significance. The prospect here was not promising.

Otto I had dragged the ancient church out of the misery of the harlot dynasty, but his influence was not long-lived. The quarrels among the Italian factions continued to trouble the papacy, and interference from the Saxons often did nothing more than add one more party to the infighting.

The pope who ends this period, Gregory V, brings this out clearly. Appointed by Emperor Otto III in 996, he was later toppled by an enemy of the emperor, who promoted a Greek minister to the papacy as John XVI. It was an unwise move.

Otto made haste back to Rome, John fled in terror, and Gregory was reinstated. Hearing of the trouble, the great hermit Nilus visited the royal court to plead that the fallen pope be spared.

'Do not darken your victory with cruelty to Pope John. He is old, and it was not his own scheming which raised him to power. Allow him to end his days peacefully in a monastery.'

Otto was moved by the plea, and he assured Nilus that his advice would be followed. Gregory V, however, had different plans.

Gregory ordered that the unfortunate John be hunted down and returned to him, and then supervised as the old man was blinded with red-hot irons, and had his tongue, ears and nose cut off. John was thrown into a narrow dungeon, his wounds left open and bleeding.

When the wounds had begun to heal the pope was brought before a council, and the deaf, dumb and blind husk of a man was formally charged with the terrible offence of disgracing the papacy! Once found guilty he was seated, facing backwards, on a mangy ass, and paraded through the streets. An empty wine-bladder was put on his head in mockery of the papal tiara that he had dared to seize. After startling, or amusing, the depraved and barbarous populace the old man disappeared forever in the depths of the dungeon.

If there can be a happy note on which to end such a story, it is the reminder that those who take up by the sword die by the sword. Gregory survived his victim less than a year, falling victim to a poisoning plot. The monster belched forth his life in the early months of the year 999.

While such was western life it is hardly a wonder that many feared the imminent end of the world. The close of the first Christian millennium was viewed with dread and consternation, and the year 1000 loomed as a terrible reminder that the things of earth have been given a limited existence only.

Aware of the guilt of their nations and themselves, few embraced the thought of Christ's return with joyful expectation. Many frightened folk donated their estates to the church and monasteries, desiring to appease an angry God and convinced that the end was so near that there was no longer a need for worldly possessions. The influence of the millennium itself in people's fears can be easily overstated, however, for it was the state of the world itself which most inspired this climate of uneasy expectation. After, as before, the turn of the millennium, dread of the imminent dissolution of the world order remained.

When the Story Continues

Emerging from the disastrous tenth century, we shall see the church swept forward on a surging tide of intellectual and political renewal. We will follow the phenomenal rise of Europe, and its first great age of triumph over its Muslim neighbours. We will see the completion of the missionary task in Europe, with the conversion of the last pagan states, and witness the mighty movements of reform within the western church. We will watch the papacy's rise to its greatest height – and then the series of devastating blows that brings it back to earth.

Summary

Fifth century

- Jerome completes his work on the Vulgate, the Latin translation of the Bible.
- Gladiatorial combats are banned following the martyrdom of Telemachus.
- The empire's power declines, and Rome is captured by the Goths in AD 410.
- Augustine is the most significant of the 'Fathers'.
- Patrick undertakes his mission to Ireland.
- There is increased emphasis on prayer to saints and respect for relics.
- The Council of Chalcedon clearly defines the theology of the Incarnation – Christ is fully human and fully divine.
- Egypt, Syria and Persia slowly become independent of the churches of the capital cities, Constantinople and Rome.
- Rome is flooded with barbarians and the western empire is finally destroyed.
- The Franks are converted in AD 496.

Sixth century

- Vandal Arians persecute Christians in North Africa.
- Justinian revitalizes the empire, wins back many lands and codifies Roman law.

- Benedict pens an authoritative law code for monasteries.
- Jacob Baradaeus organizes the Syrian church.
- Brendan and other Irish monks explore the North Atlantic.
- Columba founds the monastery of Iona and labours for the conversion of Scotland.
- Gregory sends Augustine on a mission to the English.

Seventh century

- Arianism finally becomes extinct.
- There are Christian missionaries in China, AD 635, and the Scriptures are translated into Chinese.
- Mohammed founds the new religion of Islam.
- Muslims conquer Persia, Syria, Egypt and North Africa. Byzantines, with the aid of Greek fire, repel the Muslim advance.
- Northern England is converted to Christianity.
- There is conflict between Roman and Celtic Christians.
- English Christians begin a mission to the Netherlands.

Eighth century

- The Muslims conquer Spain.
- Boniface undertakes his mission to the Germans.
- Charles Martel defeats the Muslims at Tours.
- There is controversy over the use of pictures in worship, the 'Iconoclastic' period.
- Pepin founds a new Frankish dynasty.
- Charlemagne inaugurates a new period of learning, the Carolingian Renaissance.
- Many Saxon pagans are forcefully baptized.

Ninth century

- Charlemagne founds the Holy Roman Empire.
- Viking power expands.
- Anskar goes on a mission to Denmark and Sweden.
- Cyril and Methodius minister to central Europe.
- The Muslims conquer parts of Italy and make attacks on Rome.
- The Photian Schism – a quarrel between Patriarch Photius and Pope Nicholas divides Greece and Rome.
- The popes promote the False Decretals in order to boost their own power.
- There is chaos as civil wars tear the new empire apart.
- Alfred the Great of Wessex subdues the Danes, codifies Common Law and translates significant literature into Anglo-Saxon.

Tenth century

- The papal pornocracy.
- The convent of Cluny is founded.
- Henry the Fowler restores order in Germany.
- Athelstan unites England.
- John XII – the tyrant pope.
- Dunstan leads the English monastic revival.
- Nilus and Romuald revive Italian monasticism.
- Otto founds the Saxon Empire.
- Russia is converted.

Bibliography

Many authors of the fifth to eighth centuries are found in the two series of *Nicene and Post-Nicene Fathers*, first printed in 1886 – but still available (*ANF, NPNF*[1] [First Series] and *NPNF*[2] [Second Series]) in reprints by Hendrickson (Peabody, MA, 1994) and Eerdmans (Grand Rapids, MI, 1985–87); or in the more recent *Fathers of the Church* (FC; Washington, DC: Catholic University of America Press, 1947–). There are no references cited for many of the later chapters in the present volume, as the primary sources are often numerous and generally not available in English. For more information on the general history of the period, *The Cambridge Medieval History* (Cambridge: Cambridge University Press, 1911–32), with its extensive bibliographies, is a good place to begin. For detailed discussion of the early missionaries, K.S. Latourette, *A History of the Expansion of Christianity* (7 vols.; London: Eyre and Spottiswoode, 1938–47) is still indispensable. S. Baring-Gould, *Lives of the Saints* (16 vols.; Edinburgh: J. Grant, 1914) contains a wealth of biographical information, but is often unreliable on details.

Acts of the Councils, *NPNF*[2] 14.

Adomnan, *Life of Columba* (tr. A.O. and M.O. Anderson; Oxford: Clarendon Press, 1991).

Anonymous, *The Primary Chronicle*, a selection in *Medieval Russia: A Source Book, 900–1700* (ed. B. Dmytryshyn; Hinsdale: The Dryden Press, 1973, 1967).

Anonymous, *The Sayings of the Desert Fathers* (tr. B. Ward; London: A.R. Mowbray & Co., 1975).

Anonymous, *The Tripartite Life of Patrick* (tr. W. Stokes; London: Her Majesty's Stationery Office, 1887).

Anonymous, *The Voyage of Brendan,* in *The Age of Bede* (tr. J.F. Webb; London: Penguin, 1983).

Augustine, *Works, NPNF*¹ 1–8.

Bede, *A History of the English Church and People* (tr. L. Sherley-Price; Harmondsworth: Penguin, 1968, 1955).

Boniface, *The English Correspondence of Saint Boniface* (tr. E. Kylie; New York: Cooper Square Publishers, 1966).

Ching-Ching, 'The Hsianfu Monument', translated in A.C. Moule, *Christians in China before the Year 1550* (London: SPCK, 1930).

Chrysostom, *Works, NPNF*¹ 9–14.

Claudian, *Works* (tr. M. Platnauer; London: Heinemann, 1922).

Einhard, *Life of Charlemagne,* in *Two Lives of Charlemagne* (tr. L. Thorpe; Harmondsworth: Penguin, 1969).

Eugippius, *Life of Severinus*, FC, 55.

Evagrius, *Church History,* in *The Ancient Ecclesiasticall Histories of the First Six Hundred Years after Christ* (tr. M. Hanmer; London: Abraham Miller, 1636).

Gildas, *The Ruin of Britain* (tr. M. Winterbottom; London: Phillimore, 1978).

Gregory of Tours, *The Glory of the Confessors* (tr. R. Van Dam; Liverpool: Liverpool University Press, 1988).

—. *The Glory of the Martyrs* (tr. R. Van Dam; Liverpool: Liverpool University Press, 1988).

—. *The History of the Franks* (tr. L. Thorpe; Harmondsworth: Penguin, 1974).

Gregory the Great, *Dialogues*, FC, 39.

Ibn Ishaq, *Life of Mohammad* (tr. E. Rehatsek; London: The Folio Society, 1964). W. Muir, *The Life of Mahomet* (London: Smith, Elder & Co., 1894) is a full treatment of the prophet's life from the earliest sources.

Jerome, *Works, NPNF*² 6.

Leo, *Letters, NPNF*² 12.

Leontius, *The Life of St John the Almsgiver*, in *Three Byzantine Saints: Contemporary Biographies of St Daniel the Stylite, St Theodore of Sykeon and St John the Almsgiver* (tr. E. Dawes; Oxford: B. Blackwell, 1948).

Mohammed, *The Koran* (tr. N. J. Dawood; Harmondsworth: Penguin, 1956).

Mohammed, *The Koran* (tr. G. Sale; London: Frederick Warne).

Orosius, *Seven Books Against the Pagans*, FC, 50.

Palladius, *Lausiac History* (tr. W.K. Lowther Clarke; New York: SPCK, 1918).

Patrick, *His Writings and Muirchu's Life* (tr. A. Hood; London: Phillimore, 1978).

Priscus, *History*, survives only in fragments. These are translated in R.C. Blockley, *The Fragmentary Classicising Historians of the Later Roman Empire* (Liverpool: Francis Cairns, 1981–83).

Procopius, *Works* (tr. H.B. Dewing; London: Heinemann, 1914–28).

Rimbert, *Life of Anskar*, in *Anskar, The Apostle of the North, 801–865* (tr. C. Robinson; Westminster: Society for the Propagation of the Gospel in Foreign Parts, 1921).

Socrates, *Church History*, NPNF[2] 2.

Sozomen, *Church History*, NPNF[2] 2.

Theodoret, *Church History*, NPNF[2] 3. *History of the Monks* is not available in English.

Victor of Vita, *History of the Vandal Persecution*, (tr. J. Moorhead; Liverpool: Liverpool University Press, 1992).

Willibald, *The Life of St Boniface* (tr. G.W. Robinson; Cambridge, MA: Harvard University Press, 1916).

Zosimus, *New History* (tr. R.T. Ridley; Sydney: Australian Association for Byzantine Studies, 1982).

Index